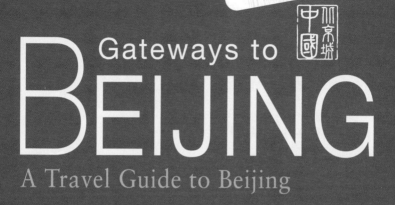

Gateways to
BEIJING

A Travel Guide to Beijing

MARK & MISTY
LITTLEWOOD

ARMOUR

Published by Genesis Books
An imprint of ARMOUR Publishing Pte Ltd
Kent Ridge Post Office
P. O. Box 1193, Singapore 911107
Email: mail@armourpublishing.com
Website: www.armourpublishing.com

12	11	10	09	08
5	4	3	2	1

Printed in Singapore

Gateways to Beijing — A Travel Guide to Beijing
ISBN 13: 978-981-4222-12-9
ISBN 10:   981-4222-12-7

Pray for Beijing — A 40-Day Guide
ISBN 13: 978-981-4222-49-5
ISBN 10:   981-4222-49-6

Package
ISBN 13: 978-981-4222-51-8
ISBN 10:   981-4222-51-8

This book is dedicated to our three children,
Luke, Ryan and Sarah.

You were all born in Beijing during the writing of this book and have a heritage in the beautiful nation of China. You are all precious gifts from above.

CONTENTS

Six

Seven

DIRECTORIES/RESOURCES

Eight

APPENDIX

ONE

Beijing History

Beijing History

INTRODUCTION

The area that is today's Beijing Municipality has a history of several thousand years. Due to its excellent geographical location, the area developed as a strategic military and trading centre in the north of China. Feudal kingdoms warred over this land, dynasties rose and fell, and the nation that is today's China has its foundations here.

The city we now know as Beijing was known by several different names in the past: Ji meaning 'thistle' or 'reeds'; Youzhou, the 'city of tranquillity'; Zhuojun, a place name; Nanjing, meaning 'southern capital'; Yanjing, the 'capital of swallows'; Zhongdu, 'middle capital'; Dadu, 'grand capital'; Khanbaliq, 'capital of the Khans'; Beiping, 'northern peace'; and finally, Beijing, meaning 'northern capital'. The history that follows is not an exhaustive one. It is, however, an overview of the key events and people who contributed to the city's historical significance and modern day development.

BEIJING — THE STATES OF JI (蓟国) AND YAN (燕国)

Archaeological evidence points to the existence of civilisation in the area surrounding today's Beijing by the late Shang Dynasty (17th century - 11th century BC). During this time, two small kingdom states, Ji and Yan, existed side by side. With the collapse of the Shang Dynasty and founding of the Western Zhou Dynasty in 1045BC, nobles or dukes were appointed as rulers over the smaller kingdom states. The Emperor Wu gave the State of Ji to the descendents of the legendary Yellow Emperor and the State of Yan to the descendents of the Duke of

Shao. The capital of the State of Ji was called Ji and is believed to have been located in today's Xuanwu District. During the Spring and Autumn Period, the State of Ji was conquered by the State of Yan. The city of Ji then became capital of the State of Yan, one of the seven powerful kingdoms existent in China during the Warring States Period (475 - 221 BC).

BEIJING — CITY OF JI (蓟)

Qin Dynasty's horse and chariot.

Conflict escalated between the various kingdoms of the Warring States Period. China was ultimately unified by the western state of Qin under the leadership of Emperor Qin Shihuang in 221BC. The city of Ji then became a strategic military and political capital of the newly-formed Guangyang Prefecture, one of 36 prefectures of China during the Qin Dynasty. It was during this period that construction of the Great Wall first began. The

joining of existing defensive walls formed a continuous line of protection against Inner Asian tribal groups to the north. The Qin Dynasty was only to last 15 years before collapsing, taking China into a brief period of unrest.

The Western Han Dynasty (206BC - 220AD) was soon established in 206BC. The city of Ji was then named the political centre of the Prefecture of Yan. Industry and commerce thrived in the city with traders from various regions coming to sell their wares in the city's markets.

During the Eastern Han period, General Zhang Kan chose Ji for his military command centre, to defend against, and launch attacks on the northern Xiongnu tribesmen. This general is also remembered for establishing large rice paddy plantations in the area of today's Shunyi District. As with earlier dynasties, the Han Dynasty finally ended with turmoil and chaos.

BEIJING — CITY OF YOUZHOU (幽州)

After the fall of the Han Dynasty, China was divided into three warring kingdoms. Ji became the capital of Youzhou Prefecture under the

Wei Kingdom (220 - 280) and was renamed Youzhou (City of Tranquility). The famous military leader, Cao Cao, took command of the city as a strategic military post in the north. He also ordered the first large-scale water conservation project in Beijing, which laid foundations for the city's future development.

A religious priest.

The Three Kingdoms Period came to an end when China was unified under new rulers during the Western Jin Dynasty (265 - 317). Buddhism was introduced to Beijing at this time with the building of the Tanzhe Temple, the earliest temple in existence in the municipality today. A well-known saying reflects the temple's early origins: "First there was Tanzhe Temple, and then there was Youzhou."

("先有潭桔寺, 后有幽州.") Later, Buddhism became popular both as a religion and as a powerful political tool.

Political instability in the Western Jin Dynasty saw a shift of China's capital from Luoyang in Central China, to Nanjing in the south. This marked the beginning of the Eastern Jin Dynasty (347 - 420) and a shift of political power which left the area vulnerable to attacks by non-Chinese peoples from the North.

In 350AD, the city of Youzhou was occupied by the Xianbei people and became capital of a non-Chinese kingdom for the first time. Political instability, continuous war campaigns and oppressive rule mark this period as one of great suffering in the north of China. Many were forced into slave labour by the foreign rulers. Youzhou struggled to develop as neighbouring peoples fought for control of the city. China remained divided under various northern and southern kingdoms until the founding of the Sui Dynasty in 581AD.

BEIJING — CITY OF ZHUOJUN (涿郡)

The Sui Dynasty (581 - 618) brought about national political unity and the administrative renaming of the city as Zhuojun. The most significant contribution to the city's development was the building of the Grand Canal which stretched almost 2,000 kilometres from Hangzhou in the south to Luoyang, and later extended to the outskirts of today's Beijing. The city underwent significant development during this period, reaching a total population of 130,000 at its peak.

Zhuojun achieved prominence for a time under the last Sui Emperor, Sui Yandi, as a military staging post for launching attacks against the Korean Korguyo Kingdom in the northeast. However, overspending, and excessive use of forced labour on overambitious projects, and a succession of failed military campaigns are attributed to the eventual collapse of the Sui Dynasty.

BEIJING — CITY OF YOUZHOU (幽州 — AGAIN)

The Tang Dynasty (618 - 907) was quickly ushered in to replace the collapsed Sui Dynasty. Historians regard this period as a high point for Chinese civilization. Arts and literature flourished, and commerce and industry prospered. Once again the city had a name change to resume its former name, Youzhou. With the presence of 31 business associations (guilds), Youzhou was a major commercial centre and military command centre in the north of China.

The Tang Dynasty Emperor, Taizong, used the city as a military base for engaging the northern tribes in battle. To honour the warriors lost in such battles, the emperor commissioned the building of a temple called 'Compassion for the Loyal' in 696AD. This same temple was later renamed Fayuan Temple. Today it is the oldest existent temple in the city area proper. Other structures from this time include the Temple of the Sleeping Buddha, the Temple of the Cloud and the White Cloud Daoist Temple.

A Tang Lady.

BEIJING — CITY OF DADU (大都)/YANJING (燕京)/YOUZHOU (幽州)

In 742, the Youzhou Administrative Area with a population of 370,000 became one of three military regions under the command of General An Lüshan. In 755, troops were dispatched to attack the Tang

Dynasty capital at Luoyang. The emperor and his concubine fled south to Sichuan, and An Lushan declared himself founder of a new dynasty, Da Yan. The city once again had a name change: Dadu. The rebellion only lasted eight years before the Tang Dynasty was restored. However, during this brief period the city was known by several names: Dadu, then Yanjing, and then back to its former name, Youzhou.

BEIJING — CITY OF NANJING (南京)

Misrule, economic instability, internal political dissension and the rise of peasant rebellions finally led to the collapse of the Tang Dynasty and the beginning of a brief period of history known as the Five Dynasties, a time when the control of China's territories was divided. The city was overthrown by Khitan tribes from the northeast in 907AD, marking the establishment of the Liao Dynasty, which ruled over the north of China. A military alliance was forged between the Tang general, Shi Jingtan and the Khitan rulers. The alliance fought to overthrow the Tang court and succeeded. In 938AD, the northern areas of China, including the city of Youzhou, were given over to

the Khitan in gratitude for their assistance. The Liao Dynasty rulers had five capital cities, from which they ruled the land, with Youzhou being a secondary capital. At this time, Youzhou was renamed Nanjing, meaning 'southern capital'.

BEIJING — CITY OF YANJING (燕京)

In 1013AD the city was renamed Yanjing. While it had achieved recognition as an important trading and strategic military base in the north of China during earlier periods, it lacked significance when compared with the grand capitals of Chang'an, today's Xian; Luoyang; and Bianliang, today's Kaifeng. During the Liao Dynasty, however, the grand and orderly city began its rise as the cultural and political centre of China.

According to the *Khitan History* 《契丹国志》[1], Yanjing had a population of over 300,000, a grand palace, well laid-out streets, splendid markets with produce from both land and sea, fine fabrics, advanced printing techniques and some grand Buddhist temples. The Liao Dynasty emperors advanced the spread of Buddhism. Some of the temples built during this time still exist today including the Tianning,

The Lugou Bridge.

Dajue and Jietai Temples. The Niujie Mosque was also built during this time.

BEIJING — CITY OF ZHONGDU (中都)

The Jurchen (or Nüzhen) people in the northeast of China rose up against the Liao rulers and founded the Jin Dynasty in 1115. Their chosen capital was close to today's Harbin. As the result of an alliance between the Northern Song and Jin, Yanjing briefly came under the jurisdiction of the Northern Song Dynasty in 1120. The Jin conquered the Liao in 1125 and then turned to attack the Northern Song armies, their former ally, forcing them to head South. The north of China then came under Jin control. The city became capital of the Jin Dynasty in 1153 and was renamed Zhongdu.

A rebuilding and expansion of the city began in 1151. More than 400,000 soldiers and 800,000 artisans were conscripted to build the city and its new palaces. Previous city walls were fortified and extended to the east and west of the earlier Liao city parameters. Forty-foot walls stretching a total of 26 miles in length surrounded the new square-shaped city. Twelve defensive gates and 910 watch towers were also built to defend the city and its inhabitants. Imperial palaces were situated within an inner imperial city and built in imitation of the Northern Song palaces in Bianliang, today's Kaifeng. Imperial gardens were also built outside the city walls. Most famous of these were the Daning Palace, later named Wanning Palace located at today's Beihai Park; and those at Xiangshan, today's Diaoyu Guesthouse and Yuquanshan. Growing in great splendour and wealth, Zhongdu had approximately 1 million people by the end of the Jin Dynasty.

Zhongdu's prosperity and grandeur did not last. In the early 13th century, Genghis Khan amassed forces in the steppes of Mongolia against the kingdoms to their south. Having defeated the Xi Xia Kingdom in western China, his forces sought to overthrow Zhongdu in 1211. The city successfully fended off the Khan's great army for a number of years until it was surrounded and starved into submission in 1215. Because Zhongdu had dared to resist Genghis Khan's cavalry forces, the city was spared no mercy. All the city's inhabitants were slaughtered and the magnificent Jin capital is said to have burnt for a whole month, leaving nothing but charred frames and streets covered with liquefied human flesh.

BEIJING — CITY OF DADU (大都)/KHANBALIQ (汗八里)

The rebuilding of the city did not come for another generation. It was in 1269 that Kublai Khan, Genghis Khan's grandson, chose the former city area to build a capital over his newly expanded

territory. Mongol armies finally overpowered and occupied the southern territories of China in 1271. This heralded the beginning of the Yuan Dynasty. The city was renamed Dadu, also known as Khanbaliq in the Mongolian language, and made capital of the Yuan Empire. The empire occupied a territory covering East Asia including today's Seoul, Hanoi and Mandalay, through Central Asia to Baghdad, and onward from Damascus to Eastern Europe.

A site north of the former city ruins was chosen for building the new capital, Dadu. An inadequate water supply was one reason for the former site of Zhongdu being abandoned. New irrigation channels were dug to bring water from the north and a well-planned city lay within the rectangular earthen walls. Streets formed a

Kublai Khan.

chessboard pattern conforming to a north-south axis. The Bell and Drum towers stood at the centre of Dadu, with the city's main commercial area located at Jishuitan.

Kublai Khan drew inspiration and technical help from Chinese, Muslim and Mongolian architects and engineers for the design and building of the new city. His walled palaces were described in Marco Polo's accounts of the city as being grand and resplendent, of which nothing in Europe could compare. Nonetheless, many Mongolian princes preferred to live in Yurts which could be seen throughout the city and palace grounds.[2]

Some of the city's oldest *hutongs* date back to this time, as do a number of significant structures remaining today. These include the Drum and Bell Towers; the Imperial School, or Guozijian; the Confucian Temple; Baita and Huguo Temples; and the Daoist centres of Baiyunguan and Chenghuang Miao. By the end of the Yuan Dynasty, the city had a population of approximately 500,000 people.

The city became a hub of industry and commerce for the Yuan Empire. Agriculture flourished in the surrounding districts. In the city and suburbs,

The Bell Tower.

industries such as silk weaving, rug making, silver and coal mining, iron smelting, liquor production and glazed tile making were well-known.

Due to the extent of the Yuan Empire, and Kublai Khan's tolerance of various cultures and belief systems, Dadu was a mixing pot for Nestorian Christians, Muslim traders, Buddhists and Daoists. Foreign traders and envoys from Central Asia and beyond were seen in the city's markets. Marco Polo and his uncles were among these. The first Catholic missionaries also arrived in Dadu at this time.

BEIJING — CITY OF BEIPING (北平)

The last years of the Yuan Dynasty were marked by natural disasters, disease, and economic and social unrest. Dissension among the Chinese towards the Mongol foreign rulers soon became widespread, leading to uprisings across China. One of these insurrections saw the southern capital of Nanjing come under control of a rebel group known as the Red Turbans in 1356. Its leader was Zhu Yuanzhang (better known by his reign name as Hongwu), a former peasant turned Buddhist monk turned rebel commander. In a bid to rid China of its foreign rulers, he sent troops from Nanjing to attack the Yuan Dynasty capital at Dadu. Rather than facing the threat of capture or death, the Mongolian emperor and his court chose to flee the city for the steppes of Mongolia, allowing the city to slip easily into Hongwu's hands in 1368. Hongwu then proclaimed the establishment of a new dynasty known as the Ming. Nanjing, in the south, was made capital. The former Yuan Dynasty palaces in Dadu were set on fire and the city was renamed Beiping, meaning 'northern peace'.

BEIJING — CITY OF BEIJING (北京 — MING DYNASTY)

Hongwu appointed his fourth son, Zhu Di, as ruler over Beiping and its surrounding areas. Zhu Di quickly consolidated his power base in the north by amassing large numbers of troops. After Hongwu's death in 1398, the title of emperor was bestowed to his grandson Jian Wen, Zhu Di's nephew. The new emperor did not trust his uncle, and sent assassins to kill him at Beiping. When the assassination attempt was unsuccessful, Jian Wen mobilized an army of 500,000 soldiers to suppress Beiping and dispose of his uncle once and for all in 1399. Their attempts to storm the city were once again thwarted by Zhu Di's army and the city's inhabitants. It is even said that the women participated in the battle by throwing down pots from the city walls onto the heads of their attackers![3]

Zhu Di then marched his armies south to attack Nanjing. He successfully unseated his nephew and took control of the throne in 1402, proclaiming himself as the third Ming Dynasty emperor under the name of Yongle. Having been a frontier commander in Beiping for many years, Yongle understood the strategic location of the city. He renamed the city Beijing (Northern Capital) and officially made Beijing the capital in 1406.

It was during this time that the basic layout of today's

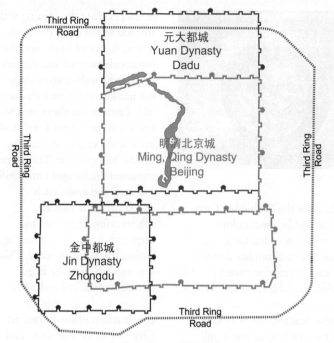

元大都城
Yuan Dynasty
Dadu

Third Ring
Road

Third Ring
Road

Third Ring
Road

明清北京城
Ming, Qing Dynasty
Beijing

金中都城
Jin Dynasty
Zhongdu

Third Ring
Road

Jin, Yuan, Ming and Qing Walls.

Beijing was formed. The building of the Ming palaces, altars and defensive walls was a massive undertaking. It is recorded that an army of 1 million guarded the city, while another 1 million were employed for the construction projects. The first phase of construction took almost two decades to complete.

The Ming capital was built on the foundations of the former Yuan capital of Dadu. While keeping the basic layout, the northern walls were moved south and the southern walls extended to today's Qianmen. Twelve-metre high and twenty-kilometre long reinforced brick walls surrounded the city area. A walled inner imperial city was built north of Qianmen Gate with another set of walls enclosing the Forbidden City at its centre. Work on the Forbidden City began in 1407 and did not finish until early 1421. As one of the most extensive palaces in the world, its design communicated the emperor's supreme power. Jonathon Spence, in his book *The Search for Modern China*

The blue tiles.

describes the Forbidden City: "Laid out in a meticulous geometrical order, the grand stairways and mighty doors of each successive palace building and throne hall were precisely aligned with the arches leading out of Peking to the south, speaking to all comers of the connectedness of things personified in this man the Chinese termed 'Son of Heaven'".[4]

Other significant Ming construction projects included the Temple of Heaven, the Altar for the Creator of Agriculture, the dredging of the Grand Canal, extending and reinforcing the Great Wall and the construction of the Ming Tombs.

The city was further expanded in 1564 with an extension of the city walls south from Qianmen Gate. The original plan was to extend the wider outer walls northward to further enclose the existing walls and add to the city's defensive layers. A lack of funds saw the project abandoned and the city took on its well-known shape, not unlike the Chinese character '凸'. The new southern area was known as the 'Outer City', and became the centre of business for the Ming capital. This layout remained unchanged until 1949.

Arts and crafts such as coloured-tile making, silk weaving, cloisonné and carpentry flourished in Beijing during the Ming Dynasty. This was partly due to the large numbers of skilled craftsmen brought to the city for the construction of the Forbidden City and its various altars and temples.

China was closed to international trade and cultural exchange for most of the Ming Dynasty. It was during this time, Italian Jesuit missionary, Matteo Ricci, found an opportunity to establish his ministry in Beijing. Taking on the role of a Chinese scholar, he won respect and admiration from court officials for his exceptional understanding of mathematics and geography. Ricci's ministry resulted in the establishment of a church in the city and foundations being laid for the Catholic Church in China. Upon his death in 1610, he was granted the highest honour of being granted a burial plot by the emperor.

By the beginning of the 17th century, rampant corruption and abuse of power by the eunuchs led to the economic and political decline of the Ming Dynasty. Natural disasters and the outbreak of epidemics, dissension and rebellions further weakened the power of the state. At the same time, external pressure grew as Manchu tribesmen took control of the areas north of the Great Wall.

Rebel leader, Li Zicheng, entered Beijing and mounted an attack on the city in April 1644 to put an end to the Ming Dynasty. His successful use of propaganda to highlight the excesses and corruption of the Ming court gained him local support for his cause. Knowing his time had come, the reigning Ming Emperor, Chongzhen, left the Forbidden City by the north gate and hung himself at the foot of Jingshan Hill. During their time in Beijing, Li's generals and troops looted and ravaged the city and therefore, lost support of the general populace. Li Zicheng ascended the Dragon Throne to proclaim himself emperor of a new dynasty on June 3, 1644. This 'reign' lasted only one day as Li and his troops fled the city on June 4, 1644, when attacked by the Manchu armies.

BEIJING — CITY OF BEIJING (北京 — QING DYNASTY)

Manchu troops found a way through the Great Wall through the Shanhaiguan Pass which had been opened to aid their expulsion of the rebel leader, Li Zicheng. Beijing came under Manchu control in June 1644. The title Qing was given to the new dynasty and Beijing was formally proclaimed capital.

The Qing kept the overall layout of the capital. One of the most significant changes was the Manchus' occupation of the northern 'Inner City'. Chinese and Hui Muslims were moved to the 'Outer City', resulting in the division of a southern Chinese city and a northern Manchu city.

The 'outer city' south of Zhengyang Gate (or Qianmen Gate) and centred around Dashilar, developed as the centre of commerce and culture — shops, medicine and craft markets, restaurants, entertainment spots (including prostitution) and guildhalls for different regional associations were built. Vendors in Liulichang sold Confucian classics, calligraphy, scrolls, paintings and other literary

Tourists visiting the Yuanmingyuan site.

works. The Tianqiao Market area was popular for its live street performances and was so named as the 'cradle of arts' in Beijing.

During this period, many old temples were restored and several new ones constructed. Buddhism once again flourished as the Manchu Shamanists adopted some of the practices of Lamaism. The Emperor Qinglong commissioned numerous pleasure grounds known as the 'Three Hills and Five Gardens' which included well-known sites such as Fragrant Hills Park, Yuanmingyuan (Old Summer Palace), and today's Summer Palace.

As with all previous dynasties, the Qing Dynasty began to decline and by the mid-19th century it was facing insurmountable challenges from both outside and within. Corruption and rebellions were seen as the most serious threats to the survival of the Qing Dynasty by many officials. However, it was the challenges brought by European traders which were to further weaken the ailing state and expose the Qing court's deficiencies.

BEIJING — CITY OF BEIJING (北京 — 1800s)

China's defeat during the Opium War of 1840 and the subsequent signing of the unequal Treaty of Nanjing marked the beginning of China's humiliation at the hands of a number of foreign nations. One of the demands placed upon China was to allow foreign envoys to have rights of residency within the walls of the capital, Beijing. When China refused to accept the terms of the treaties, which included access to foreign legations, an Anglo-French joint expedition marched into Beijing in 1860. The city came under siege and Yuanmingyuan, the Old Summer Palace, was burned to the ground on October 18, 1860. China was forced to concede to the foreigners' demands. Foreign diplomats could then reside within the inner city walls and foreign missionaries had the right to preach throughout the nation. Following the occupation of Beijing, the Qing rulers sought to bring about reforms through a programme of modernization known as 'Self-Strengthening'.

In the search for answers and in a quest for knowledge that might lead to reform, several western-styled colleges, including Peking University, were established. However, attempts to reform the government and economy were thwarted by the powerful Empress Dowager Cixi, who placed the emperor, her own nephew, under house arrest in 1898.

By the end of the 19th century, conditions in Beijing had deteriorated. Many areas of the city were dilapidated and dirty. Beggars were everywhere, as were the homeless and the old, the crippled and the sick with no one to care for them.[5]

BEIJING — CITY OF BEIJING (北京 — EARLY 1900s)

Peace in Beijing was once again disturbed with the arrival of the martial arts based movement, the Boxer Rebellion in June of 1900. Made up largely of labourers and farmers from rural Shandong, the movement rose up and swept across Northern China in an attempt to destroy foreign missionaries and their converts. The first Boxers arrived in Beijing on June 13, 1900. Placards appeared on walls throughout the city, calling for 'death to foreigners and Christians.' Churches were attacked and burned; missionaries were forced to seek protection in the foreign legation district; and local believers had to choose between apostasy and death. Railway lines and telegraph wires were destroyed as were shops with foreign imports. The movement gained momentum when the Empress Dowager Cixi lent her support by declaring a war against the foreign powers on June 21. The Boxer Rebellion was finally put down on August 14, 1900, after the arrival of a 20,000-strong, eight-nation occupation force in the city. The Empress Dowager Cixi, the Emperor Guangxu and the entire Qing court fled the city for Xian, leaving the city and its inhabitants at the mercy of the foreign troops.

The foreign troops divided the city into zones, each under the command of a different nation's forces. The Forbidden City became the command centre, and the Altar of Heaven a field gun mount. Temples and mosques were occupied and foreign troops did not hesitate to harass, loot and destroy all in the name of revenge. Several major sites and temples in Beijing were damaged by the foreign soldiers including the Summer Palace. The Boxer

Rebellion and its looting and destruction has been described as the most brutal carnage experienced since Genghis Khan torched the Jin city in 1215. As a result, a psychological scar was left on the city.[6]

Several attempts were made to reform China over the next ten years. These efforts, however, came as too little too late. The Qing Dynasty was in decline. The Empress Dowager Cixi passed away in 1908, but not before ensuring that Emperor Guanxu's nephew, Puyi, was to ascend the Dragon Throne. The last Emperor was thereby installed at the age of three with great pageantry on November 14, 1908.

The final collapse of the Qing Dynasty came in 1911

The Forbidden City Hall.

after an uprising in Wuchang (today's Wuhan), which successfully unseated the provincial governor. Within a six-week period, fifteen southern and central provinces had declared themselves independent from the Qing rulers and united to usher in a new state under the name of the Republic of China. The revolutionary leader, Sun Yatsen, became provisional president of the new republic until handing over the title to the northern Qing general, Yuan Shikai. The Qing Dynasty formally gave up control of China on February 12, 1912 when the Prince Regent Chun, signed a degree announcing the formal abdication of the throne by the boy emperor. The emperor and his family continued to reside in the Forbidden City and have access to the other formal palaces up until 1924.

Beijing remained the capital at the beginning of the Republic of China. It was not long, however, until Yuan Shikai seized absolute power from parliament and attempted to establish a new dynasty with himself as emperor on January 1, 1916. As a result of his announcement and then untimely death in June of the same year, several regions broke away from the republic under the command of warlords. China then struggled with the absence of a strong central government. Sun Yatsen's nationalist revolutionaries (Kuomintang Party) held loose control over the southern provinces while a government of sorts was maintained in Beijing.

BEIJING — CITY OF BEIJING (北京 — 1919-1928)

During this period, young intellectuals waged their own wars by challenging old Confucian culture and traditions. Old culture was blamed for China's demise and calls for a new cultural movement were made through literature. Chen Duxiu and Li Dazhao, both founders of the Communist Party of China; Lu Xun and many other key intellectuals and writers worked tirelessly in Beijing to expose the weaknesses of old Chinese society. A New Culture Movement gained momentum in 1919 when young intellectuals and students took to the streets of Beijing in protest against China's unjust treatment at the Treaty of Versailles. On May 4, 1919, more than 3,000 students gathered at Tiananmen Gate. Shouting patriotic slogans and attempting to storm a pro-

Japanese cabinet member's house, the students were soon suppressed and their leaders arrested. These actions set off a chain reaction of protests and strikes across the nation in support of the students and their cause. The government was forced to release the students, the cabinet was replaced and China then refused to sign the Treaty of Versailles. The May 4th Movement was an important event in that it marked the beginning of revolutionary nationalism in modern China. It was only two years later that the Communist Party of China was founded in Shanghai in July 1921. Amongst its leaders were Li Dazhao, Chen Duxiu and Mao Zedong, a young librarian from Peking University.

In February of 1924, Beijing came under the control of the northern warlord, Feng Yuxian. Feng, also known by many as the 'Christian General', forced President Cao Kun to resign; drove the deposed Emperor from the Forbidden City; and set up Duan Qirui as 'provisional chief executive'.

A complex set of events soon led to the Japanese government making a series of demands on China. In response, a group of nationalist students organized a protest outside the provisional chief executive's office to demand that the Japanese ultimatum be rejected. The following day more than 5,000 university students gathered near Tiananmen Gate. Making their way toward the chief executive's office, they were intercepted by police and fired upon. Forty-two students were killed in what was to become known as the May 18th Incident of 1926. As a result, Duan Qirui was forced to resign and flee the city.

BEIJING — CITY OF BEIPING (北平 — 1926-1949)

Beijing came under the control of the Manchurian warlord, Zhang Zuolin, in June 1926. Zhang proclaimed himself the Grand Marshall of the Republic of China with its legal government in Beijing. An alliance of regional warlords led by the Nationalist leader Chiang Kaishek attacked Zhang's forces and took control of Beijing on June 3, 1928. The nation's capital was moved from Beijing to Nanjing in the south. No longer the capital of China, Beijing was renamed Beiping.

In the meantime, China entered into a state of civil war. An earlier alliance forged between the Communist and Nationalist parties broke apart when the Nationalists brutally attacked Communist supporters and members in Shanghai in mid-1927.

During this same period, Japan sought to occupy Chinese territory. Northeast China had been annexed by the Japanese in 1931 and in the following year a puppet regime was established over the territory under the title of 'Manchukuo'. Most Chinese were enraged at the Japanese encroachment on Chinese territory and appalled at the Nationalists' reluctance to take tough action against the Japanese. The Nationalists, for their part, believed that China was no match for the Japanese Imperial Forces and turned their efforts instead to reigning in their Communist rivals.

Students in Beiping responded to the gradual giving over of territory to the Japanese by organizing themselves into the Beijing Students' Union. Around 6,000 students took to the streets in protest on December 9, 1935. The police responded by spraying them with fire hoses, clubbing them and making arrests. The protests once again touched a national chord, sparking further protests in other cities around the country in the following days. One week later, more than 30,000 marched in Beiping in a second demonstration.

Full-scale war with Japan finally broke out on July 7, 1937. Japanese and Chinese Nationalist forces faced each other on opposite sides of the Lugou Bridge. Shots were accidentally exchanged in what can be considered as the first battle of World War II and the beginning of China's War against Japanese Aggression.[7] Beiping, and much of the east and northeast of China, was soon occupied by the Japanese and remained under their control until 1945.

BEIJING — CITY OF BEIJING (北京 — 1949-1976)

The civil war between the Nationalists and Communists resumed soon after the defeat of the Japanese at the end of World War II. The Nationalists were quick to lay claim to the major industrial bases in the northeast and key cities, including Beiping and Shanghai. Unable to reign in the economy, they soon lost support of the general populace and with it their claims to governance over China. The People's Liberation Army marched into Beiping on January 31, 1949, without a fight.

On October 1, 1949, Mao Zedong proclaimed that the "Chinese people had stood up"

A Guard standing post in front of the Tiananmen Gate.

and announced the founding of the People's Republic of China while standing atop Tiananmen Gate. Beiping became Beijing and was made the national capital — this time, over a newly-unified nation under the command of the Chinese Communist Party.

The next ten years saw major changes in the capital. The area in front of Tiananmen Gate was cleared to become Tiananmen Square, Chang'an Avenue was built as a major artery, the Soviet-designed Beijing Exhibition Centre was completed, and many of the gates and walls were torn down to make way for new roads.

To mark the tenth anniversary of the founding of the People's Republic of China, ten major construction projects were embarked on.

These included the Great Hall of the People (built in only 10 months), the National Museum, the Beijing Railway Station, the Nationalities Cultural Palace and the Military Museum. Beijing had finally established itself as the political centre of the nation, and as such, was being built into a city that reflected its status.

Major political and social upheaval was soon to befall China. Following the failed Great Leap Forward (1958 - 1961) and the subsequent nationwide famine (1959 - 1962), Mao had been discredited by his colleagues for his disastrous economic policies. Convinced that the party and state apparatus had become entrenched with those whom he termed 'capitalist roaders', he launched a new revolution and class struggle against his, and the revolution's, enemies.

The Great Proletariat Cultural Revolution was launched in the middle of 1966 with a call to rid the nation of 'old culture, old customs, old habits and old thinking'. Young people from Beijing's middle schools and universities rose up to rid the nation of the 'four olds'. Beijing's youth began to attack, beat and kill their teachers, parents, old people, Communist Party members and government leaders in the name of a new 'class struggle'. By the end of September, a total of 33,695 households had been ransacked and 1,772 were recorded as having been killed at the hands of the Red Guards in Beijing. Some sources, however, suggest that up to half a million people may have been killed in the first month which later became known as 'Bloody August'.[8]

Red Guards across the nation attacked anything and anyone they determined as a class enemy or anti-revolutionary. Many people committed suicide by hanging or throwing themselves in the city's lakes rather than falling into the hands of the Red Guards. Temples, churches and many of the nation's cultural sites were defaced or destroyed by enthusiastic youth in the name of advancing the revolution. In Beijing, Mao stood on top of Tiananmen Gate to view massive crowds of enthusiastic Red Guards numbering up to 1 million at a time. The first and most destructive phase of the Cultural Revolution came to an end in 1971. Red Guard brigades were then disbanded by the army to avoid total social collapse.

In the next phase, young people were sent to the countryside to learn from the peasants in a re-education campaign. Many young people sent to the countryside were not able to return to their homes until the early- to mid-1980s. The Cultural Revolution would come to an end with the death of Mao Zedong in September of 1976 and the fall of the Gang of Four in November of the same year.

Before Mao's death, two further significant events took place in the capital. The first of these was the spontaneous gathering in remembrance of the late Premier, Zhou Enlai, during the traditional Qingming Festival in early April 1976. Full of emotion and armed with wreaths, banners, poems and flowers, the crowds gathered to lay their tributes at the Martyrs' Memorial. On the day of Qingming, it is estimated that hundreds of thousands of people visited the monument to pay their respects and express their outward feelings. Among the mourners were those protesting the extreme political ideologies of the Gang of Four and others boldly calling for democratic reform. With the situation beyond the control of the government, Beijing's revolutionary committee declared the gatherings illegal and began ordering the people to disband and go home. While many responded, others refused to vacate the square. At 10:00pm that night, the People's Militia began to clear the square with force. The protests were declared counter-revolutionary by the Gang of Four and blamed on the recently reinstated Deng Xiaoping.

The Tangshan earthquake of July 28, 1976 also had a lasting impact on Beijing. While heavy damage in Beijing was limited, the city of Tangshan was virtually obliterated with an official death toll estimated of over 242,000 people. Many of those who had survived the earthquake in Tianjin

and northern Hebei were left homeless and destitute and flooded into Beijing for help. Rough and makeshift housing was quickly built across the city, often in the open courtyard areas of the city's traditional *siheyuan* houses and other vacant spaces changing the look of the city's old *hutong* areas.

BEIJING — CITY OF BEIJING (北京 — 1977-PRESENT)

Following the death of Chairman Mao and the resulting end of the Cultural Revolution, China was ready for change. With the rise of Deng Xiaoping at the end of 1978, China was

A bicycle in a Hutong.

ushered into an era of political and economic reform and opening up. These winds of change came as a welcome relief from the political extremes of the previous ten years. Beijing's economy witnessed renewed growth and free markets became popular across the city as private enterprises were endorsed. Standards of living improved as the economy began to soar and industry prospered. Nonetheless, many people still struggled to process their experiences during the Cultural Revolution.

With rapid development, tensions increased across the nation as inflation began to rise and corruption amongst opportunist officials became all too apparent. Demands for government transparency, greater economic and democratic reforms circulated amongst Beijing's university students. Students first gathered to voice their concerns in Tiananmen Square at the end of 1986. For some, this was the beginning of the road toward the 1989 Tiananmen Square incident.

Student protests at Tiananmen Square began in early April 1989 to mark the passing of the former communist party leader, Hu Yaobang. The gatherings gradually grew to become a mass demonstration against corruption and a call for democratic reform. Student demonstrators won the support of many ordinary people across Beijing. At its peak, more than one million of Beijing's citizens staged their own protests by marching through the city streets. On the night of June 3rd to early the next morning, a convoy of heavily-armed soldiers advanced across the city toward Tiananmen Square. As a result, students finally gave up the Square in the early hours of June 4th. Shortly after, chaos and fighting broke out around Tiananmen Square and beyond. The exact number of how many people were wounded or killed in this incident is unknown. The final word on the 1989 Tiananmen Square incident was given by the government who declared the student demonstrations as a counter-revolutionary uprising.

In the years after 1989, Beijing began to see the effects of China's continuing economic growth. Old areas of the city gradually disappeared to make way for modern office buildings, expansive housing complexes and stylish shopping malls, significantly changing the appearance of the city. Numerous historic *hutongs*

The Beijing Olympic Games 2008 countdown clock.

and traditional *siheyuan* courtyard houses were lost in the process. The city has also continued to expand outward with new housing complexes and industrial zones built well outside of the old city area. The Fourth, Fifth and Sixth Ring Roads were completed in recent years and new highways developed to connect the suburban areas of the municipality to the city. The building of new subway lines has again become a priority with three new lines opened within one year of the 2008 Olympic Games. Construction began in late 2007 for a further six subway lines, all of which are scheduled for completion by 2012.

Beijing was named host of the 2008 Olympic Games and Paralympic Games on July 13, 2001. As a result, the city entered a new phase of development and construction.

Endnotes

[1] Beijing Cultural Bureau http://www.bjww.gov.cn/tsbj/ (Translated by Authors) Accessed: 3 Sept. 2004.

[2] Piper Rae Gaubatz, *Beyond the Great Wall* (Stanford: Stanford University Press, 1996) 40.

[3] Gavin Menzies, *1421* (London: Bantam Books, 2003) 49.

[4] Jonathon Spence, *The Search for Modern China* (New York: Norton & Company, 1999, 2nd ed.) 7.

[5] Jonathon Spence, *The Gate of Heavenly Peace* (New York: Penguin Books, 1982) 30.

[6] M.A.Aldrich, *The Search for a Vanishing Beijing* (Hong Kong: Hong Kong University Press, 2006) 150.

[7] Jonathon Spence, *The Search for Modern China* (New York: Norton & Company, 1999, 2nd ed.) 421.

[8] M.A.Aldrich, *The Search for a Vanishing Beijing* (Hong Kong: Hong Kong University Press, 2006) 52.

TWO

Overview

Overview

GEOGRAPHY AND TOPOGRAPHY

Beijing, also referred to as 'Jing' (京), is located at 39° 56' north and 116° 20' east, at about the same latitude as the cities Rome, Madrid, and Philadelphia. Bordered by Tianjin Municipality to the east and Hebei Province to the north, west and south, Beijing Municipality occupies a total land area of 16,808 km². The municipality is positioned at the junction of the North China Plain, the Inner Mongolian Plateau and Shanxi Yellow Earth Plateau, with the city proper located on the North China Plain. The resulting topography of the area is diverse with mountains to the west, north and northeast and low-lying plains in the south and east. Mountainous areas occupy 62% of the total land area of the municipality.

Over 200 rivers from the Hebei Mountains flow through Beijing across the low-lying plains toward the Bohai Sea. Principal amongst these are the Yongding (永定河), Chaobai (潮白河), Juma (拒马河) and Gou (沟河) rivers, and the northern section of the Grand Canal (北运河). The Yongding River, also known as the 'Little Yellow River' because of its sand

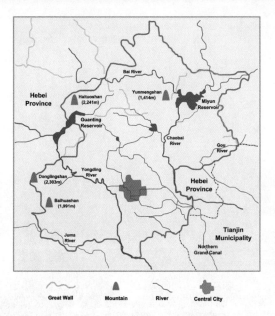

and silt content, is the longest river stretching 684 kilometres (425 miles). The northern section of the Grand Canal ends in Tongzhou District. Totally man-made, it now serves as an important wastewater channel for the city.

The surrounding mountains are divided into several distinct ranges. The Yanshan and Jundu Ranges form the northern mountainous areas, with the Taixing and Xishan Ranges to the west of the city. Separating the various ranges are the Guangou, Juyong and Gubei passes. The highest peak is Mt. Dongling (2,303 m/7,600 feet) on the Hebei/Beijing border.

Various natural and interest sites are located throughout the mountain areas, including gorges, grasslands, water reservoirs, forestry zones and multiple sections of the Great Wall.

Beijing's excellent geographical location led to its becoming a strategic military post historically. An ancient saying goes: "The area of Yan [Beijing] is strategically located. It has majestic topography, is well-positioned to control the regions around the Yangtze and Huaihe rivers to the south, and borders the desert in the north. Where better to build a military post?"

CITY LAYOUT

The layout of the city of Beijing features concentric ring roads encircling a core city area.

At the heart of the city lies Tiananmen Square with the Forbidden City to its north. The Second Ring Road is the actual first concentric ring road and follows the old Ming Dynasty city walls. The Third, Fourth and Fifth Ring Roads enclose the main city area, with a Sixth Ring Road near completion. Several highways fan out from the core city area, linking Beijing to major cities like Tianjin, Shenyang, Harbin, Shijaizhuang, Kaifeng and Chengde.

Some areas of the city are primary areas for commerce, industry, and education. For example, the main banking and finance area is found to the west of Tiananmen Square and at Xidan (西单) in Xicheng District; the main business district (CBD) is to the east of Jianguomen (建国门); the China World Trade Centre, government and foreign embassies are primarily located in Chaoyang District; the education and research facilities are mostly in the north-western area of Haidian District.

Beijing's traditional shopping areas include the pedestrian walking section of Wangfujing (王府井), Beijing's number one shopping street; Xidan (西单); and the newly reconstructed walking street of Qianmen (前门大街),

south of Tiananmen Square. Other tourist shopping areas include the markets at Xiushui Jie (秀水街市场), also known as Silk Alley; Hongqiao Market (红桥市场); Panjiayuan Market (潘家园市场); and Liulichang (琉璃厂).

Most of the city's main tourist sites can be found within the Second Ring Road. Major sites outside of the city area include the Summer Palace (颐和园); the Yuanmingyuan Palace Ruins (圆明园); the Western Hills (西山) and Fragrant Hills (香山); the Lugou Bridge (卢沟桥), known in the west as the Marco Polo Bridge; the Museum of the Chinese People's Anti-Japanese War; the Ming Tombs (十三陵), and multiple sections of the Great Wall.

The main Olympic Stadium and Village for the 2008 Olympics are located to the north of the 4th Ring Road, directly in line with the Forbidden City and Tiananmen Square. In ancient times, the meridian line was believed to have run through the Forbidden City, forming a central north to south axis through Beijing. With the Forbidden City at its centre, this imaginary line was an important feature in the layout of old Beijing. Capturing some of Beijing's traditional element, it is no doubt significant that

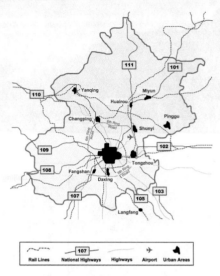

the Olympic facilities have been built on the northern part of this central axis.

Several suburban towns within Beijing Municipality exist outside of the main city area. These include Shunyi (顺义), Tongzhou (通州), Fangshan (房山), Daxing (大兴), Changping (昌平), Huairou (怀柔), Yanqing (延庆), Miyun (密云) and Pinggu (平谷).

The Beijing Capital International Airport, *the busiest in China,* is located to the northeast of the city. It is connected to the central city by expressways and a newly-built light-rail train. A secondary, domestic-only airport is situated south of the city at Nanyuan (南苑). Plans are being made for the construction of a

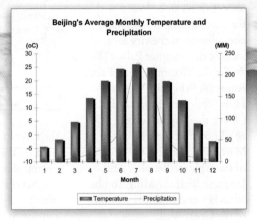

Beijing's Average Monthly Temperature and Precipitation

second international airport in 2010.

CLIMATE

Beijing, located in the North Temperate Zone, enjoys four distinct seasons with abundant sunshine. Summers are hot and humid, with more rainfall than the other seasons. The hottest month is July with temperatures reaching 38° C (100°F) and above. Winters are cold, sunny and dry with little snow. The coldest month is January, with an average temperature of -4.6°C

(23.7°F) and extreme lows of -15°C (5°F). Spring is dry and dusty, frequented by 'Yellow Winds' blanketing the city with fine sand, carried by strong winds from the Gobi Desert. Autumn is sunny and cool. Beijing has a frost-free period lasting as long as 180-200 days a year, and receives an average annual rainfall of 500mm-700mm (20-27 inches). 60% of this precipitation comes during July and August. In 2007, Beijing entered its ninth consecutive year of drought.

DEMOGRAPHICS

POPULATION: 17,140,000‡	
14ᵗʰ largest city in the world* and the second largest city in China	
Registered Population:	12,040,000‡ (2007)
Migrant worker population:	5,100,000‡ (2007)
Expected total population 2008:	17.5 million
Urban population:	83.62% 12.86 million (2005)
Rural population:	16.38% 2.52 million (2005)
Population density (urban districts)^:	22,210/km² (2005)
Number of households:	4,517,000 (2005)§
Average #/household:	2.18 persons (2005)§
Birth Rate:	6.29 % (2005)
Death Rate:	5.20 % (2005)
Natural Growth Rate:	1.09 % (2005)
Male/Female Ratio:	Male : 50.63% 7.787 million (2005) Female : 49.37% 7.593 million (2005)
Children (0 - 14):	10.2% 1.57 million (2005)
Adults (15 - 64):	79% 12.15 million (2005)
Elderly (≥65 years):	10.8% 1.66 million (2005)

	Life expectancy:	Male : 78.1 yrs (2003) Female : 81.4 yrs (2003)
	Registered Unemployment % (official):	1.4% (2003)
	Illiteracy rate:	4.9% 578,000 (2000)¥
	Pop. who have attained university qualifications:	16.8% (2000)
	% of young aged 18 - 22 who attend university:	40% (National high) (2003)
	Number of Children of Migrants in Beijing:	504,000 (2006)#
	Per Capita disposable income:	¥19,978 (US$2,528) (2006)
	Per Capita expenditure:	¥14,825 (US$1,877) (2006)
	Marriages:	170,000 couples (2006)
	Divorces:	20,000 couples (2006)
	% of Beijing's population on-line	> 30% (2006)

Total Population, Registered Population and Migrant Worker Population are based on PSB figures published August, 2007 (www.chinaview.cn 2007-08-21). All other population figures are based on 2005 data unless otherwise specified. The total population figure for 2005 was 15,380,000 with a registered population of 11,807,000.

*   United Nations Population report 2005 http://www.un.org/esa/population/unpop.htm
∧   Urban districts are listed as Xicheng, Dongcheng, Xuanwu and Chongwen districts
§   Number of households/average household size based on Registered Population
¥   Illiteracy rate is based on % of registered population 15 years of age and above at year 2000 census
Renmin University of China 2006 survey estimate

Sources: Beijing Municipal Public Security Bureau, Beijing Land and Resources Bureau, Beijing Municipal Statistics Bureau, Beijing Administration Office of Marriage, Renmin University of China

BEIJING MUNICIPAL GOVERNMENT

Beijing is the capital of the People's Republic of China and is one of four special municipalities having a status equal to that of a province. As capital of the nation, Beijing is the seat of national government, and is the place from which the Beijing Municipal Government also operates. Since 1949, Beijing's municipal leaders have had greater involvement in national politics than leaders from other localities across China.

Three distinct administrative bodies govern Beijing Municipality: the People's Congress made up of elected Communist Party deputies from each district and county in Beijing; the People's Government comprised of the Mayor and nine Vice-Mayors; and the Committee of the Chinese People's Political Consultative, an advisory body. Long-term planning and the day-to-day running of city affairs come under the jurisdiction of the Mayor. The Beijing People's Congress elects the Mayor and Party Secretary for terms of five years.

The Party Secretary of the Communist Party remains the highest position of power for the city and he holds a position in the Politbureau. Names and profiles of current Beijing Municipal Government mayors, vice-mayors, and some other officials can be found at the following Beijing government websites: http://www.ebeijing.gov.cn (English) or http://www.beijing.gov.cn (Chinese).

Corruption among government figures is an issue in the municipal and national government. As a result, the government has become vigilant in stamping out corruption through internal watchdogs and the implementation of harsh penalties for those involved in corrupt dealings.

Beijing has Sister City relationships with 31 cities such as Tokyo, New York, Berlin, Canberra and Wellington. (A complete listing of sister cities can be found in the appendix.)

Beijing is also home to 152 Foreign Embassies, 18 international organisations and 185 foreign news agencies.

CITY SYMBOLS

The flowers for Beijing are the Chinese Rose and the Chrysanthemum. The city trees are the Eastern Cedar and the Cypress.

FUTURE VISION AND LONG-TERM GOALS FOR BEIJING

In early 2004, the municipal government announced a blueprint to replace the current one-city-centre layout with a multi-polar plan to alleviate the city's current congestion and develop environmentally-friendly high-tech, industry and education zones. There are long-term goals for Beijing to become a world-class service centre (by 2020) and a historic and cultural city with sustainable development (by 2050).

BEIJING, SEAT OF NATIONAL GOVERNMENT

In addition to being the seat of the municipal government, as the capital of China, Beijing is also home to the President; the Premier of State; the Central Standing Committee of the Politbureau; the State Council; the National People's Congress; and central government ministries and commissions. There are 28 ministries and commissions centred in Beijing, including key ministries handling Foreign Affairs, Economic Policy, National Security, Defence, Health, Customs, Communications, Banking, Transportation, Agriculture, and Industry. Please note that the national government will not be further described here, as the intended focus is Beijing's Municipal Government.

DISTRICT AND COUNTY POPULATION STATISTICS (2005)[1]

District/ County Name	Total Population[2]	LandArea (km²)	Population density (per km²)	Number of households[3]	Non-registered population[4]
Urban districts	2,052,000	92.39	22,210	811,000	364,000
Dongcheng 东城区	549,000	25.34	21,665	219,000	102,000
Xicheng 西城区	660,000	31.62	20,873	262,000	118,000
Chongwen 崇文区	311,000	16.52	18,826	133,000	51,000

Xuanwu 宣武区	532,000	18.91	28,133	197,000	93,000
Near Suburbs	**7,480,000**	**1,275.93**	**23,503**	**1,773,000**	**2,092,000**
Chaoyang 朝阳区	2,802,000	455.08	6,157	655,000	840,000
Fengtai 丰台区	1,568,000	305.80	5,128	390,000	366,000
Shijingshan 石景山区	524,000	84.32	6,214	127,000	149,000
Haidian 海淀区	2,586,000	430.73	6,004	601,000	737,000
Outer Suburbs	**5,129,000**	**10,819.02**	**4,307**	**1,629,000**	**1,062,000**
Fangshan 房山区	870,000	1,989.54	437	312,000	119,000
Tongzhou 通州区	867,000	906.28	957	288,000	197,000
Shunyi 顺义区	711,000	1,019.89	697	238,000	156,000
Changping 昌平区	782,000	1,343.54	582	197,000	219,000
Daxing 大兴区	886,000	1,036.32	855	213,000	253,000
Mentougou 门头沟区	277,000	1,450.70	191	105,000	41,000
Huairou 怀柔区	322,000	2,122.62	152	120,000	53,000
Pinggu 平谷区	414,000	950.13	436	156,000	24,000
Counties	**719,000**	**4,223.2**	**337**	**304,000**	**55,000**
Miyun 密云县	439,000	2,229.45	197	182,000	35,000
Yanqing 延庆县	280,000	1,993.75	140	122,000	20,000

Administrative Districts Website Listing

• Dongcheng District	东城区	www.bjdch.gov.cn
• Xicheng District	西城区	www.bjxch.gov.cn
• Chongwen District	崇文区	www.cwi.gov.cn
• Xuanwu District	宣武区	www.bjxw.gov.cn
• Chaoyang District	朝阳区	www.bjchy.gov.cn
• Haidian District	海淀区	www.bjhd.gov.cn
• Fengtai District	丰台区	www.bjft.gov.cn
• Shijingshan District	石景山区	www.bjsjs.gov.cn
• Mentougou District	门头沟区	www.bjmtg.gov.cn
• Fangshan District	房山区	www.bjfsh.gov.cn
• Tongzhou District	通州区	www.bjtzh.gov.cn
• Shunyi District	顺义区	www.bjshy.gov.cn
• Daxing District	大兴区	www.bjdx.gov.cn
• Changping District	昌平区	www.bjchp.gov.cn
• Pinggu District	平谷区	www.bjpg.gov.cn
• Huairou District	怀柔区	www.bjhr.gov.cn
• Miyun County	密云县	www.bjmy.gov.cn
• Yanqing County	延庆县	www.bjyq.gov.cn

Sources: Beijing Municipal Public Security Bureau, Beijing Land and Resources Bureau, and Beijing Municipal Statistics Bureau.

1. Population estimates are based on the 2005 Beijing 1% Population Sample Check with a total population of 15,380,000.
2. Total population includes the registered population and estimated non-registered population.
3. Number of households is based on those households registered with the Public Security Bureau.
4. Refers to those who do not posses a Beijing residency pass (*hukou*). This primarily refers to the migrant population in the city.

ADMINISTRATIVE DISTRICTS MAP

BEIJING INNER CITY DISTRICTS MAP

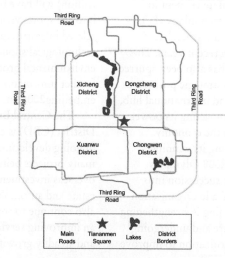

Wangfujing Street.

ECONOMICS

Beijing, the political, educational and cultural centre of China, has attracted domestic and international investment in the internet technology (IT), high-tech and science-based industries in recent years. This investment has also been spurred by Beijing's strategic position as a national and international hub, obviously impacting its power to influence the economy.

Following its winning bid for the 2008 Olympics and China's succession into the World Trade Organisation (WTO), Beijing is strengthening infrastructure and undergoing rapid modernization to improve transportation, communications, medical services and education. As of 2008, an expected total of 15 trillion Yuan (US$1.81 trillion) will have been poured into the sports venues, Olympic-related infrastructure projects, technological support and environmental protection. For further information see: http://en.beijing2008.cn.

The Central Business District (CBD) is experiencing ongoing development with many projects being funded by overseas investment. The real estate and automobile sectors also continue to soar alongside an improving service sector and steadily growing tourism market. All of these factors are bolstering the economy, making Beijing into a viable, attractive business centre.

Furthermore, industrial development zones in suburban districts and 'Satellite Towns' have strengthened the investment market in scientific, technological and intellectual resources through the 'Five High-Tech Industries': electronics and information, bioengineering and new pharmaceuticals, optical, mechanical and electrical engineering, new materials and environmental protection and multi-purpose utilization of resources. Beijing is also home to a state-owned Petrochemical Oil Refinery and the Shougang Steel Mill.

The Zhongguancun Science and Technology Park (ZSTP), dubbed as the 'Silicon Valley of China', and the Wangjing High Tech Park have attracted IT, electronics and pharmaceutical industries such as Lucent Technologies, Nortel, Microsoft, Samsung, Nokia, Sony and Lenovo.

Satellite towns, ecological belts, and development belts are functioning as bases for modern processing industries and logistics. Plans for local and overseas investment in infrastructure and service will increase productivity in these areas.

Economic growth has been at more than 11% for the past five years. In 2006, the gross domestic product (GDP) of Beijing reached 772.03 billion Yuan (US$96.5 billion), with the GDP per capita reaching US$6,210. By the end of 2005, fixed-asset investment was valued at 282.72 billion Yuan (US$35.34 billion).

Tourism is an important part of the Beijing economy. 2005 saw more than 12.48 million domestic tourists spending a total of 130 billion Yuan (US$16.25 billion), and 3.9 million foreign visitors spent a total of US$3.62 billion.

Beijing is home to the headquarters of the People's Bank of China, the Bank of China and all of China's major

Signs along Wangfujing Street.

financial institutions and insurance companies, located mostly on 'Finance Street', the area comprising Chang'an Jie (长安街) west of Xidan and the 2nd Ring Road West (西二环).

Agriculturally, Beijing produces and distributes wheat, maize, sorghum, bean and millet as staple crops. Locally grown fruits include apples, pears, peaches, grapes, apricots, watermelons, persimmons and nuts.

Rapid development has had some negative impact, resulting in several factors limiting the growth of the economy: a shortage of water, pollution and traffic congestion. An ambitious scheme to divert water from the Yangtze River in the south to the north of China aims to benefit Beijing's agriculture, industries and drinking water supplies. Government spending to clean up waterways, create green areas and improve air quality for the creation of a more desirable living environment in the city has increased significantly in recent years.

Full economic data from the Beijing Municipal Bureau of Statistics can be viewed at the following website: http://www.bjstats.gov.cn/esite. (Source for economic data: Beijing Bureau of Statistics Beijing Statistical Yearbook, 2006.)

BEIJING PEOPLE AND LANGUAGE
Beijing People

Beijing people are often characterised as being open, hospitable, confident, frank, proud, conservative, practical, and humorous. Most display an interest in political events and show some reluctance toward any change that challenges the social order or their own positions of authority. While outwardly friendly, they are at times also perceived as looking down on people from outside of Beijing. These traits are described as characteristic of the Beijing ethos known as 'Jing Pai' (京派), which has been influenced by the city's role as a political centre and home of the imperial court, aristocrats and scholars. 'Jing Pai' also reflects the Confucian ideals of social order and places value on moral correctness, tradition, personal cultivation, family and relationships. A dedication to hard work, personal diligence and attaining high personal qualifications is also held as the basis of success. *Guanxi* 关系 (personal connections) and *renqing* 人情 (mutual obligations) are cultural and personal values that have a strong influence in Beijing.

Young people are generally ambitious, independent and keen to travel abroad. They are willing to spend money, and time, on the latest technologies; and are attracted by the latest fashions and trends.

As Beijing strives to become a modern metropolis, the old social order and people's values are being challenged. Money has become a driving force and a new measure of success. Many people aim to have a good career, buy a modern apartment, own a car, have the latest mobile phone or other high-tech gadgets, enjoy a leisurely lifestyle, and have the means to travel. While rapid modernization of society calls for a reconsideration of many traditions, many of the overarching values that are unique to the people of Beijing remain firmly rooted in place as pillars of their culture.

Language

Mandarin is widely spoken in Beijing. Beijing dialect, or *Beijinghua* (北京话), while closely related to Mandarin, has a very distinct 'r' inflection; its unique phrasing and words stem from both Mongol and, more prominently, Manchu influences. People from rural counties have a distinct accent similar to the neighbouring Hebei Province. The large mix of people that make up Beijing's current population means a variety of dialects, accents and minority languages can be heard.

ARTS ASSOCIATED WITH BEIJING

Handicrafts

Beijing's finely crafted pieces of art were developed historically to meet the imperial court's demands. Of the many types of handicrafts found in the city, four are listed as the 'Four Famous Arts of Beijing': cloisonné, lacquer ware, jade carving and ivory carving. In addition, kite making, dough figurine making, 'monkey toys', sugar figurines, paper cutting, fan making, painted snuff bottles, palace lanterns, embroidery, carpets and various woodcrafts are recognised as art forms. While many of these are also found in other regions of China, those here have a style unique to Beijing.

Traditional Performing Arts

Peking Opera is the most well-known of the traditional performing arts. The opera which incorporates traditional singing, music, drama, acrobatics and at times martial arts has been popular with both the general populace and imperial families in the past. Peking Opera, with its styles of face painting, colourful costumes and unique style of singing, is one of several hundred genres of opera throughout China. Its origins lie in the merging of a number of different genres of local opera from Anhui and Hubei provinces over 200 years ago. Many operas depict folk stories and traditional legends, both fictionally and historically based. Traditionally, female actors were not permitted on the stage, so men played female roles known as *dan*. Performer Mei Lanfang (梅兰芳, 1894-1961) was well-known for his exquisite *dan* performances and also for introducing Peking Opera to the international scene in the early 20th century.

The most famous theatres where performances are held are the Zhengyici Theatre (正乙祠戏楼) (1667); the Guangdelou Theatre (广德楼戏园) (1796); and the Huguang Guild Hall Theatre (湖广会馆) (1830), which also has a museum. Performances can also be enjoyed at the Chang'an Theatre (长安剧院) and the Liyuan Theatre (梨园剧场). Peking Opera enthusiasts practise their singing skills in the city parks most days of the week.

Yangge Opera, a lesser known local opera of about 700 years old, is on the verge of extinction with only 50 surviving pieces. The opera was extremely popular historically and even performed at the Forbidden City on special occasions. Only a handful of elderly men at Baiyu Village in Mentougou District can still perform the opera. Three Yangge pieces, telling the history of old Beijing, take both day and night to complete.

Chinese Acrobatics remain one of the most popular traditional art forms found in

Beijing today. Skilled acrobats, many times only children, perform stunning and seemingly impossible feats on stage. Beijing has a long history of acrobatics and has been dubbed the birthplace of modern acrobatics performance in China. Acrobatics can be viewed in a number of places across the city including the popular Chaoyang Theatre (朝阳剧场) and Tiandi Theatre (天地剧场).

Modern Performing Arts

Beijing attracts a large number of contemporary international and domestic performances including symphony orchestras; ballet; dramas; stage shows; cultural dance and music groups; world-renowned magicians; rock bands; etc.

Literature

Numerous writers and poets have made their homes in Beijing and penned their works here over the centuries. China's most celebrated novel, the *Dream of Red Mansions* (红楼梦), also known as *The Story*

National Theatre.

of the Stone, was written by Cao Xueqin (曹雪芹) in Beijing. First published in 1791, this novel is regarded as the greatest masterpiece of traditional Chinese fiction.

Many famous writers including Lu Xun (鲁迅), Guo Moruo (郭沫若) and Maodun (茅盾) lived in Beijing and portrayed aspects of life and society of old Beijing in their works. The 20th century playwright, Lao She (老舍), is also best remembered for his satirical plays, of which *Teahouse* (茶馆) won worldwide acclaim. Several writers' former residences are preserved as museums displaying their works and other personal effects: Lu Xun Museum (鲁迅博物馆, 阜成门内宫门口); Guo Moruo Former Residence (郭沫若故居, 西城区, 前海西大街18号); Mao Dun Former Residence (茅盾故居, 东城区, 后圆恩寺13号); and Lao She Former Residence (老舍故居, 灯市口西街富强胡同).

The China Modern Literature Hall (中国现代文学馆, 朝阳区, 文学馆路45号) showcases the development of literature in modern China starting from the May 4th and New Culture Movements. Houhai (后海), Liulichang (琉璃厂) and Taoranting Park (陶然亭公园) are three other historic areas known as important places for literature, poetry and calligraphy in Beijing.

Art Museums

Numerous art galleries found throughout Beijing exhibit various styles of traditional and contemporary arts. The National Art Museum of China hosts both local and international exhibitions. The well-known Beijing Arts Institute has produced many artists in a number of fields. The pioneer of contemporary Chinese painters, Xu Beihong (徐悲鸿), has some of his most famous works displayed in the museum named after him. A short directory of the largest art museums can be found in the appendix.

Art Museums and Arts Villages

Recent years have seen a number of arts villages spring up in and around Beijing. Needing large yet affordable space to work, these arts villages have formed in rural areas and abandoned factory buildings in the suburban districts and counties of Beijing. The most well-known of these is found in the Dashanzi 798 Arts District.

Formerly derelict warehouses and factory buildings have been transformed into chic studios, exhibition spaces and apartments, giving it a 'sohoesque' type atmosphere. A listing of the most commonly known arts villages can be found in the appendix.

Arts Festivals in Beijing

Every year arts festivals attracting local and foreign artists and performers are held. A range of performances and styles of music are included in these festivals including ethnic music and dance, orchestral, drama, ballet, acrobatics, operas, jazz and rock. Some of the arts festivals focus exclusively on exhibiting the fine arts which include painting, sculpture, photography, etc. The main cultural and arts festivals held in Beijing annually include the following: the Beijing Dashanzi International Arts Festival (Spring); the Midi Rock Festival (April); the Meet in Beijing Arts Festival (May); the Chaoyang International Pop Music Festival (May); the Beijing 2008 Olympic Cultural Festival (July); the Green Beijing Rock Festival (August); the Beijing International Cultural Tourism Festival (Autumn); the Minority Arts Festival (September); and Art Beijing (October).

CULTURAL DEVELOPMENT

As a result of Beijing's rich cultural heritage, the city has been known as the 'cradle of the masters of all arts' in China. These arts, folk customs and culture are the result of a diverse mix of cultural influences. Various northern minority groups and tribes have added to the cultural development of the city: the Khitan (Liao Dynasty); Nüzhen (Jin Dynasty); Mongols (Yuan Dynasty); and the Manchu (Qing Dynasty). The early Ming Dynasty also brought strong cultural influences from the Jianghuai region of Eastern China with a large number of artisans and officials moving northward during the court's move from its former capital at Nanjing. The resulting mix of cultures within Beijing's communities resulted in a unique blend of folk customs. Some of these folk customs have spread to other regions of China and become an integrated part of what is generally described as 'Chinese culture'. Over time, some folk customs have lost their prominence and have all but been totally relegated to

Chinese New Year Temple Fairs or other cultural festivals. Over 300 folk arts and crafts were found in the city up to the mid-1960s, with only 30 remaining by the end of the 20th century. An excellent display of old Beijing folk customs can be seen at the Capital Museum (首都博物馆).

Hutongs (胡同), which are traditional alleyways and *siheyuan* (四合院), or courtyard houses, are important cultural features of old Beijing. With the earliest layout of *hutongs* dating back to Kublai Khan's capital in the Yuan Dynasty, they have been an important part in the development of Beijing's culture and customs. During the Ming and Qing Dynasties, the city was also divided into northern and southern areas known as the inner and outer cities respectively. The two distinct areas of the city no doubt saw the development of different types of folk arts, performing arts, cuisines and customs. Today's Qianmen and Tianqiao (天桥), formerly in the Outer City, were well-known centres for a host of arts, crafts, tea houses, guild halls and local foods.

Temple fairs; elaborate celebrations at traditional Chinese festivals; street vendors and markets; street performers; and lively processions for weddings and funerals were all important parts of old Beijing life. Temple fairs marked significant events on the traditional lunar calendar. Originating in the Liao Dynasty, these fairs were an important part of old Beijing's social and cultural scene attracting craftsmen and performers from across the nation. Five major temple fairs stood out from the many held during the year. These were those held at the God of Earth Temple, Huashi, the White Pagoda Temple, the Huguo Temple, and the Longfu Temple. Today, temple fairs are an important part of the Chinese New Year celebrations in the city and keep alive many traditional art forms. The most

Man selling sweet potatoes.

well-known of these is held at the Altar of Earth, called Ditan (地坛).

Chinese New Year (春节) remains the most colourful and spectacular of the traditional festivals still celebrated in Beijing. Red couplets are pasted on doorways, houses are cleaned, children receive red packets, families partake in traditional banquets and welcome in the New Year with fireworks. The Lantern Festival (元宵节), Qingming Festival (清明节), Dragon Boat Festival (端午节) and Mid-Autumn Festival (中秋节) are also celebrated.

Lanterns as festive decorations.

The Tianqiao Triangle Market (天桥三角市场), located in Xuanwu District, was an important area for street theatre and folk arts in the late part of the Qing Dynasty. As the centre of the southern 'Outer City' during the Ming and Qing Dynasties, the area became well-known as a cradle of folk arts, producing top performers and

troupes in a number of areas. These included two-man comic acts, cross-talk, acrobatics, Peking Opera, puppet plays, performing monkeys, martial arts, traditional operas, comedy, contortionists and balancing acts. Today, Tianqiao remains as an area known for its cultural arts in Beijing, and a taste of old Tianqiao can be experienced at the Tianqiaole Teahouse (天桥乐茶园, 宣武区, 天桥市场, 北纬路113号. Tel: 63040617; Open 9:00 to 21:00; performances at 19:30 to 21:00).

As in many other parts of China, tea houses and guild halls have been centers for arts and cultural development. Of the few existing traditional teahouses, the Laoshe Teahouse has become one of the most famous as an entertainment venue for both locals and foreigners. For more about the Laoshe Teahouse, visit the following website: http://www.laosheteahouse.com.

BEIJING CUISINE

Beijing cuisine has been subjected to a wide range of outside influences. Shandong entrepreneurs are said to have dominated the restaurant scene in Beijing during the 19th century. Other influences include Mongolian Hotpot (lamb); barbecued meat

Lady selling corn.

(Manchu); Islamic Halal cooking; and the cuisine styles from Zhejiang, Jiangsu, and particularly Shandong. People tend to prefer salty flavoured food and many dishes contain leeks, garlic and spring onions. Dumplings, steamed breads and pancakes are local staples.

With a history of over 600 years, the most famous local specialty of Beijing is Peking Duck (北京烤鸭). Thin slices of meat, usually with the skin and fat intact, are rolled in a thin pancake with spring onions or leeks, and plum sauce. The two most famous Peking Duck specialty restaurants in Beijing are Quanjude (全聚德) (www.quanjude.com.cn) and Bianyifang (便宜坊) (www.bianyifang.com).

Imperial Cuisine, or Court Cuisine, has its origins in the Qing Dynasty imperial palace kitchens. Meticulously prepared and often using rare or expensive ingredients, the style was reserved for the emperor

and his family. A small number of restaurants today serve imperial cuisine to the public including Fangshan Restaurant in Beihai Park and the Ting Li Guan Pavilion for Listening to Oracles in the Summer Palace.

More than 250 different kinds of traditional local snacks can be found at small vendors in residential areas, hutongs, the well-known Donghuamen Night Market (东华门夜市), and at more famous restaurants such as Duyichu (都一处), Nanlaishun (南来顺) or Beijing 9 Traditional Snack Restaurant in North Houhai. The area around Qianmen (前门) and the hutongs off Dashilar have also traditionally been famous for sampling a range of local snacks. Some of the most well-known snacks include: *zhimaqiu* (芝麻球 sesame balls); *wandouhuang* (豌豆黄 bean flour cakes); *douzhi* (豆汁 mung bean milk); *ludangun* (芦荡滚 pastries made

Food on a stick.

of glutinous millet flour and sugar); *chatang* (茶汤 millet or sorghum flour custard); *aiwowo* (艾窝窝 steamed cone-shaped sticky rice balls); *jiaoquan* (焦圈儿 crispy fried dough ring); *babaofan* (八宝饭 eight-treasure rice); Beijing *chaogan* (北京炒肝 fried liver); and *guanchang* (灌肠 sausage). Various kinds of local *jianbing* (煎饼 fried pancakes); pea flour cakes; small corn buns; walnut cakes; peanut candy; Beijing honeycomb; and candied hawthorn fruit (糖葫芦) are also common treats in the city. Other snacks, not regarded as local to Beijing, include roasted sweet potato; roasted chestnuts; *youtiao* (油条 fried dough sticks); various kinds of *mantou* (馒头 steamed bread); *jiaozi* (饺子 dumplings); and *yangrou chuan* (羊肉串 lamb skewers).

Muslim boy.

MINORITIES

Beijing has historically been home to a mixture of different peoples and cultures. Early influences from peoples other than the predominant Han Chinese include the Khitan (Liao Dynasty); the Nüzhen (Jin Dynasty); Mongols (Yuan Dynasty); and the Manchu (Qing Dynasty). Each of these groups established the city as their capital and influenced the development of the city.

Today, Beijing has an ethnic population of approximately 586,000 (2000 Census). This accounts for 4% of the total population. All of the 56 officially recognised ethnic groups in China are represented in Beijing. According to official statistics, the largest minority groups resident in the city are the Manchu (250,286); Hui (235,837); Mongol (37,464); Korean (20,369); Tujia (8,372); Zhuang (7,322); Miao (5,291); Uyghur (3,129); Tibetan (2,920); Yi (2,000); Dong (2,000); and the Bai (2,000). Actual figures for some of these groups may be larger due to their unregistered status. While Manchu people are officially the largest minority group present, they have become largely assimilated with the predominant Han Chinese.

70% of minorities live in, or in close proximity to, the inner city districts. Xuanwu District has traditionally had the largest grouping of Hui Muslims in Beijing, centred around the Niu

Jie Mosque in a predominately Muslim community.

SOCIAL ISSUES
Migrant Workers

Migrants building wall.

Beijing has a large 'floating population' mainly made up of unregistered migrant workers coming from rural areas to look for work. Currently totalling over 5.1 million people in Beijing, migrants make up almost 30% of the city's overall population. This influx has obviously placed excess pressure on Beijing's infrastructure and resources such as housing, jobs, transportation, water and electricity.

The majority find jobs as maids, restaurant staff, basic maintenance workers and street cleaners; or on construction sites; or doing other 'high-risk/low-pay' jobs. Over 75% of migrants are aged between 15-39 years, and 61% of the total is male. Most migrant labourers typically receive 800 *yuan* or

less per month and live in small, and often substandard housing. Large communities of migrants can be found in many of the city's outskirts, living in poor housing areas. In addition to housing issues, migrants struggle to find adequate, affordable healthcare and vaccinations, increasing their risk for disease. AIDS is of particular concern in migrant communities.

Childcare and the education of migrant children is another challenge. Over 240,000 of these children reside in Beijing (2004). In 2003, the government directed all schools to take in children of migrant parents and lessen the fees. About 70% of migrant children attend schools. However, some workers find the cost of public school fees too high and send their children to migrant schools (often substandard and unregistered), or they simply forgo formal education altogether. Up until 2005, there were an estimated 299 migrant schools in Beijing.

Migrants at station.

Early 2006 saw the launch of the Coalition for Migrant Children (CMC) in Beijing. Their vision is to significantly improve the quality of life for migrant children through social and educational programs. For more information: www.cmc-china. org or contact them directly through the following e-mail address: info@cmc-china.org.

Many migrants are treated poorly and are taken advantage of. Some have faced the problem of having their wages withheld or unpaid. The city government has helped to recover unpaid wages. Employers of migrants have been asked to provide pensions, unemployment insurance, and industrial injury. Some websites have been launched to help migrants understand their rights, although many do not have access to the internet.

In 2000, the Municipal Public Security Bureau (PSB) made claims that migrants committed 60 - 65% of crimes in the city. Migrants who cannot find work in the city have sometimes had to resort to theft in order to survive or get enough money to return to the countryside.

Aging Society
Because of the decline in the birth rate and the availability

of better health care, Beijing's elderly population is increasing. In 2005, the elderly population was 1.66 million (10.8% of the total population). An increasing number are left to live alone by their adult children. With this trend, specialised health care, elderly assistance programs and quality old age nursing and retirement homes need to be developed.

Elderly women.

One-Child Policy
The implementation of the one-child policy has been successful in lowering the population

growth rate. Most children in Beijing under age 20 are without siblings. Parents and grandparents spoil many of these children, leading to the title 'little emperors'. A growing number of young couples prefer to remain childless, claiming that raising a child is too expensive in Beijing.

Family Issues

The rate of divorce in Beijing is increasing. In 2006, there were approximately 20,000 divorces. Domestic violence is also prevalent and on the rise. Few services are available for family counselling or support for victims of domestic violence. Pre-marital sex and non-married couples living together are becoming widely accepted in Beijing. Most people still disapprove of homosexuality.

Unemployment

The municipal government faces pressure to create new jobs and keep the unemployment

rate low. The restructuring of certain industries to make them competitive in newly opened markets has meant large job losses in recent years. The number of migrant workers looking for work has also put pressure on the job market.

Youth Depression

23.66% of university undergraduate students in Beijing suffered from depression in 2006. Academic and family pressures are compounded by their concerns about finding work. In response to this issue, the government has launched a

program known as Sunshine in Your Heart (心灵阳光工程) in conjunction with the Red Cross Society of China. The program has been designed to provide lectures, camps and resources to help students cope with the pressures they face and find hope. For more information, visit the following website: http://www.nphe.org/english/gcjs.htm.

HIV/AIDS

While the number of reported cases of HIV/AIDS is still relatively small, growth in the number of new cases being reported each year is raising concern among health authorities. By the end of 2006, there were 3,462 reported HIV/AIDS cases in Beijing. Actual numbers are estimated to exceed 12,000. Migrant workers and university students are seen as two potentially vulnerable groups. Of the 633 new reported cases in Beijing during 2006, 77% (491) were migrant workers. Public HIV/AIDS prevention education programs have been initiated to raise people's understanding about the risks of unprotected sex and needle-sharing. In July 2004, HIV treatment drugs began to be covered by local government health insurance for Beijing residents.

Drug Abuse

Drug abuse and trafficking is becoming increasingly common in Beijing. The illegal distribution of party drugs such as 'ecstasy' and 'P' has become a problem in nightclubs and bars. The Municipal Anti-Drug Committee states that drug trafficking has expanded to rural areas and spread over all walks of life. The government is tackling the overall drug problem by targeting drug traffickers.

INFRASTRUCTURE AND URBAN PLANNING

A rapid increase in the city's population coupled with swift economic growth has placed great pressure on the transport infrastructure. With rising incomes, more people in Beijing can afford cars. By the middle of

2007, there were already three million vehicles in Beijing with another 30,000 being added to the roads each month. As a result, traffic congestion and resulting delays are a major problem in Beijing. Expansions of subway and light-rail lines are expected to alleviate the traffic problems.

An over-concentration of key government offices, commercial districts, and public institutions in the inner districts draws a large working population to central Beijing. Areas around Tiananmen Square, Qianmen and Dazhalan have a high population density with over 60,000 people per km². This overcrowding issue has forced the government to take action by relocating residents and industry bases. However, in the attempt to alleviate the inner city overcrowding, historic housing districts, *hutongs* (alleyways) and *siheyuan* (courtyard houses) are being demolished, raising concerns about the protection of historic and cultural sites.

The new housing areas in the suburbs and satellite towns around Beijing lack commercial and industrial enterprises necessary for employment. Therefore, some of the residential areas have been labelled 'sleeping cities',

or 'bedroom communities', due to the fact that large numbers of people commute into the city centre for work each day, and only 'sleep' in the suburbs. The unequal development of different city districts has been a long-standing problem. An old saying in Beijing goes: "The east gathers the rich, whilst the west the powerful; in the south, the poor; and in the north, the humble". The ongoing construction of multiple urban centres, ecological belts, and development belts are expected to alleviate the current problems and ensure future sustainable development.

注意 Note:

Beijing has fourteen satellite towns. These include: Tongzhou (通州), Yizhuang (亦庄), Huangcun (黄村), Liangxiang (良乡), Fangshan (方山), Changxindian (长辛店),

Menchengzhen (门城镇), Shahe (沙河), Changping (昌平), Yanqing (延庆), Huairou (怀柔), Miyun (密云), Pinggu (平谷) and Shunyi (顺义). Efforts are being made to develop industry in these satellite towns to provide jobs and alleviate overcrowding in central Beijing.

ENVIRONMENTAL ISSUES
Water Shortages
Eighty-five reservoirs serve the city's needs but successive years of drought have resulted in an acute water shortage. The city's per capita annual water supply has dropped to less than 300 cubic metres (only ⅛ of the national average). This places it well short of the globally acknowledged water shortage benchmark of 1,000 cubic metres per capita. Water conservation and water diversion projects are expected to help meet some of the shortages. However, the gap between Beijing's water demand and supply is likely to remain a problem with the increased population and industrial demands. Two-thirds of the city's surface water supply comes from the Miyun (密云水库) and Guanting (官厅水库) Reservoirs. Pollution from upstream cities and industry has, however, meant that Guanting Reservoir may not supply drinking water.

Pollution
Beijing has a severe pollution problem stemming from coal burning, industrial pollution, vehicle emissions and dust clouds from construction sites. Up to 80% of the rainfall in Beijing during 2006 was classified as acid rain. The city is surrounded on three sides by mountains making it difficult for accumulated air pollution to dissipate. Harsh weather days, made up of smog or dust storms, account for almost 30% of the year.

Most wastewater is treated. Several rivers and canals around the city have undergone clean up projects and major water polluting industries have been closed down. Water pollution is not nearly as big a problem as it once was in Beijing.

Beijing continues to face a growing problem with desertification. As the climate has become drier and water supplies in the region have decreased, desert areas are encroaching on some outer areas of the municipality. Dust and sand storms are a major source of irritation. Sand from surrounding deserts is picked by strong winds and blown into the city affecting air quality.

To combat pollution, heavy polluting industries including the Shougang Steel Mill, Beijing's number one industrial polluter, have been removed from the city. Green areas are being built, as well as low emission natural gas heating plants for winter heating.

HEALTH

Beijing boasts some of the best healthcare and medical research facilities in the country. As of 2005, there were 692 hospitals and healthcare centres in Beijing municipality at the county level and above. Disease prevention and treatment remain as the two main objectives of the Municipal Health Bureau. To achieve these goals, medical research facilities have invested in new AIDS labs, infectious disease reporting clinics, and emergency treatment stations. The SARS scare of 2003 has resulted in greater transparency in the reporting and controlling of infectious disease outbreaks.

Community health services in local communities were established in 2007 with 10,000 home medical service workers active throughout the city. These services mean that patients are able to seek medical help from a local community health team instead going to a hospital.

In Beijing, the average life expectancy is 80.07 years (2006) — 78.1 years for men, and 81.14 years for women. Up to 80% of Beijing residents die of chronic diseases related to smoking, excessive alcohol consumption, poor diet and obesity.

Today, the increase in the number of HIV/AIDS patients is a major concern. Another issue of concern is the lack of clean drinking water due to old pipes throughout the city. Safe drinking water projects have been initiated by the municipal authorities.

Fitness clubs and gyms have become increasingly popular in Beijing as incomes have risen. These are in addition to the informal morning exercise groups found throughout the city's parks and open areas within housing complexes. As of 2003, there were more than 3,800 registered exercise groups with more than 1.3 million people in attendance each morning.

EDUCATION

Beijing, with its 82 universities and 115 research institutes, is a very important centre of education for China, especially in the areas of technical and practical skills. As a result, Beijing has the strongest technical capability in China in terms of the number of technical personnel, engineers, and scientists engaged in research and development. Sixty-eight universities and tertiary colleges are located in Haidian District.

Children begin school at the age of six, and there are nine years of compulsory education. A growing number of private primary and secondary schools attract many parents, who desire the highest quality education for their children. As a result, Beijing residents spend a large percentage of their household savings on education. Much pressure is therefore placed on children to perform and secure entry into university.

Sixty-nine of Beijing's universities and tertiary institutes accept foreign students. There were a total of 26,309 foreign students enrolled in the city's universities in 2005.

Beijing also has 23 special education schools — 17 for mentally challenged, five for hearing impaired and one for the blind.

Students and intellectuals in Beijing have made significant contribution to modern history and social movements in China, acting as a 'prophetic voice' calling for reform.

The Beijing Municipal Commission of Education is located at 109 West Qianmen Dajie, Beijing 100031. For further information, see: http://english.bjedu.gov.cn

MEDIA

Major Chinese language newspapers published in Beijing include: *People's Daily* 人民日报 (www.people.com.cn); *Beijing Evening News* 京报 (www.ben.com.cn); *Beijing News* 新京报 (www.thebeijingnews.com);

Beijing Star Daily 北京娱乐信报 (www.stardaily.com.cn); *Beijing Youth Daily* 北京青年报 (www.bjyouth.com.cn); and *Beijing Morning Post* 北京早报.

English language papers include: *China Daily*, *Beijing Weekend* and *Beijing Today*. Several English and Japanese magazines for tourists and resident foreigners are published on a monthly basis. These include: *City Weekend*, *Beijing This Month*, *Beijing Talk*, *That's Beijing*, *Metrozine*, and *Beijing Walker* ウエネバー北京版 (Japanese). Other language publications include the *Beijing Review* (published in English, French, German and Japanese).

Beijing Television (BTV) currently has ten channels, BTV 1-10. China Central Television (CCTV) broadcasts numerous channels including CCTV 1-12, Kids, News, Music, French and Spanish. CCTV 9 is the only English language channel broadcast by either BTV or CCTV. Many complexes and areas of the city now have Digital Cable TV. Foreign channels, including CNN, HBO, ESPN, Star Movies, and Star Sports can be received in some housing complexes in Beijing via satellite or cable.

There are approximately 20 radio stations in Beijing. Three have programs in English. These include: *Hit FM* (FM88.7), *Easy FM* (China Radio International FM81.5) and *Radio 774* (AM774).

RELIGION

The religions of Buddhism, Daoism (or Taoism), and Islam have been influential in the historical and cultural development of Beijing. In addition to these religious influences, traditional Chinese beliefs such as *Fengshui* (geomancy), ancestor worship, and superstitious beliefs in evil spirits, guardians and deities were all prevalent in the past, and are still influential today. The city's north-south layout is believed to be in accordance with *fengshui* principles to ensure protection from evil spirits. Historically, and presently, the Chinese lunar calendar,

A Chinese door guardian.

based on the movement of the stars and planets, determined auspicious times for getting married, having children, and many other important affairs of family and state. Currently, many hold beliefs made up of aspects from both Daoism and Buddhism, coupled with Confucian philosophies and animist superstitions.

Religious influence has lessened since the founding of the People's Republic of China in 1949. During the Cultural Revolution, all religious beliefs were denounced and a number of temples and religious sites were destroyed by over-zealous Red Guards.

Today, most people in Beijing claim to hold no religious belief. Secularism and materialism are more prevalent throughout society. Many young people state a belief in themselves, or in a quest for enjoying life. However, some have a curiosity, even a hunger, toward spirituality. Many people continue to burn incense or offer money when visiting a temple or other historic religious site hoping they will be blessed with good luck. In trying to cope with a competitive modern society, many young people are looking for values and meaning.

Since 1978, the Chinese government has recognised

Chinese "Fu" charms.

Buddhism, Daoism, Islam, Protestant Christianity and Catholicism as official religions.

Buddhism
Buddhism has perhaps had the greatest influence in the city. It first appeared in the region during the Western Jin Dynasty, and continued to thrive with many of the existent temples in Beijing being built during the Yuan and Ming periods. The Qing Dynasty emperors held strong Buddhist beliefs. The Emperor Qianlong restored a number of monasteries and built temples in the Summer Palace and other imperial gardens. By the end of the Qing Dynasty (1911), there were over 500 Buddhist temples in Beijing.

First built over 1600 years ago, Tanzhe Temple is the oldest temple. Today several temples are national and regional centres for Buddhism: Guangji

ESTIMATES OF RELIGIOUS AFFILIATION IN BEIJING		
Non-believing or Atheist:	92.8%	(13,500,000)
Buddhist:	3.4%	(≤ 500,000)
Muslim:	1.7%	(250,000)
Chinese Religions:	1%	(150,000)
Christian (protestant):	0.9%	(120,000)
Catholic:	0.2%	(40,000)

A statue of the Buddha.

Temple is headquarters of the China Buddhist Association, Fayuan Temple serves as China's Buddhist College, and Guanghua Temple is the headquarters for the Beijing Buddhist Association.

Yonghegong (Lama Temple) and the Yellow Temple, home of the Tibetan Buddhist College, are two important centres of Tibetan Buddhism.

According to the Chinese Academy of Social Sciences, Buddhism is experiencing growth with many young people and professionals being attracted to the religion. A number of Buddhist websites have been set up, and it has a growing influence through art exhibitions and international cultural performances which depict Bodhisattvas and other Buddhist images as representative of Chinese culture.

Daoism

During the Tang Dynasty, Bai Yun Temple was built for the Quanzhen and Longmen sects of Daoism. It prospered as a key centre of Daoism for the north

A Daoist temple.

of China until being destroyed by fire in 1202. In 1224, during the Yuan Dynasty, the Mongol Emperor Genghis Khan, invited the priest Qiu Changchun to rebuild the temple. Located west of the Forbidden City, it became the centre for Daoism in China, a place where China's rulers could seek divination and insight for the nation. Today, it is headquarters for the China Daoist Association and one of the most important temples for Daoists in China.

Islam

A Hui vendor.

Islam spread to Beijing during the 10th century. The Niujie Mosque, also known as Niujie Libai Si, built during the Liao Dynasty in 996, is Beijing's largest and oldest mosque. Several mosques were built during the Yuan Dynasty because many Muslims entered the city during that time. Islam developed quickly during the Qing Dynasty with more than 30 mosques built between 1644 and 1829.

The majority of Muslims in Beijing are Hui, with a smaller number being Uygur or from other groups. There are 68 active mosques in the city. Muslims celebrate their own festivals and have their own customs. There are a number of Hui kindergartens, schools, shops, restaurants and abattoirs. The headquarters of the Beijing Islamic Association is located at Dongsi Mosque, with the China Islamic Association Headquarters located at 103 Nanheng Xijie, Xuanwu District (宣武区, 南横西街103号).

Christianity

Approximately 1% of the population is estimated to be Christians based on the church survey conducted by the Religious Affairs Bureau (RAB) in 2003. (Note: Comprehensive statistics on the Church in Beijing are not available.) About 30,000 are members of the officially-sanctioned Three-Self Churches, while about 90,000 attend unregistered house churches, although a number of believers attend *both* registered Three-Self Churches *and* unregistered house churches.

The abovementioned RAB Report indicated that there are at least 3,000 house church fellowships in Beijing. Most are described as small fellowships with an average of 20-30 members. There is only a limited amount of networking and cooperation seen among house churches in Beijing, due to both internal and external factors relating to security, as well as competition with other groups.

The Three-Self Church has 10 large churches serving approximately 30,000 members. Funded in part by the Beijing Municipal Government, two churches (located in Fengtai and Chaoyang) were constructed

A cross.

in 2005, the first to be built in Beijing since 1949. Clergy and lay workers are mostly trained at the Yanjing Theological Seminary (燕京神学院).

The church in Beijing has experienced steady growth over the years since 1989. Many intellectuals and students came to faith following the Tiananmen incident. As a result, a number of fellowships exist among intellectuals, students and business people. Some universities also have well-established fellowships and Christian unions on campus. As a result, Haidian (海淀区) and Chaoyang (朝阳区) Districts have a significant number of house churches and fellowship groups made up of young people. Solid Bible teaching, leadership training and discipleship of young believers remain the greatest needs expressed by Christians in Beijing.

For your reference, the Chinese Christian Council of Beijing is located at 181 Dongdan Bei Da Jie, Dongcheng District (东城区, 东单北大街 181 号). The Yanjing Theological Seminary (燕京神学院) is located at Dianhe Road, Qinghe Township, Haidian District, Beijing 海淀区, 清河镇, 淀河路. Tel: 010-62904272 ext 8005 or 8015.)

The Nantang Cathedral.

Catholicism

Catholics in Beijing number at least 40,000 with 15 meeting locations. Several stately cathedrals stand as landmarks in the city, bearing testimony to the early beginnings of the Catholic mission in Beijing. Several of these old cathedrals mark the location of early Jesuit mission bases from the early 17th century. The existing church buildings mostly date from the period after the Boxer Rebellion in 1900, replacing those earlier buildings which were damaged or destroyed at that time. Priests are trained at the National Seminary of the Catholic Church in China, opened in 2006 in the Daxing District. The largest seminary in China,

it is jointly run by the Chinese Catholic Patriotic Association and the Chinese Catholic Bishops' Conference.

OVERVIEW OF MISSION AND CHURCH HISTORY IN BEIJING

Early Beginnings

Legend holds that the Apostle Thomas first brought the gospel to China from India in 62AD. However, no evidence adequately supports this belief. Most historians, therefore, point to the later date of 635, when the Nestorian missionary Olopen is recorded to have brought the gospel to the Tang Dynasty capital at Chang'an, today's Xian. The church was established at a time when Buddhism was also becoming widespread. As such, the Nestorian Church was equated by some as being related to Buddhism and was later severely persecuted by the Tang Dynasty

Nestorian Christians.

East West dialogue.

Emperor Wu Zong in 845. Nestorianism (景教 Jingjiao) was re-introduced to China at the beginning of the Yuan Dynasty. Prior to this period, there are no existing historical records of Christian activity in Beijing.

Kublai Khan and the Nestorians (1268-1294)

Christian history in Beijing began with the arrival of Nestorian believers to the area at the beginning of the Yuan Dynasty. Also known as the Church of the East, the Nestorians established a presence in the Yuan capital at Beijing, then known as Khanbaliq, or Dadu (大都). Significant numbers of the imperial family and nobility

of the ruling Mongols were Nestorian followers, including Kublai Khan's mother and many of the ruling Khans' wives. The Mongolian rulers, however, tolerated other religions and practised Islam and Buddhism in addition to the Nestorian faith. It was in 1268 that Kublai Khan (1260-1294) established his capital at Dadu, allowing the building of several Nestorian churches in the city, including one adjacent to the imperial palace in 1275. In 1278, Kublai Khan established a department to deal with Christians in his empire with the Nestorian, Ai-Hsueh, as its first president.

During this period, cultural relations between China and Europe began to develop. The accounts of Marco Polo's travels to Dadu and other regions of China are well known. At about the same time, a Uygur-born Nestorian priest, Rabban Bar Sauma, and his student, Rabban Bar Markos, left Dadu on a personal pilgrimage to the Holy Land. Setting out from the Monastery of the Cross, in today's Fangshan District in 1276, they travelled the ancient Silk Road to Persia to pay their respects to the Patriarch of the Nestorian Church. From Persia, Bar Sauma was sent to Europe in 1287 as an envoy of the Persian Khan (Arghun Khan), in an attempt to secure an alliance against the Mamluks who were then occupying the Holy Land. His journey took him to the Vatican in Rome, where he received the Eucharist from Pope Nicholas IV at Easter, and then onward to Bordeaux and Paris in France where he shared mass with Edward I of England and King Philip IV of France. Bar Markos remained in Persia and was elected Patriarch of the Nestorian Church with the title of Patriarch Yaballaha III. He was the first and only China-born-Uygur patriarch of the Nestorian Church. Although Bar Sauma did not reach the Holy Land, his journey through Europe (1287-1288) is historically significant for intercultural relations between China and Europe, earning him the title of 'The Chinese Marco Polo'.[1]

The First Catholic Mission in China (1294-1369)

In 1266, Kublai Khan sent a message to the Pope in Rome requesting a hundred men of learning, devoted to Christianity, and capable of "[proving] to the learned of his dominions by just and fair argument that the faith professed by Christians is superior to and founded on more evident truth than any other."[2] Two Dominican Friars were sent, but they did not reach Dadu.

In 1289, Pope Nicholas IV sent a Franciscan mission from Rome to Khanbaliq led by Giovanni da Montecorvino. He reached Khanbaliq (Dadu) in 1294, only to learn that Kublai Khan had just died. The succeeding emperor, Temür, while showing no interest in Christianity nevertheless favoured Giovanni and supported his efforts to establish a church in the city. Despite facing enormous opposition from the Nestorians, Giovanni managed to build the first Catholic Church in 1299. Growth through his work continued with the building of a second church in 1305 and a third by 1318. Also in 1305, Giovanni sent a letter to the Pope requesting help, claiming that he had already won more than 6,000 converts. He also stated that he would have baptized more than 30,000 converts had it not been for the opposition of the Nestorians. In 1307, Pope Clement V sent seven more Franciscans to join the work (although only three arrived), and consecrated Giovanni da Montecorvino as the first Archbishop of Beijing and Patriarch of the Orient.

Giovanni died in 1328, but the news of his death did not reach the Pope for five years after his passing. Friar Nicholas de Botras was appointed as the new Archbishop of Beijing but did not arrive in Dadu, and his fate remains unknown to this day.

The last documented Christian mission from Rome to the Mongol court in Dadu was led by the Franciscan John of Marignolli along with thirty clergy. Arriving in 1342, Marignolli met with the Khan several times before withdrawing from the city in 1345, sensing the impending rise in anti-Mongol sentiment and violence in China.

The collapse of the Yuan Dynasty and rise of the Ming Dynasty in 1368 saw the destruction of the established churches in Beijing. A failure by both the Nestorians and the Franciscan Catholic Mission to make Christianity indigenous among the Han Chinese was one reason for their demise. This was due, in part, to the fact that the early churches did not use the Chinese language but favoured the language of the ruling Mongols. For example, the New Testament and some hymns had been translated using colloquial Mongol text rather than Chinese. The Chinese Ming Dynasty rulers, who were opposed to all foreign influence, immediately began vigorous persecution of the Christians. Within a decade they destroyed the established churches and expelled all believers, effectively putting an end to the earliest beginnings of the Church in Beijing.

Matteo Ricci and the Jesuit Mission in Beijing (1601-1717)

In 1601, the Jesuit Catholic priest, Matteo Ricci, arrived in Beijing. Having learned the Chinese language of the court, become a master in the Chinese classics, and displaying impressive skills in mathematics and astronomy, he was well received by the literary class and officials. Wearing the robes of a scholar and winning favour with local mandarins, Ricci began his mission in Beijing with the express aim of winning the emperor and high-ranking officials to Christ. While Ricci and his colleagues were kept from meeting the emperor by the powerful eunuchs, they did see several influential scholars and mandarins come to faith. Among them are the well-known mathematician, scientist and court official, Xu Guangqi, and famous geographer, Li Zhizao. The Jesuit's vast understanding of advanced mathematics, astronomy and map-making from Europe were well received by the imperial court, giving the Jesuits great favour and social standing. As a result Ricci and the Jesuits were granted property and residency in Beijing. With help from Li Zhizao, Ricci translated and compiled a number of works, which helped advance Chinese knowledge of contemporary mathematics and science. He also wrote several Christian apologetic works in Chinese. Among these, *A True Disputation about God* and *Ten Paradoxes* became powerful works in the early advance of the gospel in China. During his years in Beijing, over 100 converts were won each year. Ricci died in Beijing in 1610 and was honoured with the granting of a burial site by the Emperor. The work of Matteo Ricci marked the beginnings of a continuous and indigenous Catholic presence in China.

After the death of Matteo Ricci, the Catholic Church in Beijing and across China continued to flourish. Succeeding Jesuit priests and Chinese converts continued the work of Ricci by reaching out to the imperial court. A serious miscalculation by Chinese astronomers in predicting an eclipse in 1610 led to an invitation for the Jesuits to reform the Chinese calendar. This edict was fiercely opposed by the eunuchs and was not given serious attention until the arrival of the German Jesuit Adam von Schall to Beijing in

MATTHEVS RICCIVS MACERATENSIS QVI PRIMVS E SOCIETA
ESV E VANGELIVM IN SINAS INVEXIT OBIIT ANNO SALVTIS
1610 ÆTATIS. 60.

Matteo Ricci.

1630. Following the overthrow of the Ming Dynasty and formation of the Qing Dynasty in 1644, von Schall quickly made a good impression on the new Manchu rulers. Emperor Shunzhi is recorded as having visited von Schall 24 times to discuss both 'spiritual and temporal matters'. The emperor later appointed him as President of the Board of Mathematicians. The Qing court also granted the Jesuits funds to build a church in Beijing on the site of Matteo Ricci's former house and chapel.

By the late 17th century, French Jesuits had won respect and were invited as advisors to the Qing Emperor. As a sign of appreciation for their help in negotiating a suitable treaty with Russia, the Treaty of Nerchinsk in 1689, Emperor Kang Xi issued an edict of tolerance toward the Christian faith in 1692.

It was also during this period that the Russian Orthodox Church was established in Beijing by the Russian Albazin community, previously taken captive by the Czar's army in 1685. Among them was the Russian Orthodox priest Maksim Leontbev, who brought with him the icon of Saint Nicholas and a number of Russian Bibles. Emperor Kang Xi showed his favour

toward the Russian Orthodox community by granting them the use of a Buddhist temple (*Guangdi Miao*) at Dongzhimen as a place of worship. They then rebuilt the temple into what was to become the first Orthodox Church in Beijing. The Russian Imperial Court later supported the founding of St. Nicholas Church and gifted the holy vestments for worship. The former site is today on the grounds of the Russian Embassy and, as such, is inaccessible.

The Rites Controversy (1704-1724)

As the Catholic mission in China grew, Franciscans, Dominicans and other Catholic orders arrived in China. In contrast to the Jesuits, they took a direct and uncompromising approach to evangelism and theology. The Mendicants quickly came to criticize Matteo Ricci and the Jesuits' tolerance and adaptation of Confucian rites being practised by Chinese converts. They protested to the Pope that the Jesuits had propagated a tainted form of Christianity.[3] The ensuing Rites Controversy escalated when Pope Clement XI issued a decree in 1704 prohibiting any act of reverence being shown toward Confucius or the dead by believers. A papal mission was subsequently sent from Rome to Beijing to inform the emperor of his decision. Emperor Kang Xi was offended by the Pope's envoy (Charles Thomas de Tournon) and rejected the decree by issuing an edict governing the missionaries' presence in China. The Red Edict (1706) clearly stated that if any missionaries wished to remain in China, they must obtain an imperial permit, which was issued only to those who agreed to abide by the practices of Matteo Ricci.[4] Angered by the ongoing arguments between the missionaries and Rome, Kang Xi finally instructed the Board of Rites to prohibit Catholicism entirely in 1717.

In 1724, the succeeding emperor Yong Zheng stated his objection to the western religion and called for the expulsion of all missionaries, except those fulfilling key positions at the imperial court. As a result, a wave of persecution came against missionaries and Chinese believers throughout China. Only a few old Jesuits remained

The Emperor Kang Xi.

in the imperial court as artisans, but were no longer trusted as advisors. The following emperor, Emperor Qianlong, issued a further edict in 1736 which prohibited the teaching of Christian doctrine, under the penalty of death. A subsequent and severe wave of persecution swelled during the reign of the Emperor Jia Qing (1796-1820), with church buildings being confiscated or destroyed. China was again closed to foreign missions, leaving the existing Catholic communities under the direction of lay workers.

The First Protestant Missions in Beijing (1861-1900)

Missionaries were only able to enter Beijing again following the Opium Wars (1840-1860) and the signing of the Unequal Treaties forced on China by Britain, France, Germany, America, and several other nations. These Treaties not only granted trading rights, concession ports and compensation for foreign losses, but also granted the right for missionaries to work in China under the protection of the foreign legations. In 1846, Emperor Dao Guang ordered all buildings previously owned by Christians to be returned to their owners. It was not until 1860 that former Catholic churches in Beijing were finally placed in the hands of Lazarist missionaries. European Catholic missionaries were the first to enter the city.

It was some time after missionaries had arrived in other parts of China that Protestant missions were established in Beijing. Dr. William Lockhart, of the London Missionary Society, arrived in Beijing in 1861 to open a mission hospital. He was soon joined by Joseph Edkins who transferred from Tianjin the following year.[5] The year 1862 also saw the arrival of the Anglican missionaries, John Shaw Burdon and Samuel Isaac Joseph Schereschewsky.[6] Both used their positions at the British and American legations to build relationships with high-ranking Qing government officials. Burdon was quickly recommended to lecture at the Translation Bureau of the Qing Foreign Ministry. At the same time he rented a local house to set up a primary school to use as a base for spreading the gospel. Through these efforts, the first Protestant church was founded in Beijing in 1862.

Schereschewsky also attempted to establish a primary school, but was forced to close it a short time after. In 1867, he purchased a Buddhist temple, which he converted into a church and primary school. After marrying the American missionary, Susan Waring, they also set up a medical clinic from which they shared the gospel with their patients. After a number of years with only 20 converts, they handed the mission to the British in 1876.

W.A.P. Martin also arrived in the city in 1863, with a vision to establish a permanent mission in the city. Martin described Beijing as "the fountain of political influence for the whole empire" and, as such, the key to winning the nation.[7] His vision was to use education as a means to win the influential classes and government to Christ. He secured a small property to build a school and mission hospital. Martin's school and initial missionary endeavours were slow and attracted suspicion from both the government and aristocracy. As a result, most of his students and converts came from among the very poor and needy rather than his targeted upper classes. However, after several years of labour, his school began to flourish and his sphere of influence with high-level officials began to widen.

By the late 19th century, several denominational missions and overseas missionary organizations became established in the city, building western-style mission schools, orphanages, hospitals, colleges and churches in addition to their efforts in evangelism and church planting. Foreign missionaries ran churches and directed programmes, mostly with overseas funding, and conscripting local Chinese as co-workers. While the missionaries were respected and had a growing number of converts, many Chinese resented their presence, equating their endeavours and the Christian faith with western imperialism.

The Boxer Rebellion (1900)

The tide of anti-foreign and anti-Christian sentiment peaked in 1900 with the advent of the *Boxer Uprising*. This martial arts-based movement, mostly farmers and labourers recruited from rural Shandong, rose up in response to aggravations supposedly caused by foreign

Boxer Rebellion.

missionaries and their converts. Sweeping across Northern China, attacking and killing missionaries and Chinese Christians in their path, the first Boxers arrived in Beijing early June, 1900. Placards appeared on walls throughout the city, calling for "death to foreigners and Christians".[8] Churches were attacked and burned, missionaries were forced to seek protection in the foreign legation, and local believers had to choose between apostasy and death. Many Chinese Christians in Beijing refused to deny their faith and were subsequently beheaded or burnt alive in their homes. The movement escalated further after the Empress Dowager Cixi lent her support by declaring war against the foreign powers. Several hundred Chinese were martyred, including 222 from the Russian Orthodox Church.[9] The attack against foreigners and Chinese Christians in Beijing was finally put down in August 1900, with the arrival of an eight-nation occupation force of 20,000 soldiers.

Growth of the Church in Beijing (1900-1937)

The years following the Boxer Uprising saw the decline and overthrow of the Qing Dynasty, the formation and

rise of political movements and the rapid growth of mass nationalism rising from the May 4th Movement of 1919. Accompanying these changes came a period in the 1920s when Christianity again came under attack, this time from intellectuals schooled in Social Darwinism and those revolutionary activists fired up with nationalist sentiment and new communist ideals. It was during this period that the protestant church in Beijing saw an increase in the number of believers and began to grow more diverse in its appearance. New mission groups formed, independent traditional and Pentecostal churches were established, and Chinese Christian leaders took leadership positions in churches. Some leaders chose to distance themselves altogether from foreign mission structures and support. An independent, indigenous Christianity was beginning to form, which was autonomous in its operations and local in vision, goals and leadership.

The Church under Japanese Occupation (1937-1945)

During Japan's eight-year occupation of China (1937-1945), churches in Beijing were able to continue, albeit under Japanese supervision. The Japanese, concerned about the churches' reliance on foreign direction and support, attempted to coerce the churches to sever all ties with foreign missionaries. In 1942, Japan entered into war with most of the nations from which the missionaries had come. All foreigners and missionaries were rounded up and placed in internment camps across China, forcing churches and missions to exist on their own. The Japanese occupying forces, hoping to gain better control of churches, attempted to create a unified Protestant Church in China. Following a succession of Japanese-organized meetings, the North China Christian Union (NCCU) was formed in Beijing in late 1942.[10] While the NCCU allowed individual denominations to keep their own identities and properties, the movement was seen as a contributing step to achieving the ideals of an indigenous church. Although the union did not achieve all that the Japanese had envisioned, churches nevertheless came under local leadership and achieved a closer cooperation among denominations. The independent pastor and teacher, Wang Mingdao (王明道), was one of the few in Beijing to put up bold resistance against Japanese pressure to join the union. [11]

The Church in New China (1949-1966)

By 1949, there were 64 protestant churches and organizations from various denominational backgrounds in Beijing. These included the YMCA and YWCA, Salvation Army, Chinese Church for Christ, Chinese Anglican Church, Assemblies of God (from Norway, Sweden and USA), Presbyterian Church, Seventh Day Adventist Church, Union Church, Oriental Mission of America and the Bible Society. In addition to these were many independent Chinese churches and movements which included the True Jesus Church, founded by Paul Wei in 1917; the Christian Tabernacle, founded by Wang Mingdao in 1925; the New Holy City Church, founded by Sun Yongnian in 1926; the Christian Meeting Place, founded by Meng Xiangzhao in 1936; Funeidajie Church, founded by Yuan Xiangchen [Allen Yuan] in 1946; and Dongdadi Church, founded by Peng Honglian in 1947.[12] At this time, there were 65 Catholic and 72 Protestant church buildings spread across Beijing.

Dongtang Cathedral.

The founding of the People's Republic of China in 1949 raised new concerns as to how the Church would fare under a Communist regime. The new government, determined to build a China free from all foreign interference, viewed Christianity as an agent of western imperialism. Foreign missionaries and clergy were, therefore, soon expelled and Catholics and Protestants alike came under close scrutiny. While not immediately closed down, churches were forbidden to engage in street preaching and evangelism.

In 1950, the new government began to dialogue with a small group of key protestant leaders, representative of those who had shown support toward the new government. The formation of a national protestant church, which was patriotic and independent from all foreign support, was proposed. Its founders envisioned the Three-Self Patriotic Movement of Protestant Christians as the realization of the long-held ideal of an indigenous Chinese church, which was self-governing, self-supporting and self-propagating. As a bridge between the government and protestant churches, many viewed the Three-Self Patriotic Movement (TSPM) as the sole means for the church to continue under the new communist government. The TSPM was formerly inaugurated in 1951 under direction of the Religious Affairs Bureau and the United Workers Front as the governing body for Protestant Church activities in China. By 1955, however, all churches were ordered to come under the TSPM or be closed down.

In Beijing, a number of independent pastors, including Wang Mingdao, Allen Yuan and other key leaders refused to recognize the highly-politicized TSPM as a legitimate ecclesiastical authority. Their refusal to submit and join the TSPM led to them being denounced as 'unpatriotic and anti-revolutionary'. Wang Mingdao and his wife were first arrested and imprisoned on August 7, 1955. They were later freed and incarcerated indefinitely in 1958, along with Allen Yuan and nine other independent leaders. The eventual arrest and imprisoning of all non-TSPM leaders brought about a growing distrust and bitterness toward the government-sponsored TSPM.

From 1951 to 1966, denunciation campaigns affected all sectors of society, including the Three-Self Church. Various evangelical clergy and influential theologians within the movement were denounced, humiliated and sent to labour camps. Some were labelled as rightists for their earlier refusal to agree to the so-called 'Chinese Christian Manifesto' of 1950. Others were denounced for prior association with western missionaries and organizations. As time went on, the accusation campaigns and ideological criticism of the church intensified. In 1958, denominations were abolished with all churches coming under Three-Self governance and doctrine. Denominations were no longer free to practise specific traditions and churches in Beijing were merged, bringing the number of official churches in the city to four only.

During this same period the Catholic Church also felt the brunt of the government attacks. With foreigners making up almost 80 percent of its clergy and bishops, missionaries directing church education, and all followers answerable to the Pope in Rome, Catholicism was immediately viewed as a threat. Chinese Catholic leaders had already shown an uncompromising attitude toward the new Communist government by encouraging believers not to cooperate with the new state. It was, therefore, not long before the government began confiscating church properties, seizing church-run schools, orphanages and hospitals, and labelling Catholicism as 'unpatriotic'. A Chinese Catholic Patriotic Association was only established in 1957. The association was established on the same 'three-self principles' used for the TSPM. This, however, meant that Catholics could no longer look to the Vatican or the Pope as the head of the Church. While many Catholic leaders did join the association, and were appointed as bishops, many refused to break their allegiance to the Pope and took their faith and congregations underground.

The Cultural Revolution (1966-1976)

The Cultural Revolution ushered in a dark and difficult period for the Church across China. All religious activities were forbidden, churches were confiscated and turned into theatres, schools or warehouses, pastors were imprisoned,

Bibles and hymnals were burned, and believers became targets for persecution. During the first phase, armed Red Guards swarmed across Beijing harassing, humiliating and often killing Christians and anyone they perceived to be rightists. Christians were beaten and their Bibles confiscated and destroyed. Surviving believers, if known, were later sent to work in factories, the countryside, or coal mines as part of their re-education. In the early 1970s, Chairman Mao's wife, Jiang Qing, even boldly declared that Christianity in China has been confined to the historical section of the museum. She went on to say that there were no Christians left in China. Time proved that she was wrong, as remaining Christians continued to meet quietly in their homes. In 1971, two churches were allowed to open in Beijing as places of worship for the foreign embassy community only.

Reform and a New Era (1978-2005)

The death of Chairman Mao in 1976 marked the end of the Cultural Revolution and the beginning of a new era for China. It was not long before the Gang of Four were arrested and Deng Xiaoping led China into a period of reform starting

Haidian Christian Church.

in 1978. Christians who had survived the various purges began to gather in homes and share their faith. Having survived a period of harsh persecution, they emerged with a greater depth of faith and boldness than had ever been seen in China. Imprisoned leaders, such as Wang Mingdao and Allen Yuan, were soon released and returned to Beijing, giving inspiration to many in the emerging house churches.

The Three-Self Patriotic Movement (TSPM) and Chinese Catholic Patriotic Association (CCPA) were re-established in 1979. Protestant Christianity and Catholicism (non-aligned

to the Vatican) were again recognized as two of the five approved religions in China. The Chinese Christian Council (CCC) was established in 1980 as a sister organization to the TSPM, with responsibility for reopening Protestant churches and seminaries, for supervising the spiritual and theological direction of the church and overseeing the printing of Bibles. Believers were expected to join the officially sanctioned and reopened churches. Many Christians, however, continued to meet in unofficial house churches, preferring the greater depth of discipleship and closeness of fellowship.

House churches continued to grow quickly in the early 1980s as a whole generation was coming to terms with the void left from the Cultural Revolution. Believers in Beijing were estimated to number up to 20,000. House churches, however, continued to face pressure to register or be closed down. The Anti-Spiritual Pollution Campaign (1983-1985) seriously affected the unregistered groups, with many leaders being detained. A period of relative freedom and openness followed and house churches enjoyed an interlude from government opposition.

Many intellectuals and students came to faith in Christ in the period following the Tiananmen Square incident (June 1989). Both TSPM and unofficial churches were inundated with young people, and new groups formed around universities. Fuelled by government concerns for maintaining social stability, a full-scale campaign against all unregistered house churches and other 'criminal agents' began the following year.

The early years of the 21st century have continued to see a steady growth in the number of believers. In 2004, the local government allowed the CCC to begin the construction of two new church buildings in Fengtai and Chaoyang districts.

In March 2005, a new bill was passed on the governing of Religious Affairs in China. Unregistered groups were urged to register with the Religious Affairs Bureau without having to come under the governance of the Three-Self Church.

Endnotes

[1] Sir E.A, Wallis Budge, trans. *The Monks of Kublai Khan, Emperor of China* (1928) http://chass.colostate-pueblo.edu:80/history/seminar/sauma/sawma1. htm Accessed: 8 December, 2006.

[2] William Marsden, trans., ed. *The Travels of Marco Polo the Venetian* (re-edited by Thomas Wright) p.6 http://www.china-institut.org/bibliothek/ The%20Travels%20of%20Marco%20Polo.PDF Accessed: 8 December, 2006.

[3] Vincent Cronin,. *The Wise Man from the West.* (London: Harvill Press 1955 rpt. 1999) 280.

[4] Vincent Cronin, Ibid., 282.

[5] Handlist to the London Missionary Society / Council for World Mission Archive Collection (CWM/LMS) 1764-1940. (The Library School of Oriental and African Studies, July 1994, updated 2003) 121 www.cwmission.org.uk/ upload/cwm_guide.pdf Accessed: 8 December, 2006.

[6] Wang Yuhua, *A Brief History of Christianity in Peking* http://www.sinofile. net/saiweng/swpage.nsf/(Pages)/history?opendocument Accessed: Accessed: 8 December, 2006.

[7] Peter Duus, "Science and Salvation in China: The Life and Work of W.A.P. Martin (1827-1916)" in *American Missionaries in China: Papers from Harvard Seminars,* ed. Kwang-Ching Liu (Harvard, 1966) 22.

[8] Father Geoffrey Korz, *The Chinese Martyrs of the Boxer Rebellion* http:// www.orthodox.cn/saints/korz_en.htm Accessed: Accessed: 8 December, 2006.

[9] Father Geoffrey Korz, Ibid.

[10] Timothy Brook, "Toward Independence: Christianity under the Japanese Occupation, 1937-1945" in *Christianity in China — From the Eighteenth Century to the Present*, ed. Daniel H. Bays (Stanford: Stanford University Press, 1996) 333.

[11] Daniel H. Bays, "The Rise of an Indigenous Chinese Christianity" in *Christianity in China — From the Eighteenth Century to the Present*, ed. Daniel H. Bays (Stanford: Stanford University Press, 1996) 268.

[12] Philip Yuen-Sang Leung, *Conversion, Commitment and Culture: Christian Experience in China, 1949-1999*. http://www.cuhk.edu.hk/his/2002/chi/staff/ leung/confu_christ/christ06.htm Accessed: 8 December, 2006.

THREE

Preparing to
Come to Beijing

Preparing to Come to Beijing

PASSPORTS

All nationalities are required to hold a passport valid for six months from your arrival in China. Check with your home country regarding relevant passport regulations and application procedures.

VISAS

Travellers are required to apply for a visa before entering China. (Those holding passports from Japan, Singapore and Brunei, staying in China for less than 15 days are granted visa-free entry). Visa application should be made at a Chinese Embassy, Consulate, or visa office. Many travel agents can also handle applications on your behalf.

If you plan to travel through Hong Kong first, travel agencies there can arrange visas within one working day for single and double entry tourist (L) visas. The China Visa Office in Hong Kong is located in

the China Resources Building, Harbour Drive, Wanchai.

注意 Note:

Visa regulations and conditions frequently change. Check with your nearest China Embassy, a website or with a travel agent for current information prior to making visa applications.

BRIEF INTRODUCTION TO CHINESE VISAS

L) *Tourist Visa*

A tourist visa is 1-3 month visa for visiting or touring in China. Single and double entry tourist visas can be obtained.

F) *Visit/Business Visa*

Six-month multiple entry visas are issued for business, short-term study or other visits by invitation. For many passports, application for an (F) visa can be processed through most travel agents in Hong Kong without the need of supporting documents. Chinese Embassies and Consulates outside of Hong Kong usually need to see an invitation letter from an authorized Chinese company or government department, or other company documents specifying the scope of your intended business in China. An (F) visa may only be issued if you have already been to China on a prior occasion or hold valid invitation letters.

注意 Note:

Travel agents in Hong Kong are currently unable to process (F) visas for a number of countries including the United States, India, and Indonesia, unless accompanied by an official invitation letter.

注意 Important Note:

Students and work permit holders changing from (X) or (Z) visas to an F visa may be required to prove completion of employment or study. This can be in the form of a graduation diploma or letter from your employer or school.

X) *Student Visa*

Long-term study visas may be issued to foreigners accepted for study at a Chinese university or recognized school in China for six months or more. An (X) visa will be issued by an Embassy or Consulate of the People's Republic of China upon presentation of the university acceptance letter and JW202 visa authorization notice issued from the Ministry of Education. The JW202 is usually sent with the admission letter from the receiving university.

It is also possible to arrive in the country on a tourist visa (L), and then change to a student visa (X). This will cost a little more to process but may be more convenient. A health check is required and a temporary residency permit will be issued in your passport. In most cases this allows multiple entries into China.

G) *Transit Visa*

A transit visa is available for many international passports. This can be applied for upon arrival at the Beijing Capital International Airport for passengers holding an onward ticket for an international flight departing Beijing within 24 hours of arrival. Check with your closest Chinese Embassy, Consulate or knowledgeable travel agent in your home country for full details and qualifying countries and passports.

Applying for a Visa

When you apply for a Chinese visa you need to have the following:

- A valid passport with at least two blank pages.
- One or two recent passport-sized photo(s).
- A completed application form.

注意 Notes:

- Application forms are available through your nearest Chinese Embassy or Consulate and often available on Chinese Embassy websites.
- The cost of a visa varies according to the nationality of the passport holder and place of application.
- Visa fees are waived for holders of passports from Bosnia and Herzegovina, Bulgaria, Maldives, Pakistan, Poland, Slovakia and Yugoslavia. (Note: An application for a visa still needs to be made.)

Visa extensions

Tourist visas (L) can be extended in China for up to one month each time, with a maximum of two extensions. Multiple-entry visit business visas (F) can only be extended with an official seal of a registered work unit/company or through a visa agency. All applications for visa extensions need to be made before the visa expires, otherwise you face a fine. It is recommended that you take your passport to the Foreigners Visa Section of the Public Security Bureau and allow at least five working days for the application to be processed. Take into account public holidays during which the visa office will be closed.

All visa extension applications must be accompanied with a Registration Form of Temporary Residency (临时住宿登记表) as well as photos. If staying at a hotel, ask for a copy of the registration made when you arrive. If you are resident in Beijing, you must show the form you received when you registered with your local area PSB. Make two photocopies of your passport personal details page, current visa and the temporary residency form. You may be required to hand these in with your visa extension application.

In Beijing, the Foreigners Visa Section of the Entry-Exit Bureau of the Beijing Municipality Public Security Bureau (市公安局出入境管理中心) is located at 2 Andingmen Dajie (安定门大街2号), 600 metres east of the Yonghegong Metro Station (雍和宫). The Entry-Exit Bureau office is open Monday to Saturday, from 8:30am to 4:30pm. The office is closed on Sundays and official holidays.

A visa enquiry hotline for both Chinese going overseas and for foreigners seeking information about visa requirements and extensions is available in Chinese and English. The 24-hour number is 8402-0101.

注意 Note:
Attempting to leave China on an expired visa will result in a hefty fine.

WHAT TO BRING
Luggage

Whenever possible, pack everything into one bag. Rolling suitcases are suitable especially in large cities and towns or when travelling around China by air. However, backpacks will likely be more practical if you are planning on travelling overland by bus and train. It is recommended to have luggage with locks or zippers that can be secured with small padlocks. A daypack is useful for short trips, day outings and for use on long train rides.

A belt pack is good for carrying around small items such as maps, pens, notebook, etc. However, don't use it for valuables such as money, passports and airline tickets as it may be an easy target for pickpockets. Carry your valuables in a money belt worn under your clothes. Whatever you bring, make it small and light wherever possible.

Clothing

In major cities, fashion reigns supreme. Some foreigners unfamiliar with the scope of reforms in China in recent years have been surprised to see the latest hairstyles and good fashion sense. Many people, especially those in cities, dress up for special occasions and sometimes just for leisure outings. However, everyday dress codes do remain practical and informal. Chinese in interior cities and regions dress more practically still. Do bring at least one set of dress clothes

and a jacket and tie (for men) for planned or unexpected banquets, business meetings and formal exchanges. Women can wear either dresses, dress suits, or dress pants. Most Chinese businessmen dress formally.

What you pack depends on where you are going and what the season is. Jeans and other casual clothing are practical and acceptable for travel and most informal situations. For everyday wear, your clothing should be neat and clean. Low cut or revealing clothing is not acceptable in China.

If you plan on doing a lot of walking or visiting mountains and villages, a pair of good walking shoes is essential.

In winter, be prepared for almost unbearable cold in the north. Heavy woollen sweaters, thermal underwear and thick jackets are a must. Good sweaters and jackets are relatively cheap in China. You are, however, best advised to bring warm clothes to start with if you plan to travel during winter. The best advice for handling the cold is to follow the lead of the locals who layer their clothes to keep warm. They will, for instance, wear two pairs of socks, thermal underwear, two sweaters, and a jacket. Do note that most hotels, department stores, and shopping

Disposable contact lenses are available in big cities. It will likely be more convenient to bring a supply with you. If you do wear contacts, it is also recommended you bring glasses. Dust and pollution in some seasons may cause irritation and force you to temporarily abandon the use of your contact lenses. Likewise, if staying long term, bring your eye prescriptions with you.

Bring a full supply of any prescription medicines for your time. Filling a prescription at a Chinese pharmacy will be challenging unless you speak good Chinese.

centres are kept incredibly warm in winter, sometimes overly so.

In summer, the lightest of clothes will do for daytime wear. However, a light sweater or jacket will be useful in the hills at night, in some buildings or on train journeys with air conditioning. Remember that summer is also the wettest season of the year. A waterproof jacket or umbrella is essential.

Personal Necessities

Most basic hygiene and pharmaceutical items can be found in major cities. However, a good choice of deodorant/anti-perspirant and dental floss remains hard to find. Contact lens cleansing solutions and mosquito repellent are readily available in most cities but may be hard to find in smaller towns across China.

Sterilizing Hand Gel/ Wet Ones/Toilet Paper

Sterilizing hand gel is useful for cleaning your hands when no water is available. Likewise, moisturized wipes are another practical option for cleaning almost anything e.g. for wiping off dirty tables or seats. Bring small packets of tissue for the toilets, especially if you are heading into remote areas or when you travel by bus and train.

Pocket Knife/Spoon/ Mug/Flashlight

A small pocket knife, spoon, and large mug will be useful for long train journeys. Hot water is provided on the train for making instant noodles, tea or coffee. A flashlight/torch may be helpful for smaller towns with insufficient power and going to the bathroom at night.

Optional Extras

Many Chinese appreciate postcards, stamps, odd-looking foreign coins, key rings and other small items as gifts from foreign friends. Family photos and pictures of your home country are also greatly appreciated when meeting Chinese friends.

Film can be bought in all major cities and smaller towns. Check the expiry date on the box. You may prefer to bring specific film with you. Fast speed film, slide film and professional film may be difficult to find outside bigger cities.

A pack of cards, or other card games like Uno, will be popular with Chinese and help to fill the time on the longer train journeys. Chinese love playing cards and will probably be hard to beat.

If you are doing a lot of travelling, a tube of Shower Gel will be less messy to pack than a regular bar of soap.

A SUGGESTED PACKING CHECKLIST

- Passport with valid visa
- Phone numbers and email addresses in case of emergency
- Photocopies of passports, visas, immunization records, and a note of any medical conditions or allergies
- Extra passport photos
- Cash (for exchange)
- Money belt or pouch
- Airline tickets
- Notepad
- Pens
- Music Player, CDs, MP3/ MP4 players, I-Pod or other

portable entertainment devices

- Compact Chinese dictionary or phrasebook
- Alarm clock
- Flashlight/torch
- Extra batteries
- Day pack, a small backpack, or purse
- Sleeping bag, if you are travelling to remote areas
- Toiletries (e.g. toothbrush, soap, shampoo, deodorant, etc.)
- Medicine (e.g. cold and flu, anti-diarrhoea, etc.)
- Hand-sanitizer or antibacterial wipes
- Travel tissues in packs
- Travel hairdryer (220 volts)
- Digital camera or a camera with film
- Small gifts from your home country (inexpensive is fine)
- Clothing
- Raincoat/poncho and umbrella
- Good walking shoes
- Shower shoes/flip-flops
- Towel and washcloth
- Reusable water bottle
- A string to hang up laundry (laundry powder/soap is available in China)
- Sunglasses
- Hat
- Sun block
- A photo of your family to show Chinese friends

WHAT NOT TO BRING
Items of Value
If you plan to use public transportation around China, items of value can be a burden and are potential targets for theft, which is a common problem. Decide if you really need an item before taking the risk.

Sensitive Materials
Do not bring in any books, articles or DVDs that are in any way critical of China e.g. any books or articles on the 1989 Tiananmen incident, Tibetan independence movements, Taiwan independence or other sensitive issues. Also avoid bringing any unnecessary address books, letters or briefing materials/books with you. Some Christian literature translated into Chinese is unsuitable. Seek advice on what materials are appropriate to give to Chinese friends. You may bring a personal Bible for your own use.

WHEN TO VISIT
Autumn and spring are the best seasons to visit Beijing. Temperatures are generally warm and days fine. Summers are hot and wet while winters are very cold and dry. March and April are often plagued with severe sand storms known as the 'Yellow Winds'. During sand

storms, it is strongly advised to either stay indoors or wear a mask, if you must venture outdoors.

PUBLIC HOLIDAYS AND FESTIVALS

Take note of when main national holidays and festivals fall. Chinese New Year, the summer school holiday months of July and August and the Golden Holiday week of October 1st are peak periods for travel. Getting train tickets and hotel bookings at those times can prove difficult. Wherever possible, plan ahead and book travel arrangements early, with an agent when necessary. For up to a month either side of Chinese New Year, flights to and from China are fully booked.

CHINESE HOLIDAYS AND FESTIVALS 2008

January 1	New Year's Day	1 day national holiday
February 7	Chinese New Year	3 day national holiday
February 21	Lantern Festival	
April 4	Qingming Festival	1 day national holiday
May 1	International Labour Day	1 day national holiday
June 8	Dragon Boat Festival	1 day national holiday
July 1	Communist Party Founding (87th)	
August 8	Beijing Olympic Games begin	
September 14	Mid-Autumn Festival	1 day national holiday
October 1	National Day (59th)	3 day national holiday
October 7	Double Ninth Festival	

CHINESE HOLIDAYS AND FESTIVALS 2009

January 1	New Year's Day	1 day national holiday
January 26	Chinese New Year	3 day national holiday
February 9	Lantern Festival	

April 5	Qingming Festival	1 day national holiday
May 1	International Labour Day	1 day national holiday
June 27	Dragon Boat Festival	1 day national holiday
July 1	Communist Party Founding (88th)	
October 1	National Day (60th)	3 day national holiday
October 3	Mid-Autumn Festival	1 day national holiday
October 26	Double Ninth Festival	

CHINESE HOLIDAYS AND FESTIVALS 2010

January 1	New Year's Day	1 day national holiday
February 14	Chinese New Year	3 day national holiday
February 28	Lantern Festival	
April 5	Qingming Festival	1 day national holiday
May 1	International Labour Day	1 day national holiday
June 16	Dragon Boat Festival	1 day national holiday
July 1	Communist Party Founding (89th)	
September 22	Mid-Autumn Festival	1 day national holiday
October 1	National Day (61st)	3 day national holiday
October 16	Double Ninth Festival	

GETTING TO BEIJING
International Air

Beijing has daily flights from many major European and US gateway cities. Flights between various Asian countries are daily. There are also weekly or more frequent flights to and from Australia, South Asia, Africa, Central Asia, Mongolia, North Korea as well as the Middle East. Hong Kong to Beijing has almost 20 flights each day.

An International Departure Tax of ¥90 should be included in your ticket. Children under 12 years are exempt from paying departure tax.

Most international flights arrive and depart from Terminal 3. An automated light rail system links Terminal 3 with Terminal 2 for transfers between international and domestic flights.

Train from Hong Kong

Taking the train to/from Hong Kong can be one of the most rewarding ways of travel to and from Beijing. If you have the time, you will be rewarded with views of China's countryside, pass through several cities and have the opportunity to make Chinese friends. The journey takes about 27 hours and operates on alternate days. Passengers have the choice of hard sleeper, soft sleeper and deluxe sleeper. Tickets can be bought in Hong Kong at the Hunghom Railway Station in Kowloon, KCR stations at Mong Kok, Kowloon Tong, and Shatin, or through CTS and other travel agents. Return tickets from Beijing can be purchased in Hong Kong up to 60 days in advance. Bookings in Hong Kong can be made online with the KCR directly: http://www.it3.mtr.com.hk/B2C/frmIndex.asp. In Beijing, tickets can be bought at the Beijing West Railway Station up to 20 days in advance. Trains from Beijing to Hong Kong arrive and depart from Beijing West Railway Station (北京西站).

T98 Hunghom, Kowloon
— Beijing West Station

T97 Beijing West Station
— Hunghom, Kowloon

Hard Sleeper		
Upper: HK$574	Middle: HK$587	Lower: HK$601
Soft Sleeper	HK$934	
Deluxe Sleeper	HK$1,191	

Consignment of Luggage: HK$ per 5 Kg/$8.90 + handling fee.

International Trains

Several trains connect Beijing with Moscow, Ulan Bator, Pyongyang and Hanoi. The most famous of these is the Trans-Siberian Express, taking six days to complete. The train takes you through North East China and across the expanse of Siberia and on to Moscow. The Trans-Mongolian Express links Beijing and Moscow via Mongolia.

International train tickets can be purchased at China International Travel Service (CITS) inside the Beijing International Hotel (北京国际饭店), 5 minutes walk north of Beijing Station or through select travel agents.

You need to plan in advance for visas, purchasing tickets and meeting other requirements for China and other nations. Dedicated books and websites are available for your information.

International Boats

While Beijing has no port of its own, there are ferries from the neighbouring Tanggu Port (唐古) to Kobe, Japan and Inchon, Korea. Tanggu is located fifty kilometres east of Beijing and about 30 minutes by direct train. Tickets can be bought in Tanggu for either boat at the pier, or at the CITS office at the Beijing International Hotel (北京国际饭店).

Kobe-Tanggu

The complete journey takes about 48 hours and prices start at 20,000 Yen for a one-way ticket. Up to 40% discount is offered for return tickets.

Bookings can be made in Kobe with travel agents or directly from: China Express Line, 4-5 Shinkocho, Chuo-ku, Kobe 6500041 Japan Tel: (81) (78) 3215791

Inchon-Tanggu

There are two ships per week, a journey of 24 hours. Enquiries and bookings can be made through United Travel Service (UTS) or other travel agents in Korea.

Domestic Air

A vast range of domestic flights connect Beijing (PEK) with most major cities and tourist areas throughout China. Fares are set by the Civil Aviation Administration of China (CAAC). Discounted fares of up to 60% can be found through agents or directly through the various airline websites. Tickets can also be bought in advance through booking services such as www.elong.com or www.ctrip.com. Examples of one-way, full-price fares, less departure and fuel taxes: Shanghai: ¥1130; Guangzhou: ¥1700; Xian: ¥1050; Kunming: ¥1810. Note: Prices are subject to change.

Domestic departure tax of ¥50 should be included in your ticket. Children under 12 are exempt from paying departure tax.

注意 Note:
Flights with China Southern Airlines (CS) and Xiamen Airlines (MF) depart from and arrive at Terminal 1. All other domestic flights depart from the domestic sections of Terminal 2 and 3 unless otherwise specified.

A second domestic airport to the southeast of Beijing is being developed. Nanyuan Airport (NAY) (南苑机场) currently offers a limited number of domestic flights. Located in Fengtai District, NAY provides an air link for the southern Beijing districts and nearby counties of surrounding Hebei to destinations including Harbin, Dalian, Wuxi, Sanya, Hohhot, Chengdu, Chongqing, Urumqi and Hailaer.

Domestic Trains

Trains link Beijing to most major cities through an extensive network of rail lines crisscrossing the whole nation.

Taking the train is cheaper than flying and offers a safe, fairly comfortable journey with panoramic views of rural China. You will also encounter a whole range of people, and have experiences you would miss if you only travelled by air. Trains vary from short-hauls to Tianjin (2 hours) to long-haul journeys e.g. to Shanghai (11.5 hours), Guangzhou (24.5 hours), Wuhan (12 hours), Xian (12 hours), Harbin (11 hours), Kunming (45 hours) and Lhasa (46.5 hours).

Bullet train services, with a D coding, have been introduced on a number of key routes. These luxury trains travel at top speeds of 200km per hour: Beijing to Tianjin takes 1 hour, Harbin 8 hours, Qinhuangdao 2 hours, Shenyang 4 hours, Zhengzhou 5 hours, Jinan 3.5 hours and Hankou 8.45 hours. Tickets can be purchased for both first and second class seats in advance.

Non-stop express trains designated with a Z coding are offered between Beijing and several cities: Shanghai, Nanjing, Suzhou, Hangzhou, Yangzhou, Hefei, Changsha, Wuchang, Hankou, Xian, Changchun, and Harbin. Most Z trains have luxury soft sleeper cars, and a limited number of hard or soft seats on select routes.

Daily trains run from Beijing to Lhasa, Tibet via the Qinghai-Tibet railway. Ticket prices start at 389 (hard seat) to 813 (hard sleeper) and 1,262 (soft sleeper). Foreign travellers are required to present Tibet Travel Permits at the time of ticket purchase.

The main stations for most express and fast trains are Beijing (北京站), Beijing West (北京西站) and Beijing South (北京南站). Tickets can be bought at any station or at ticket offices throughout the city. It is important to note which station your train is scheduled to depart from. Tickets currently go on sale five days in advance for hard seat, soft seat, hard sleeper and soft sleeper, and 20 days in advance for D-class seats and Z-class soft sleeper tickets. Main stations have dedicated foreigner booking counters. Tickets can also be booked by phone reservation (9510-5105 Chinese only) but may require an additional booking fee.

The four main classes: hard seat, soft seat, hard sleeper, and soft sleeper:

- *Hard Seat* has fairly comfortable hard upright benches (plastic or padded seats on new trains). Although the hard seat option is cheap, the trains can become unbearably crowded and noisy. It is recommended for short journeys of only a few hours.

- **Soft Seat** offers more space, a set number of passengers and comfortable seats with a reclining back. The Soft Seat option is not available on long distance trains, but is a good option for a longer day journey of about 6-10 hours.
- **Hard Sleeper** is the preferred option for most travellers on long-distance and overnight routes. There are rows of three-tiered bunks with pillows and blankets. Compartments are open, which means you are part of a larger community of about 66 people in the one car.
- **Soft Sleeper** has four comfortably padded bunks in a closed compartment with a door. This is the most comfortable option for train travel, but is often not much cheaper than flying. Some of the Z trains provide personal TV screens with a selection of in-house movies.

Long-distance trains all have dining cars. The food is generally expensive for what you get. Train attendants also bring white meal boxes regularly through the train, which are basic but mostly palatable. The best option is to take food with you e.g. fruit, bread, crackers, nuts, instant noodles and other snacks. Water, Coke and other drinks are available on the train and on station platforms.

Bus

Buses serve as the main link between rural and urban China and are the only way to get to many areas of China. Long-distance bus stations are located throughout the outskirts of Beijing. Buses go to many small cities and towns, both locally and throughout the Northern, North Eastern and Eastern regions of China. They range from old, smoke-belching, rust-stained vehicles, to an assortment of sleeper buses and luxury Volvo and Daewoo coaches. Online schedules are available in Chinese at http://www.checi.cn/checi/cn. Main long-distance bus stations are as follows:

Dongzhimen 东直门长途汽车站	Tel: 6467-1346 6723-7328
Location: NE Beijing — close to Dongzhimen Metro station.	

Beijing South Railway Station 北京南站长途汽车站	Tel: 6303-4307
Location: Beside Beijing South Railway Station.	

Lizeqiao 丽泽桥长途汽车站	Tel: 6340-3408 6347-5092
Location: SW Beijing West 3rd Ring Road South. Bus: 811, 901, 541, 50, 300, 323, 324	

Zhaogongkou 赵公口长途汽车站	Tel: 6722-9491 67237328
Location: S. Beijing, South 3rd Ring Road. Bus 17, 300, 927, 368	

Lianhuachi 莲花池长途汽车站	Tel: 6346-4027
Location: West 3rd Ring Road. Bus: 6, 50, 309, 340, 323, 324, 300, 901	

Bawangzhi 八王坟长途汽车站	Tel: 800-8100770 8771-8844
Location: SE Beijing, West Dawang Road.	

Beijiao 北郊 - 德胜门外长途汽车站	Tel: 8284-7096
Location: N. Beijing, Deshengmenwai Dajie	

Liuliqiao 六里桥长途客运站	Tel: 6386-1262 6386-1264
Location: Liuliqiao Bridge (South) Bus: 6, 50, 323, 324, 300	

Muxiyuan 北京木樨园长途汽车站	Tel: 6726-7149
Location: Fengtai District, Muxiyuan. Bus: 17, 2, 300, 377, 926, 324, 341, 366, 40	

Jiulongshan 九龙山长途汽车站	Tel: 6776-2443
Location: West Dawang Lu. Bus: 31	

Sihui 四惠长途站长途汽车站	
Location: Opposite of Sihui Metro Station (Line 1).	

Tianqiao 天桥长途汽车站	
Location: 32 Beiwei Lu, Xuanwu District	

ACCOMMODATION IN BEIJING

A wide range of hotels, service apartment facilities, budget hotels and hostels can be found in Beijing. You should be able to find accommodation that fits your budget and needs. It is best to arrange accommodation before you arrive, especially during peak travel seasons. Hotel rooms can either be arranged through a travel agent in your home country, directly through a travel agent in Beijing or via the internet. Online booking services include: www.ctrip.com; www.elong.com; www.chinahotels.net; and www.hostelcn.com.

SAFETY CONCERNS

It is generally safer to travel through China than in many other developing nations. However, it is recommended you take precautions to protect yourself and your belongings, especially on public transport and in crowded places. With dramatic urbanization, China has seen a corresponding increase in crime over the past few years. While violent crimes against foreigners are rare, pick-pocketing and theft are common.

To protect yourself and belongings:

- Make photocopies of your passport, airline ticket and any other important documents. Leave a copy with friends or family at home, and keep a copy with you as you travel, preferably in a separate location from the originals. Should you lose these documents, you at least have a copy of the details necessary for getting a replacement. Keep records of Travellers' Cheques serial numbers separate from where you carry them.
- Never leave passports, money or valuables in hotel rooms and dormitories. Use the room safe or safety deposit box at reception, whenever available, or carry such items in a money belt/

pouch worn under your clothes. A belt pack worn outside your clothes is an easy target for pickpockets in crowded places.

注意 Note:
Chinese law requires foreigners to carry passport identification at all times. A photocopy of your passport and visa may suffice. However, original passports will be required for any official business, including changing money at a bank, taking domestic flights and checking in at hotels.

- Lock your bags and rooms whenever possible. Small padlocks are readily available in stores throughout China.
- Women should not walk alone at night. Always have a companion or stay with others as a group.
- It is suggested you buy a travel insurance package with coverage for loss of belongings and air tickets, liability protection, and full health cover.

If you do have something of value stolen, it is important to file a loss report at the nearest Public Security Bureau (PSB). They are likely to ask many questions concerning the circumstances before issuing an official report on the crime. The chances of seeing lost items recovered may be slim. However, depending on your policy, you may be able to make a claim with your travel insurance company by having an officially stamped loss report from the PSB.

In the case of an accident, theft of passport, illness or other emergency requiring additional assistance, contact your nearest home country embassy or consulate. They will give advice on what steps to take. Bring all embassy and consulate contact details with you for each country represented if travelling as a group. See the Directories Section.

HEALTH MATTERS
General Health Sense
Protecting your health begins with using your common sense!

全国药品零售企业统一标志

Most travellers in China experience few health problems other than coming down with common coughs and colds or a simple case of travellers' diarrhoea. However, it is important to remember that many areas of China may not meet basic hygiene standards. The following are simple common sense recommendations to keep you in good health:

- Never drink tap water, or water straight from untreated sources. Drink only boiled or bottled water, or other sealed drinks.
- Use disposable chopsticks when eating in small, basic restaurants. Most restaurants provide disposable bamboo or balsawood chopsticks. If you feel it necessary, carry a pair of your own.
- Avoid eating food from unlicenced street vendors.
- Avoid buying already cut fruit or allowing a street vendor to cut it for you.
- Where possible stay away from restaurants that are obviously lacking in cleanliness, or those that do not have running water.
- Regularly wash your hands with soap and water and/or with a sterilizing hand-gel.
- Take all practical measures to avoid being bitten by mosquitoes in affected areas. Wear light-coloured clothing with long sleeves and pants. Apply a mosquito repellent. Use mosquito coils or electric mosquito pads when needed. Keep window screens shut and use a mosquito net if one is provided.
- Limit your eating of shellfish and other seafood. New regulations on handling of seafood have improved hygiene standards, however many water areas around China are still affected by pollution.
- Be especially careful when crossing roads or riding bicycles. Do not assume that you will always have the right of way at pedestrian crossings or that vehicles will give way or even be on the

correct side of the road.

- Avoid handling live poultry or being close to where poultry is kept.
- Avoid playing with live animals, especially dogs, cats and monkeys which can all harbour rabies and other infectious diseases.
- To prevent fungal infections in the feet, use plastic sandals in bathrooms and other public areas of hotels or hostels. Dry your feet well after showering.
- Use wisdom in taking public transport. Where possible, do not board overcrowded long-distance buses, trucks, boats, or take vehicles which are obviously unsafe.
- Avoid swimming in fresh water rivers and lakes where Bilharzias is found. This warning specifically applies to the central Yangtze River basin.

Health Preparations

- Bring adequate supplies of any prescription drugs, asthma inhalers, and non-prescription medications you may need for your stay in China.
- If you are pregnant or travelling with young children, consult with your doctor for advice and precautions before setting

out. Many airlines require pregnant women to carry a current doctor's letter permitting travel during pregnancy.

- Insulin-dependant diabetics are advised to carry a doctor's letter authorizing any need to carry syringes and needles.
- Wear good UV screening sunglasses and sun block in summer months and high altitude areas.
- Take daily multi-vitamins.

First Aid Kit

It is recommended that you assemble and bring a medical kit for basic first-aid. It doesn't need to be too large, but should include basic items such as the following:

☐ Band Aids or gauze bandage with adhesive tape ☐ Thermometer ☐ Tweezers ☐ Scissors ☐ UV lotion ☐ Insect repellent ☐ Antibiotic ointment ☐ Antiseptic agent (e.g. Dettol) ☐ Diarrhoea medication (Lomotil or Imodium) ☐ Rehydration

mix for severe diarrhoea
▪ Paracetamol (Tylenol) ▪
Ibuprofen or aspirin for pain
and fever ▪ Antihistamine
(useful as decongestant for
colds or allergies) ▪ A course of
antibiotics (consult your doctor
for advice) ▪ Cold/flu tablets ▪
Cough/throat lozenges ▪ Multi-
vitamins

Pharmacies in China's larger
cities have a range of medicines
available making it easy to
replace some of the above items
as needed.

注意 Note:

Antibiotics and antihistamines
are no longer available in
China without a prescription.
Watson's in Beijing, Shanghai and
Guangzhou have a good range
of vitamins, throat lozenges and
other non-prescription health
products.

Vaccinations and Immunizations

注意 Note:

Before considering any
vaccinations, it is important to
consult with your local physician
or travel medicine clinic. The
following information is given as a
guideline only.

Basic recommended
immunizations include: Tetanus
& Diphtheria (Td), Oral Polio,

Tuberculosis (BCG), Hepatitis
A and Hepatitis B. Begin
arranging immunizations at
least four to six weeks before
departure. Some injections
require a series of two to three
shots over several weeks or
months. Many immunizations
also require booster shots after
a few years. Check with your
doctor.

Risks for contracting
Cholera or Typhoid are very
low for most travellers to China.
It is best to take preventative
measures by being attentive
to basic hygiene for food and
water.

Malaria is not a significant
problem in China. There is no
need for malaria prophylactics
unless you travel to high-
risk areas. The World Health
Organization (WHO) states
there is no risk in urban areas
or the densely populated plains
areas of China. There is a low
to very low risk of malaria in
extreme rural areas of Hainan,
Yunnan, Fujian, Guangdong,
Guangxi, Guizhou, Sichuan,
Anhui, Hubei, Hunan, Jiangsu,
Jiangxi and Shangdong during
summer months and year
round below latitude 25°N. If
you are spending more than
a few weeks in these areas,
anti-malarial prophylactics are
recommended. For Hainan
and Yunnan, Mefloquine is

recommended. For the other provinces, Choloquine is recommended. Doxycyclin may also be effective. Check with your doctor for advice.

Japanese Encephalitis is a mosquito-borne disease, found primarily in rural areas of Eastern China during summer. A vaccination is available, however, it is generally only recommended for those staying long-term or short-term travellers spending extended periods of time in affected rural areas. As with malaria, the best advice for prevention is to take measures against being bitten by mosquitoes.

For updates on current health risks and preventative measures for travel in China check with the WHO or the US Centre for Disease Control (CDC) online. Their web addresses are as follows:

- <http://www.who.int/csr/don/archive/country/chn/en>
- <http://www.cdc.gov/travel/eastasia.htm>

Medical Insurance

It is highly recommended you take out comprehensive travel or medical insurance. Insurance will most times assure that you receive quality healthcare and treatment in the event of an emergency. A good insurance package will probably provide for evacuation to a more fully-equipped hospital either in China or outside, should the situation demand it. While hospital treatment in China is not exorbitant, it will still cost several thousands of yuan for basic treatment and a short stay in hospital. Keep all receipts (English if possible) for any medical treatment to ensure reimbursement from your insurance company.

Coughs and Colds

Coughs and colds are prevalent throughout China and are the most common health annoyance for most travellers. Bring a basic supply of your preferred cough, cold and throat lozenges or medicines. Quality locally-produced cold medicines are also available at most pharmacies. Watson's in Beijing have a limited range of western throat lozenges and cough drops.

SARS and Bird Flu

Since the sudden outbreak of Severe Acute Respiratory Syndrome (SARS) in 2003, stringent screening measures and preventative plans have been established in China. Following the containment of the original outbreak, no new cases of SARS have been reported since early

2004. While the likelihood of your suddenly contracting an isolated case of SARS is extremely unlikely, it is advised that you are at least aware of the main symptoms during a declared outbreak. If you have a fever consistently over 38°c (100.4°F), accompanied by a cough, sore throat and/or difficulty breathing, you should immediately go to a hospital or clinic for examination by a doctor.

In late 2004, the WHO issued warnings regarding the potential outbreak of a Human Bird Flu pandemic originating in Asia. While no proven human-to-human cases of bird flu are known to date, concern remains over the potential for the virus to mutate. There is little risk to travellers whose activities do not include visits to poultry farms, poultry markets or involve the handling of live foul or other at-risk birds. Keep a watch on all government-issued travel warnings regarding Bird Flu. For current information, check the WHO website. Individual countries may post travel advisory information on their government websites.

Hospitals

Many large cities have dedicated clinics and wards for foreign patients at the main hospitals.

The facilities are generally good with an adequate quality of healthcare provided. Communication often remains the biggest problem for many foreigners. Smaller cities and rural towns have basic hospitals and clinics only, and can only be relied upon for emergency care. Any need for extensive medical consultation or surgery should be sought in large cities such as Beijing, Shanghai, and Hong Kong, or in your home country.

Beijing and several other major cities have private joint venture or wholly foreign-owned medical clinics for foreigners, expatriate businessmen and their families. These offer high standards of health care by foreign and local doctors, but the costs are high for the self-paying patient.

CULTURAL ISSUES

The complexities of Chinese values, beliefs and worldview, and reasons behind certain behaviours are extensive. This section is not an exhaustive commentary on culture, but it is a list of tips on some common behavioural differences between Western and Chinese cultures. Your time in China will be enriched if you acknowledge some of the following guidelines.

Practice general cultural sensitivity:

- Understand the importance of guanxi (关系), which means 'relationships/connections'. Many times it's who you know when it comes to getting things done.
- Understand that the Chinese are generally a group culture. The group, or collective, is more important than the individual. Group opinion is important and Chinese people often follow the crowd.
- Understand the need for saving face and not losing face. Do not embarrass Chinese friends in any way.
- Some values important to the Chinese include respecting family and elders, friendship, hard work, peace/harmony, loyalty, knowledge/value of education, and respect for tradition.

When eating out at a Chinese restaurant or formal banquet:

- Always order and eat as a group, not individually. One person may order for the whole group.
- A banquet meal will often follow a set order: cold dishes will be served first, followed by hot dishes, soup, and then fruit for dessert. Rice is not usually served at a banquet, as banquet food is special and rice is an ordinary, everyday staple.
- Wait until everyone is seated before starting to eat. It is traditionally polite to let the oldest or most honoured person start eating first.
- If you are guest at a banquet, don't be surprised if your host serves you by putting a few pieces of food in your bowl.
- It is considered rude to help yourself first and serve only yourself. The same is true of serving tea. Pour tea for others before yourself. It is impolite to pass dishes across the table.
- If you touch some food with your chopsticks, you should try your best to pick it up and put it on your plate or in your mouth. Try not to touch all the food, just the food you intend to take. It is also fine to use a spoon to take food into your bowl. If you accidentally drop food

on the table, do not pick it up. Just leave it on the table.

- Try everything that is served. Even if you don't like it, you have at least given it a try. This will satisfy most hosts.
- Avoid mixing foods together. Each dish is a delicacy in its own right and should be enjoyed as such.
- Avoid playing with your chopsticks. Never stab your chopsticks upright into a bowl of rice. Traditionally, this was a sign of hostility and resembles incense sticks used at a funeral rite or in ancestral worship.

- When finished eating, place your chopsticks on the table neatly. Throwing them down haphazardly can be taken as a sign of disrespect and dissatisfaction with the meal.

When visiting Chinese homes:
- Always take your shoes off at the door. It is considered rude to wear your street shoes inside. Usually, slippers (house shoes) will be offered for you to wear.
- It is polite to bring a small gift with you. A basket/bag of fruit, candy or cookies is

appropriate. Fruit should not consist of only four pieces, as four in Chinese has a similar pronunciation to the Chinese word for death . Small tokens from home (e.g. postcards, key rings, etc.) are great gifts for your host. If you do happen to bring flowers, make sure they are not white. White symbolizes death and may be considered as a bad omen.

- When giving or receiving gifts, use two hands. In times past, this showed you were not being deceitful by concealing your other hand. Now, it is just a polite gesture.
- If you are given a gift, do not open the gift immediately, unless your friend insists on it. Opening it may imply that you are more interested in the gift than in your friend.
- You will likely see your hosts receive the gift you have brought and place it aside without opening it. If you want them to open your gift, insist on it and they will happily oblige.
- You will likely be offered tea and snacks. It is common to refuse offers for a drink or food the first couple of times. Many times a cup of tea or hot water will be put in front of you even though you did not ask for it. You are not obliged to finish it. Likewise, if you don't want any more, then don't finish your cup.

Meeting with Chinese:

- Shaking hands is not necessary, but is becoming more common. When greeting a much older person or someone in high authority, use a two-handed shake as a sign of respect.

- Many times Chinese will offer their name card upon introduction. It is proper to offer and receive name cards using two hands, holding the corners of the name card between your thumb and forefinger. You should immediately take a moment to study the card. The name card represents the person and should therefore be given respect. If you intend to do business in China then it would be to your advantage to prepare name cards before setting out.

- When calling a friend to come over to you, beckon them with your hand facing down. Beckoning with your hand up can be considered impolite, and in the past was used by people in authority.

- In business and formal social environments most people greet each other using their last name followed by their title. For example:

> Teacher Li = Lǐ Lǎoshī
> Manager Wang = Wáng Jīnglǐ
> Mr. Huang = Huáng Xiānsheng
> Mrs. Zhang = Zhāng Tàitai

- Chinese will almost always downplay a compliment for something they have done. In complimenting their English, they will often respond, "No, my English is very poor!" Likewise, if praising someone for a meal they have cooked or on clothing they are wearing, they are likely to say something like, "No, no, this is not very good." Many don't want to be seen as proud by saying 'thank you'. Confucian thought still influences people to value modesty.

- Be prepared for many questions, especially as they get to know you. Questions about your age, family, income, how much you paid for something, and likes and dislikes are common. For many Chinese, it is their way of showing they are interested in getting to know you. Likewise, you should not hesitate in asking your Chinese friends similar questions. If you are not comfortable answering some questions e.g. regarding income, then you may politely reply, "I earn enough to live."

- Chinese place great importance on saving face. Likewise, they will often find it hard to say no, so as to save you losing face. Instead, Chinese may find an excuse or come up with a new suggestion instead. In some business circumstances you will be told one thing only to find out the truth later. This practice will often be used to save embarrassment for you or them, rather than to intentionally deceive you.

When taking public transport:
- Wear shoes on the train when walking around or sitting with your feet on the floor. Do not wear shoes on bunks. Slip them out of sight under the lower bed at night.
- On the subway or bus, offer your seat to the elderly, families with small children, pregnant women, and those with disabilities.

Expecting the unexpected:
- Spitting is common. Despite the occurrence of SARS, many people still spit. In addition, you may see the odd person blowing their nose into the drain, nearby garden or garbage bin. Throwaway tissues are, however, widely used. For many Chinese, a foreigner using a cloth handkerchief to blow their nose and then

average Chinese. You will likely be offered either a beer or a glass of wine when you are at the dinner table. It is perfectly acceptable to politely refuse alcohol and choose a soft drink, juice or tea instead.

- Spitting chicken bones or other bones on the tablecloth or floor is quite acceptable.
- Burping may be unacceptable in many cultures. Here, no one minds when a companion burps. It is seen as a natural bodily function, and there is no need to suppress it.

put it back into their pocket is very unsanitary.

- Smoking is almost universal for all Chinese men. It is common to have people smoking at the next table in a restaurant, as well as in many other public places. You may also find a new friend offering you a cigarette. There is no obligation to accept it. You can politely say no, and will often receive admiration for taking care of your health by not smoking. It may be considered rude to ask someone to stop smoking, unless you know them well or there are signs posted suggesting that smoking is not permitted.
- Drinking alcohol has no negative connotation to the

- Chinese show respect toward older people. Older people will often be treated, listened to and given preference to over and above younger people.
- Guys & Guys/Girls & Girls holding hands. It is common

and normal for friends of the same sex to hold hands or put their arms around each other. This does not indicate any tendencies as we may think of in the west, but is simply a normal sign of friendship. While it is becoming more common to see a young couple holding hands or showing affection in public, it is still considered inappropriate by many of the older generation.

ONE FINAL TIP

- Relax and enjoy getting to learn their culture. Be interested in China. Be a learner! No one expects you to be perfect. Most Chinese anticipate that your culture will be different and they will be curious about you. Your new friends will usually be very forgiving should you do things differently. Enjoy the new experience to the fullest!

FOUR

Practical Information
for Visiting Beijing

Practical Information for Visiting Beijing

ARRIVING IN CHINA:
Immigration and Customs

Whatever way you enter China, you are required to go through immigration and clear customs. The process is usually straightforward provided your passport has a valid visa, and an arrival card has been completed. A health declaration form is required at most ports of entry and you usually submit this before you line up at the immigration counters. For those arriving as tourists, the purpose of visit should be marked as 'leisure'.

Customs is located after the baggage claim area at the airport or directly after the immigration counters at most cross-border check points. Unless you have articles that must be declared, you should go through the green channel. Luggage is not usually hand-checked, although you may be required to have it x-rayed.

注意 Note:
Bringing in any agricultural products, including fresh fruits and vegetables, is prohibited. All health declaration forms, arrival cards and customs declaration forms are in English and Chinese.

For those needing to apply for a transit visa, you will need to go to the 'Visa Upon Arrival' counter before going through the abovementioned process.

DEPARTING CHINA:
Airport Security Regulations

China has implemented new screening measures for all hand-carry baggage on international flights. All liquids, gels, pastes and aerosols in containers (including tubes, bottles, cans and jars) must not exceed

国际 / 港、澳、台到达
Int'l / HK, Macao, Taiwan Arrivals

100ml. These items must be kept in a transparent re-sealable plastic bag. The plastic bag can have a maximum size not exceeding 20 x 20cm (8 x 8 inches), and must be presented for inspection separate from all other hand-carried items. Exceptions to the above limits are made for medications (accompanying prescriptions or medical certificates necessary); baby food; baby formula; and any special dietary foods. All of the above items exceeding 100ml may be put in checked baggage.

GETTING TO/FROM THE AIRPORT
Capital International Airport (PEK) (首都机场) is 27 kilometres, or 16.8 miles, northeast of the city centre.

Taxis are the fastest and most convenient way of getting to and from the airport. An average fare from the airport to the city is about ¥80 - 150 including road tolls (currently ¥10).

注意 Warning:
You may be approached by taxi drivers or touts as you exit the arrivals hall. You are strongly advised not to take these taxis. They are illegal operators and will likely ask a fare several times higher than you would pay in a metered taxi. Line up at the taxi stand for a metered taxi.

An **Airport Express Rail** links the Capital International Airport (Terminals 2 and 3) to Dongzhimen (东直门) with a stop at Sanyuan Qiao (三元桥). The total travel time to Dongzhimen is about 16 minutes and costs ¥20 for a one way journey.

Airport buses are available for a number of routes. Buses operate every 15 to 30 minutes and cost ¥16. They depart the airport near the taxi stands.

Airport Bus (机场巴士民航客班车)

Buses from the Beijing Capital International Airport to Tianjin also depart from the airport bus departure point on

BUS ROUTES

1 线

Fangzhuang — Airport (方庄 – 机场)
First Bus: 06:00. Last Bus: 19:30.

Fangzhuang (Guizhou Mansion) – Dabeiyao (China Southern Airlines Hotel) – Airport
方庄 (贵州大厦) – 大北窑 (南航大酒店) – 机场

Airport — Fangzhuang (机场 – 方庄)
First Bus: 08:00. Last Bus: 22:30.

Airport – Liangmaqiao – Hujialou – Dabeiyao (China World Trade Centre) – Panjiayuan – Shilihe (Jingduan Mansion) – Fangzhuang (Guizhou Mansion)
机场 – 亮马桥 – 呼家楼 – 大北窑 (国贸) – 潘家园 – 十里河 (京端大厦) – 方庄 (贵州大厦)

2 线

Xidan — Airport (西单 – 机场)
First Bus: 06:00. Last Bus: 19:30.

Xidan (Civil Aviation Building) – Dongzhimen (50m E. of the bridge) – Jingxin Mansion West Gate – Airport
西单 (民航营业大厦) – 东直门 (桥东50米) – 京信大厦西门 – 机场

Airport — Xidan (机场 – 西单)
First Bus: 08:00. Last Bus: until last flight.

Airport – Sanyuanqiao – Dongzhimen – Dongsishitiao – Xidan (Civil Aviation Building)
机场 – 三元桥 – 东直门 – 东四十条桥 – 西单 (民航营业大厦)

3 线

Beijing Rail Station — Airport (北京站 – 机场)
First Bus: 06:00. Last Bus: 19:30.

Beijing Rail Station (International Hotel) – Dongzhimen (50m E. of the bridge) – Jingxin Mansion West Gate – Airport
北京站口 (国际饭店) – 国贸桥 (南航大酒店) – 三元桥 (京信大厦)机场

Airport — Beijing Rail Station (机场 – 北京站)
First Bus: 08:00. Last Bus: until last flight.

Airport – Yuyang Hotel – Dongdaqiao – Chaoyangmen – Beijing Rail Station
机场 – 鱼阳饭店 – 东大桥 – 潮阳门 – 北京站

	Gongzhufen — Airport (公主坟 – 机场) First Bus: 06:00. Last Bus: 19:30. (Xinxing Hotel) – Friendship Hotel (North gate) – Beitaipingzhuang (50m E. of the intersection) – Anzhen Mansion – Airport 公主坟 (新兴宾馆) – 友谊宾馆 (北门) – 北太平庄 (路口东50米) – 安贞大厦 – 机场
4 线	Airport — Gongzhufen (机场 – 公主坟) First Bus: 08:00. Last Bus: 23:00. Airport – Int. Exhibition Centre – Xibahe – Anzhenqiao – Madianqiao – Beitaipingzhuang – Jimenqiao – Friendship Hotel (North gate) – Beijing TV – Zizhuqiao – Hangtianqiao – Gongzhufen (Xinxing Hotel) 机场 – 国际展览中心 – 西坝河 – 安贞桥 – 马甸桥 – 北太平庄 – 蓟门桥 – 友谊宾馆 – 北京电视台 – 紫竹桥 – 航天桥 – 公主坟 (新兴宾馆)

	Zhongguancun — Airport (中关村 – 机场) First Bus: 07:00. Last Bus: 19:30. Zhongguancun (Si Qiao) – Aeronautics and Astronautics University (North Gate) – Huixin Xijie (Anwei Mansion) – Huixin Dongjie (China Petroleum Group) – Airport 中关村 (四桥) – 北航 (北门) – 惠新西街 (安微大厦) – 惠新东街 (中国石化集团) – 机场
5 线	Airport — Zhongguancun (机场 – 中关村) First Bus: 08:30. Last Bus: 21:30. Airport– Wangjing (Huajiadi) – Xiaoying – Yayuncun (Anhui Bridge) – Xueyuan Qiao – Zhongguancun (Si qiao) 机场– 望京 (花家地) – 小营 – 亚运村 (安慧桥) – 学院桥 – 中关村 (四桥)

a regular schedule throughout the day.

Flight arrivals and departure information can be viewed on the Beijing Capital International Airport website. http://en.bcia.com.cn/

Nanyuan Airport (NAY) (南苑机场), Beijing's developing secondary domestic airport, is located in Fengtai District to the southeast of the city. Buses from the Civil Aviation Building in Xidan (西单民航大厦) depart on a fixed timetable. They cost ¥16, or are free if you have a ticket for a scheduled flight on that day.

For more information and current schedules on bus services and times, make inquiries with the airline.

Tricycles.

GETTING AROUND BEIJING

Beijing's public transport system is often crowded but fairly efficient. An extensive network of buses, convenient subway lines, light rail Metro lines and taxis serve the city's main transport needs. Getting across town can however, take some time given the size of the city and the increasing number of privately-owned cars on the roads.

Taxis

For many visitors, taxis are the most convenient way of getting around the city. Rates are set by the Transport Administration of Beijing and are according to the meter unless otherwise negotiated with the driver prior to setting off. Flag fall rates are ¥10 (¥11 after 11pm) for the first three kilometres. Per kilometre rate is set at ¥2.00/km for the first 15 kilometres and ¥3.00/km after that. Waiting

time and any road tolls add to the final fare payable. A limited number of luxury cars charging ¥3.00/km are also available. Not all taxi drivers understand English. If you are not sure of the name of your destination in Chinese, have it written out in characters, or have it clearly marked on a Chinese or bilingual map for the driver.

注意 Note:

Taxis cannot accept credit cards.

Buses

An extensive network of buses enables you to connect with most corners of the city and beyond. However, finding the bus or connecting buses you need may be a problem. Signs at bus stops are only in Chinese. Getting a hold of a local transport map or map book with marked bus lines may help. Buses can be incredibly crowded during peak rush hours. You will need to push hard and squeeze in tight to get on or off. Most buses in Beijing have ticket conductors. Simply tell the conductor where you want to get off and they will sell you a ticket accordingly. Prices vary from ¥1(1元) - ¥6(6元).

Metro

The city's underground and light rail Metro system is an efficient

way of getting to many of the city's main tourist sites and downtown areas. The Beijing Metro system currently consists of the underground Metro lines 1, 2, 4, 5, and 10; and the Line 13 and Batong (八通) over-ground light rail lines.

Line 1, stretches from East to West along Chang'An Avenue (长安街) and beyond to Pingguoyuan (苹果园). Major stops on Line 1 include the World Trade Centre (国贸); Wangfujing Shopping Street (王府井); Tiananmen Square (天安门广场); and Xidan Shopping Street (西单). This line connects with Line 2 at Jianguomen (建国门) and Fuxingmen (复兴门) stations.

Line 2, often referred to as the Blue Line or the Loop Line, circles the inner circle of the city providing quick access

Metro Station sign.

to Qianmen (前门), Beijing Railway Station (北京站), Jianguomen (建国门), Dong-zhimen (东直门), Yonghegong (雍和宫), Jishuitan (积水潭), Xizhimen (西直门), and Fuxingmen (复兴门). The whole loop takes about 40 minutes to complete.

Line 4 winds its way from the northwest of the city to the south connecting the following key sites: the Summer Palace (颐和园); the Old Summer Palace (Yuanmingyuan Station 圆明园); Qinghua University (at Yuanmingyuan Station 圆明园); Peking University (at Yuanmingyuan Station 圆明园); Zhongguancun IT area (at Zhongguancun Station 中关村); the China National Library (at Baishiqiao Station 白石桥); and the Beijing Zoo (动物园). It then heads east through Xizhimen (西直门) and Xinjiekou (新街口) before heading south once again passing Ping'anli (平安里); Xidan (西单); Taoranting Park (陶然亭); and Beijing South Railway Station (北京南站). Line 4 terminates at Majialou (马家楼) in Fengtai District, in the south of the city. (The first phase of this line is due to be operational by mid 2009.)

Line 5 starts at Puhuangyu (蒲黄榆) in Fengtai District (丰台区), passes the Temple of Heaven East Gate (天坛东门) and the Hongqiao Market (虹桥市场) at Tiantan East Station (天坛东门). It runs under Dongdan (东单); Yonghegong Lamasery (雍和宫); and Ditan Park (地坛 at Yonghegong Station (雍和宫) on the Second Ring Road, before heading north toward the Third Ring Road Hepingxi Overpass (和平西桥). Line 5 then runs under the Yuan Dynasty Capital Wall Relics Park (北土城东路), crossing the Fourth Ring Road north to eventually terminate at Taipingzhuang North (太平庄北).

Line 10 forms a semi-circle arc across the north and east of the city following under Zhichun Road (知春路) in the north and the 3rd Ring Road in the east. Beginning west of Suzhou Street (苏州街) near the Beijing Foreign Studies University, the line heads east underneath Zhichun Road (知春路) to Panda Roundabout (熊猫环岛) and the China Ethnic Culture Park/China Nationalities Museum (中华民族园). It then heads south past the Lufthansa Centre at Liangmahe (亮马河), the China Agriculture Museum (农展馆), and the China World Trade Centre (国贸), the Panjiayuan Market (潘家园市场) before terminating at Songjiazhuang (宋家庄). The first phase of Line 10 is due to be operational by August 2008.

Line 13 is a light rail extending in a loop from Xizhimen (西直) to Dongzhimen (东直门) and winding through the northern suburbs of Haidian (海淀区) and Chaoyang Districts (朝阳区).

The Batong Line (Line 8) connects the outlying eastern suburban district of Tongzhou (通州区) with the Sihui (四惠) and Sihuidong stations (四惠东) of Metro Line 1.

An Olympic Branch Line (due to be operational by August 2008) is an extension of Line 10, connecting Panda Roundabout (熊猫环岛) to the Olympic Centre (奥体中心); Olympic Park (奥林匹克公园); and National Forest Park (森林公园).

Tickets can be bought at Metro Station ticket offices. Ticket prices are currently set at ¥2 for any destination on the network. Distance-based fares are scheduled to be introduced in the future.

BEIJING RAIL STATION TO BEIJING WEST STATION

Until such time as a planned light rail connects the two stations, passengers needing to

METRO MAP

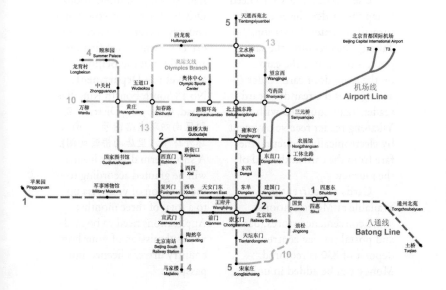

connect between the two have the option of taking taxi or bus. Buses between the two stations include the 802, 209, 703, 821, and 848.

注意 Note:

Be especially attentive for pick-pockets on buses between these two stations.

YIKATONG (BEIJING SUPER-PASS) 一卡通

The *Yikatong* Card (一卡通), also referred to as the Beijing Superpass, is an electronic payment card for use on Metro lines, buses, taxis and other services. The *Yikatong* serves as a rechargeable, electronic stored value card for cashless payment.

Users taking the Metro need to tap the card at the electronic turnstile to enter the station. Taking a bus requires the same process of tapping the card on the front door card reader and again at the rear door card reader. Taxis equipped with an Yikatong reader receive payment by electronically deducting the fare from the card at the end of the journey.

Cards are currently available at Metro stations, some convenience stores, banks and postal service centres. A deposit of ¥30 is required. Money can be added in units of ¥10, with a minimum of ¥20 and maximum of ¥1,000.

Car Rental

For foreigners staying a limited time in the city, renting a car with a driver is the best option. Car rentals can range from hiring a car with driver for a day, to weekly or monthly contracts. Taxi drivers are often willing to negotiate a full-day hire. Costs will depend on distances covered and whether it involves travel outside of the city. For weekly or monthly hire, available drivers with cars can sometimes be found in classified sections of any of the free English magazines or by contacting a car rental firm.

It is not possible to drive in Beijing using an International Driver's License or your home country driver's licence. A local driver's license must first be applied for at the **Beijing Traffic and Vehicle Department**, No 18 South Fourth Ring East Road, Chaoyang District (朝阳区南四环东路18号 — 南四环外环十八里店南桥西南侧). A short-term driver's licence will be granted according to the duration of your visa up to a total of three months. Applications need to be made with submission of your home country driver's licence and passport.

Tour Bus Lines

There are numerous tour bus options in Beijing. A tour bus dispatch center is located opposite the south west corner of Tiananmen Square. Other major tour lines include:

Tour Line 1 (游1路)
(06:00 - 10:00)
Qianmen (前门) → Badaling Great Wall (八达岭长城) → Juyongguan Great Wall (居庸关长城) → Dingling Tomb (定陵) → Changling Tomb (长陵) → Jiulong Leisure Park (九龙游乐园).

Tour Line 2 (游2路)
(06:00 - 10:00)
Beijing Railway Station (北京站) → Badaling Great Wall (八达岭长城) → Juyongguan Great Wall (居庸关长城) → Dingling Tomb (定陵) → Changling Tomb (长陵) → Jiulong Leisure Park (九龙游乐园).

Tour Line 3 (游3路)
(06:00 - 10:00)
Dongdaqiao (东大桥) → Badaling Great Wall (八达岭长城) → Juyongguan Great Wall (居庸关长城) → Dingling Tomb (定陵) → Changling Tomb (长陵).

Tour Line 4 (游4路)
(06:00 - 10:00)
Beijing Zoo (动物园) → Badaling Great Wall (八达岭长城) → Juyongguan Great Wall (居庸关长城) → Dingling Tomb (定陵) Xizhimen (西直门) → Badaling Great Wall (八达岭长城) → Juyongguan Great Wall (居庸关长城) → Dingling Tomb (定陵)".

Tour Line 5 (游5路)
(06:00 - 10:00)
Qianmen West (前门西) ➔
Badaling Great Wall (八达岭长城) ➔ Juyongguan Great Wall (居庸关长城) ➔ Dingling Tomb (定陵) ➔ Changling Tomb (长陵) ➔ Jiulong Leisure Park (九龙游乐园)

Tour Line 6 (游6路)
(06:00 - 10:00)
Xuanwumen (宣武门) ➔
Mutianyu Great Wall (慕田峪长城) ➔ Hongluo Temple (红螺寺) ➔ Yanqi Lake (雁栖湖)
    Dongsishitiao (东四条) ➔
Mutianyu Great Wall (慕田峪长城) ➔ Hongluo Temple (红螺寺) ➔ Yanqi Lake (雁栖湖)

Tour Line 7 (游7路)
(07:00 - 10:00)
Qianmen (前门) ➔ Tanzhe Temple (潭柘寺) ➔ Shihua Cave (石化洞) ➔ Jietai Temple (戒台寺).
    Fuchengmen (阜成门) ➔
Tanzhe Temple (潭柘寺) ➔
Shihua Cave (石化洞) ➔ Jietai Temple (戒台寺)

Tour Line 8 (游8路)
(07:00 - 10:00)
Qianmen (前门) ➔ Longqingling (龙庆岭) ➔ Badaling Great Wall (八达岭长城) Yongdingmen (永定门) ➔ Longqingling (龙庆岭) ➔ Badaling Great Wall (八达岭长城)

Tour Line 9 (游9路)
(06:00 - 10:00)
Qianmen (前门) ➔ Ming Imperial Wax Palace (明皇蜡像宫) ➔ Dingling (定陵) ➔ Ming Tombs Reservoir (十三陵水库) ➔ Mangshan Park (蟒山公园) ➔ Jiulong Leisure Park (九龙游乐园)

Tour Line 10 (游10路)
(06:00 - 08:00)
Fuchengmen (阜成门) ➔ Yunju Temple (云居四) ➔ Shidu (十渡) Qianmen (前门) ➔ Yunju Temple (云居四) ➔ Shidu (十渡)

Tour Line 12 (游12路)
(06:00 - 08:00)
Xuanwumen (宣武门) ➔
Bailongze (白龙潭) ➔ Simatai Great Wall (司马台长城).
    Dongsishitiao (东四十条) ➔
Bailongze (白龙潭) ➔ Simatai Great Wall (司马台长城)

Tour Line 14 (游14路)
(06:00 - 08:00)
Exhibition Center (展览馆) ➔
Jinhai Lake Park (金海湖公园)
    Dongdaqiao (东大桥) ➔
Jinhai Lake Park (金海湖公园)

Tour Line 16 (游16路)
(06:00 - 08:00)
Xuanwumen (宣武门) ➔
Hongluo Temple (红螺寺)
➔ Qinglong Gorge (青龙峡) Dongdaqiao (东大桥) ➔

Hongluo Temple (红螺寺) →
Qinglong Gorge (青龙峡)

Tour Line 18 (游18路)
(06:00 - 07:00)
Xuanwumen (宣武门) → Pan
Shan (盘山)

BEIJING MAPS/ GUIDEBOOKS

One of the best maps in English
is the *Beijing Tourist Map*, which
marks streets and tourist sites in
English and Chinese and shows
some of the main bus routes.
Another excellent map book for
bus routes across the city is the
*Beijing Gong Jiao Cheng Che
Zhi Nan Di Tu Ce* (北京工交乘
车指南地图册) — available in
Chinese only.

Bilingual free maps (*City
Map of Beijing* 享爱北京)
published by *Beijing Weekend*
and the *Beijing Official Guide*
published by the Beijing
Tourism Administration are
available at most four- and
five-star hotels.

Some locally-produced
guidebooks focus less on where
to stay and where to eat giving
greater detail to historical and
cultural aspects to the city.
The Insider's Guide, published
yearly by *That's Beijing*, has
excellent information for those
staying long-term. Other
small guides for families with

kids, health, sports and service
directories are published by
both *That's Beijing* and *City
Weekend*. Guide books can be
bought at the Foreign Languages
Bookstore at Wangfujing (王
府井), the Friendship store and
many hotel bookshops.

Further information on
restaurants, shopping, entertainment and local interest articles
are published free every month
e.g. *That's Beijing, City Weekend, Beijing Talk, Beijing This
Month and Time Out Beijing*.
These are available at large hotels and hostels and at many of
the coffee shops and restaurants
frequented by foreigners. China's English newspaper, the China Daily, is available throughout
the city at most newspaper
stands. *Beijing Weekend* is a
supplementary English paper
published by China Daily every
Friday. It has a greater focus on
news from around the city as
well as from around China.

CURRENCY

China's national currency is
Renminbi (RMB), The People's
Money. The basic unit of RMB
is the yuan (commonly referred
to as kuai), which is divided into
ten jiao (also called mao), which
are again divided into ten fen.
1 yuan 元 (1 *kuai* 块) = 10 *jiao*
角 (10 *mao* 毛) = 100 *fen* 分

The People's Bank of China issues Renminbi in paper notes of 1, 2, 5, 10, 20, 50 and 100 *yuan*; and smaller 1, 2 and 5 *jiao*. Coins are in denominations of 1 *yuan*, 5 *jiao*, 1 *jiao*; and one, two and five *fen*.

The Chinese Yuan has recently been allowed a greater freedom of movement, in relation to a basket of foreign currencies. Check the internet or banks for current exchange rates.

注意 Note:

There is no tipping in China.

EXCHANGING MONEY

Renminbi (RMB) is not yet a fully convertible currency. This means aside from moneychangers and some banks in Hong Kong, Singapore, Malaysia, and else-where around Asia, you may not easily have access to RMB prior to arriving in China.

All major foreign currency and travellers' cheques can be changed at the Bank of China, exchange counters at larger hotels, money exchange bureaus at some friendship stores, or the occasional large department store.

Currency rates at airport, border and hotel exchange counters are official rates regulated by the People s Bank of China. Rates at various exchange counters at the airport, hotels and banks should not vary, although they do reserve the right to charge a service fee. Travellers' cheques fetch a slightly higher rate than cash in China and provide an added bonus of security when travelling. Many hotels offer currency exchange for hotel guests only.

When changing money you are usually required to show your passport. Then you are issued a receipt with your name, nationality and passport number shown on it. This receipt (or an ATM receipt) should be kept if you anticipate the need to change RMB to a foreign currency when leaving China. At the moment, exchanging money from RMB back to a foreign currency can only be done at an exit port exchange counter.

At Beijing Airport

There are banks with money exchange counters both inside the luggage claim area and outside the International Arrivals security area. Banks at the airport reserve the right to charge a fee for transactions less than the equivalent of US$500. Reliable automatic exchange machines are also found inside and outside the security area for exchanging major currency banknotes to Renminbi. Note that a transaction fee may be deducted. ATM machines accepting international debit and credit cards are also available throughout the airport. Look for the Visa, MasterCard, Cirrus, Plus or Visa Link logos.

BANKING
Banking hours: 9.00am to 5.00pm from Monday to Friday, 9.00am to 11:30am on Saturdays. Sunday is a public holiday. However, many banks in Beijing are open for personal services, including currency exchange, on Saturday and Sunday.

注意 **Note:**
Not all banks offer currency exchange services. While more banks are being authorized, it is better to head straight to the nearest Bank of China.

USE OF CREDIT/ DEBIT CARDS

In China's major cities, many big hotels, international airlines, international medical clinics, some of the larger up-market department stores and expensive restaurants accept major international credit cards. Most small shops and other places of business are unable to accept credit cards at all, so their usefulness in China is fairly limited. The use of foreign-issued debit and credit cards at select ATM machines is possible in larger cities. Look for an ATM showing the Visa, MasterCard, Plus, Cirrus or Visa Link logos. However, be aware that many machines limit the number of withdrawals you can make per day and have limits on the amount of RMB you can withdraw each time. Some machines only handle local bank cards. Cash advance on a credit card is also accepted in some five-star hotels, and main branches of the Bank of China in most cities. However, there may be an added service charge by the local bank when making a cash advance transaction over the counter.

ELECTRICITY

220 volts, 50 cycles AC. Note: Many appliances from the US

and other countries using 110 volts cannot be used unless they are dual voltage or plugged into a transformer. Check carefully to make sure your appliances are set to the right voltage, are dual voltage or plugged into a transformer.

A three-pronged angled pin design.

A two-pronged flat pin design.

Plugs come in two main designs three-pronged angled pin (same as Australia/New Zealand), and two pronged flat pin (American-style without the grounding pin). Adapters can be found in many electrical stores or department stores in China. Good quality power strips with universal sockets can be bought in most cities.

WATER

Do not drink water straight from the tap or faucet in any

location. In many cities the water supply may come via old and dirty pipes. Drink boiled, filtered or bottled water only, even though water in Beijing is generally safe. Brushing your teeth should be done with purified drinking water or use boiled water that has been left to cool.

Thermos flasks of boiled water are provided to make tea, coffee or noodles on trains and at most hotels and university dormitories. Soft drinks, fruit juices and bottled water are readily available and are safe to drink. Large bottles of purified drinking water can also be bought at local supermarkets. Always make sure you drink enough water, whatever the season, especially if the climate is dry.

TOILETS

When you visit China, you will likely encounter a whole range of toilet facilities. Most hotels have western-style toilets, which can usually be rated as pretty good to excellent. Public toilets generally consist of squatty potties and, on rare occasions, may be nothing more than a trench. Most have low walls separating each stall, but may not necessarily have doors. Generally the toilets are clean

enough to use, even though they may be basic. Some charge a fee of 5 mao to 1 yuan and may even give a couple of sheets of toilet paper. However, it is best you always have a packet of tissues on hand as most don't have any paper at all. Some older public toilets have separate areas specified based on what you need to do. Furthermore some systems cannot handle toilet paper. Generally, if you see a basket next to the toilet, then that is where used toilet paper should be placed.

If squatty potties are a problem for you, then you might want to go to the nearest Kentucky Fried Chicken or McDonald's restaurant, or to a star-rated hotel. In the lead-up to the 2008 Olympics, Beijing has embarked on a toilet upgrade campaign.

The following characters might be worth remembering:

MEN　男
WOMEN　女

LONG-DISTANCE TELEPHONE CALLS

Making international calls from China using International Direct Dial (IDD) is expensive, around US$3 per minute. Hotels may also add an additional service charge for any long-distance calls made from your room. One of the cheapest options for making long-distance calls is to use an IP Card (**IP卡**), which charge as little as ¥2 per minute (approximately US 25 cents) for international calls, and ¥0.30 per minute for domestic calls. Several companies issue IP cards, and all offer comparable rates and service. IP Cards, available in ¥50, ¥100, and ¥200 values, are found at post offices, convenience stores, hotels, stationery shops, newspaper stands and many small street vendors. Cards are usually discounted. ¥100 cards can often be bought at a price as low as ¥30 at many stands. Check with your hotel first to see if you are able to use IP cards from your room and ask which card you can use.

注意 Note:
IP cards can only be used in the province/municipality where you purchase them. IP Cards cannot be used with a mobile phone.

Dialling internationally, you will need to dial 00, then the country code, area code and finally the local number you are calling. To make a domestic call, you will need to dial 0 before the area code.

Another option for making international calls is using a service from your home country. Check with your local company for rates before leaving home.

China's Country Code : 86
Beijing Area Code   : 010

MOBILE COMMUNICATIONS

Pre-paid SIM cards are available in China for GSM and CDMA mobile phones. These are great for short-term visitors or those with limited long-term mobile phone use. Setting up your

hand phone with a Chinese SIM card provides you with a local number, and gives your China-based friends an easy way to call you without incurring international charges. It will also often be cheaper than paying roaming charges from your home country. Most overseas handsets use the GSM 900/1800 systems and can be used in China.

注意 Note:
China uses the 900/1800 GSM systems. Many mobile phones from the US *cannot* be used in China unless they are tri-band capable handsets compatible with the 900/1800 GSM systems. For US subscribed tri-band phones, it will be necessary to have your phone 'unlocked' by your service provider *before* leaving home.

Two main companies offer GSM mobile communication services: China Mobile and China Unicom. Both charge ¥0.6 per minute for local calls. Roaming throughout China is available. SIM Cards and recharge cards can be bought at telecommunications shops, some post offices, markets, convenience stores and magazine vendors.

China Mobile issues ***Shenzhouxing*** (神州行) SIM cards. The set-up package and recharge cards come with clear and easy to use instructions in English and Chinese. SIM cards vary in cost depending on the number. An unpopular sounding number (usually containing the number 4) can start at as low as ¥30, with no value added. To activate the SIM card you will need to purchase and activate a recharge card by following the instructions on the card. These come in values of ¥50, ¥100, ¥200, and ¥500. English operator assistance is available by calling 1860.

China Unicom offers a similar package and rates with their ***Ruyitong*** (如意通) SIM cards. *Ruyitong* is easy to use with bilingual services. Set up and recharging is the same as for China Mobile. Be sure to purchase recharge cards for *Ruyitong* (如意通). English operator assistance is available by calling 1001 from your Unicom-connected cell phone.

CDMA services are available with China Unicom only. Set up cost is the same as GSM SIM cards. CDMA offers cheaper calls and exceptional clarity. Dedicated CDMA handsets are required to connect to the CDMA system. SIM cards and CDMA phones can be bought at China Unicom service centres and many mobile phone shops.

For those wanting to set up a long-term subscription, you will need to go to either company, China Mobile or China Unicom, with your passport and have a permanent address in Beijing. A deposit of ¥500 is generally required for foreigners. Both China Mobile and China Unicom offer several attractive long-term packages with free incoming calls and competitive rates. Check both companies for a package which suits you.

Xiaolingtong

A local system known as *Xiaolingtong* (小灵通) is available in Beijing as well as several other cities. *Xiaolingtong* offers cheaper call rates,

although signal coverage and quality is not as broad. The handsets and numbers can be purchased at cell phone shops and CNC service centres.

INTERNET/E-MAIL

Internet cafés are often small, dimly-lit rooms with a number of computers providing basic services. These cafés are frequently filled with young people playing online games or chatting. They provide reasonably reliable access to the web at the low cost of ¥2 - ¥6 per hour. Bring your passport or a valid ID, as some places require registration. A refundable deposit of ¥20 is usually required. Some hostels and hotels have their own Internet Cafés for guests.

注意 Note:
Internet Cafés are usually identified by the characters 网吧.

It is advised that you wash your hands carefully after visiting an Internet café. Health authorities advise the frequently used keyboards at Internet cafés may harbour germs for a number of infectious diseases.

Many four- and five-star (some three-star) hotels offer in-room LAN ports for connecting your laptop. A per-day rate will apply unless it is included in your room-rate. Ensure that you have a firewall and anti-viral software when connecting to any LAN or Wireless services.

An increasing number of coffee shops and small western restaurants are beginning to offer free wireless access for customers.

POSTAL SERVICES

Post Offices are found throughout China on main streets, at airports, near railway stations and some major tourist locations. They are easily identifiable by a green signboard with gold lettering in English and Chinese. Post offices are open seven days a week 9:00am-5:00pm. Some hotels sell stamps, envelopes and postcards.

Postcards sent internationally by airmail are ¥4.50 regardless of their destination.

An international airmail letter will vary in price according to zones.

	Zone 1	Zone 2	Zone 3	Zone 4
≤ 20g	¥5.00	¥5.50	¥6.00	¥7.00
+ 10g	¥1.00	¥1.50	¥1.80	¥2.30

7 January 2004

Zone 1   Neighbouring countries, including Japan
Zone 2   All other Asian Nations and territories
Zone 3   Europe, USA, Canada, Australia, and New Zealand
Zone 4   Other North American countries, South America, Africa, and Pacific Islands

Letters to Hong Kong, Macau and Taiwan are ¥1.50 (≤20g). Postcards are ¥0.80.

Local Mail is ¥0.60 (each 20g) local or ¥0.80 (each 20g) inter-provincial.

Packages can also be mailed from post offices by surface or air. Boxes can be bought at the post office. Packages must be packed at the post office so they can be inspected. You are not permitted to send CDs, DVDs, cassette tapes, videotapes, undeveloped film or other media storage devices via post from China. Main post offices also offer Express Mail Service (EMS), money transfer services, and banking.

A souvenir stall in Beijing.

SHOPPING

Beijing is a great place for shopping. On any given day, you can enjoy a variety of shopping experiences from buying things off the sidewalk to exploring a market or purchasing an item in an up-scale boutique in a mall. One of the more concentrated areas for shopping is the Wangfujing Shopping Street (王府井大街).

Tourists usually find their way to at least one of several popular markets e.g. Xiushui Jie (秀水街) or Silk Alley; Hongqiao Market (红桥市场) also called the Red Bridge Market; Yaxiu Market (雅秀市场); Panjiayuan (潘家园); and Liulichang (琉璃厂). The Silk Alley, Red Bridge Market and Yaxiu Market all offer a wide variety of goods such as clothing, handbags, jewellery, accessories, toys, souvenirs, and silk. The Panjiayuan and Liulichang markets are known for their array of antiques and collectibles.

If you are interested in buying antiques or jade, it is a good idea to get advice about whether the piece is a genuine article or a reproduction. A knowledgeable person may also advise you about what the purchase price should be, so you do not get cheated. Not all antiques can be taken out of the country as some articles are protected under customs regulations. If you are a serious buyer, you will probably find this out as you go.

In most markets and street stalls, bargaining is acceptable and expected. When in doubt, ask a local what a fair price for a particular item should be. Some Chinese friends may even be happy to help you with bargaining. This is a skill that should be cultivated, and it can be quite fun.

In department stores and grocery stores, prices are fixed. Arguing with shop attendants and bargaining in these establishments are not acceptable. Follow the lead of the locals. If they seem to be bargaining, then it is probably fine for you to bargain too.

One final note: Take note of your luggage allowance. Do not buy more than you are allowed to carry home.

LOST PASSPORTS

Losing a passport can be a stressful experience while being away from home in any country. However, like most things in China, there is a procedure to follow for getting a replacement passport and visa.

A choice of various antiques for visitors to choose from.

Police station.

Step 1

Go to the local PSB office closest to where your passport was lost or stolen to file a loss report. The PSB will issue a Certificate of Loss Report. Taking your Registration Form of Temporary Residency (临时住宿登记表 — available from your hotel front desk) and a copy of the lost passport (if available) will help.

Step 2

Go to the Entry-Exit Bureau to apply for a Loss Certificate of a Passport. Bring with you:

- The PSB Report (from step 1)
- Two passport sized photos
- Registration Form of Temporary Residency
- A valid form of ID (e.g. copy of lost passport, driver's licence)
- Any other official Chinese issued documents you may have such as Work Permit, Foreign Expert Certificate, or Student ID

You will be given a form to fill out and then you will be issued a Loss Certificate of a Passport.

In Beijing, the Foreigners Visa Section of the **Entry-Exit Bureau of the Beijing Municipality Public Security Bureau** (市公安局出入境管理中心) is located on the second floor, 2 Andingmen Dajie (安定门大街2号), 600 metres east of the Yonghegong (雍和宫) Metro Station.

Step 3

Take all the documentation received from steps 1 and 2 to your home country embassy or consulate. You will need to have some form of valid ID for entrance and proof of identity in applying for a new passport. Again, a photocopy of your original passport will help. A driver's licence is helpful. You may need to have family or friends fax copies of documentation, including a birth certificate, to the embassy. You will also need to bring at least two passport photos for the application. It may pay to call or check the website of your embassy or consulate prior to going. As a replacement passport may take time, some countries issue a temporary travel document.

Step 4
Take the newly issued passport or temporary travel document, and all other documents from steps 1 and 2 back to the Entry-Exit Bureau to apply for a visa. Two passport photos and your Registration Form of Temporary Residency are required.

BRIEF CHINESE MENU
Food is important in Chinese culture. Take this handy menu with you to Chinese restaurants for easy ordering. Try a variety of dishes. Enjoy your meal!

MENU

Pork, Beef and Lamb

Sweet and Sour Pork	古老肉	Gǔ lǎo ròu
Twice Cooked Pork	回锅肉	Huí guō ròu
Peanuts with Pork	花生肉丁	Huā shēng ròu dīng
Diced Pork with Hot Peppers	辣椒炒肉	Là jiāo chǎo ròu
Muxu Pork	木须肉	Mù xū ròu
Minced Pork Fried with French Beans	干煸扁豆	Gān piàn biǎn dòu
Fried Chilli Pork Chops	香辣猪扒	Xiāng là zhū bā
Spare Ribs in Wine Sauce	酒醉排骨	Jiǔ zuì pái gǔ
Stewed Spare Ribs with Tomato Sauce	茄汁炆排骨	Qié zhī wen pái gǔ
Sliced Pork with Vegetable Shoots	菜蓬滑肉片	Cài peng gǔ ròu piàn
Mustard Green with Ham	云腿芥菜胆	Yún tuǐ jiè cài dǎn
Shredded Pork in Spicy Garlic Sauce	鱼香肉丝	Yú xiāng ròu sī
Beef with Oyster Sauce	蚝油牛肉	Háo yóu niú ròu
Beef Iron Plate	铁板牛肉	Tiě bǎn niú ròu
Stir-fried Beef with Lychee	荔枝炒牛肉	Lìzhī chǎo niú ròu
Stir-fried Ox Ribs with Pineapple	菠萝牛仔骨	Bōluó niú zǐ gǔ
Lamb Skewers	羊肉串	Yáng ròu chuān

Chicken, Duck and Pigeon

Chicken, Peanut and Chillies	宫爆鸡丁	Gōng bào jī dīng
Fried Chicken with Peppers & Onion	辣椒炒鸡肉	Là jiāo chǎo jī ròu
Steamed Chicken with Ginger Sauce	清蒸鸡肉	Qīng zhēng jī ròu
Shredded Chicken & Green Peppers	青椒鸡丝	Qīng jiāo jī sī
Chicken Cubes with Cashew Nuts	腰果鸡丁	Yāo guǒ jī dīng
Steamed Chicken with Salted Sauce	香妃鸡	Xiāng fēi jī
Chicken Fried with Chilli Peppers	辣子鸡丁	Làzi jī dīng
Chicken in Sweet and Sour Sauce	糖醋鸡块	Táng cù jī kuài
Shredded Roast Duck with Jelly Fish	赛海蜇拌火鸭	Sàihǎizhēbànhuǒyāsī
Honey Chicken with Ginger Shoots	蜜糖子姜鸡	Mì táng zi jiāng jī
Curry Chicken with Apple	苹果咖喱鸡	Píng guǒ gālí jī
Duck Wings with Coriander	香荽鸭翼	Xiāngsuī yāyì
Deep-fried Pigeon in Spiced Sauce	卤炸乳鸽	Lǔ zhá rǔ gē
Peking Duck	北京烤鸭	Běijīng kǎo yā

Seafood

Whole Steamed Fish	清蒸鱼	Qīng zhēng yú
Fish Head Soup with Black Beans	黑豆煲鱼头汤	Hēidòu bāo yú tóu tāng
Deep-fried Snapper	干炸多春鱼	Gānzha duō chūn yú
Fried Fish with Onion	洋葱煮鱼	Yángcōng zhǔ yú
Baked Fish with Chilli And Salt	椒盐焗鱼	Jiāoyán ju yú
Crab Meat in Chicken Broth	清汤蟹肉	Qīng tāng xiè ròu
Fried Crabs in Chilli Sauce	辣椒炒蟹	Làjiāo chǎo xiè
Fried Shrimp Balls & Sesame Seeds	黑白分明	Hēibái fēnmíng
Prawns in Garlic Sauce	蒜蓉蟠龙虾	Suànróng pán lóngxià
Shrimps and Broccoli Soup	菜花虾羹	Càihuā xiā gēng
Rice Crisps with Seafood	三鲜锅巴	Sānxiān guōba

Vegetables

Dou Miao (green vegetable)	豆苗	Dòu miáo
Morning Glory with Garlic	大蒜空心菜	Dà suàn kōng xīn cài
Sword Beans	素烧刀豆	Sù shāo dāo dòu
Bak Choy and Mushrooms	香菇菜心	Xiāng gū cài xīn
Fried Egg Plant	素烧茄子	Sù shāo qiézi
Eggplant Casserole	鱼香茄子暴	Yú xiāng qié zi bào
Shredded Potato with Green Peppers	青椒土豆丝	Qīng jiāo tǔ dòu sī
Lettuce Fried in Oyster Sauce	蚝油生菜	Háo yóu shēng cài
Chinese Cabbage Fried with Garlic	蒜容炒白菜	Suànróng chǎo bái cài
Broccoli Fried with Garlic	蒜容炒西兰花	Suàn róng chǎo xī lán huā
Stir-fried Corn and Pine Nuts	松仁玉米	Sōng rén yù mǐ
Home Style Doufu	家常豆腐	Jiā cháng dòu fu
Spicy Doufu (mapo doufu)	麻婆豆腐	Má pó dòu fu
Doufu & Mushrooms	蘑菇豆腐	Má gū dòu fu
Fried Vegetables with Shrimp Paste	马拉盏炒菜	Mǎlāzhǎn chǎocài

Steamed Egg Custard & Minced Pork	肉碎蒸滑蛋	Ròusuì zhēnggǔdàn
Fried Vermicelli in Hot Bean Sauce	素香粉丝	Sùxiāng fěnsī
Stir-fried Bean Sprouts	清炒豆苗	Qīng chǎo dòu miáo
Lotus Root	莲藕	Lián ǒu
Dried Oysters and Black Moss Soup	发财好市汤	Fācài hǎo shì tāng

Soup

Hot and Sour Soup	酸辣汤	Suān là tang
Corn and Egg Soup	粟米羹	Sù mǐ gēng
Tomato and Egg-drop soup	蛋花香茄汤	Dàn huā xiāng qíe tàng
Fish Ball Soup	鱼丸汤	Yúwán tāng
Wonton Soup	馄饨汤	Húntún tāng
Potato and Black Mushroom Soup	薯仔煲冬菇汤	
Pork Thick Soup	肉羹汤	Ròu gēng tāng
Seaweed Soup	紫菜汤	Zǐcài tāng
Meat Ball Soup	貢丸汤	
Egg & Vegetable Soup	蛋花汤	Dànhuā tāng

Eggs

Scrambled Eggs with Tomatoes	西红柿炒蛋	Xīhóngshì chǎo dàn
Scrambled Eggs w/ Tomatoes, Peppers, Onions	西红柿,青椒, 洋葱,炒蛋	
Scrambled Eggs with Peppers	青椒炒蛋	Qīng jiāo chǎo dàn
Onion Omelette	洋忽煎蛋	Yáng cōng jiān dàn

Rice, Noodles and Dumplings

White Rice	米饭	Mǐ fàn
Fried Rice (Yangzhou Style)	扬州炒饭	Yángzhōu chǎo fàn
Mantou (Steamed Bread)	馒头	Mán tóu
Jiaozi (Dumplings)	饺子	Jiǎo zi
Guotie (Fried Dumplings)	锅贴儿	Guō tiē'r
Spring Rolls	春卷	Chūn juǎn'r
Beef Noodles	牛肉面	Niú ròu miàn
Xinjiang Style Noodles	炒面片	Chǎo miàn piàn
Fried Noodles with Vegetables	蔬菜炒面	Shū cài chǎo miàn
Fried Rice Noodles	炒米粉	Chǎo mǐfěn
Wonton & Noodles	馄饨面	Hún tún miàn
Dan Bing (egg cakes)	蛋饼	Dàn bǐng
You Tiao (deep fried bread stick)	油条	Yóu tiáo
Soybean Milk	豆浆	Dòu jiang

Dessert

Pulled Silk Banana	拔丝香蕉	Bá sī xiāng jiāo
Glutinous Rice Sesame Balls	芝麻球	Zhī ma qíu
Bean Paste Cake	绿豆糕	Lù dòu gāo
Red Bean Cake	红豆糕	Hóng dòu gāo

Taro Cake	芋头糕	Yù tou gāo
Custard Tart	蛋塔	Dàn tá
Sweet Soup Balls	汤圆	Tāng yuán

Drinks

Green Tea	绿茶	Lù chá
Chrysanthemum Tea	菊花茶	Jú huā chá
Jasmine Tea	茉莉花茶	Mò lí huā chá
Eight Treasures Tea	八宝茶	Bā bǎo chá
Black Tea	红茶	Hóng chá
Coca-Cola	可口可乐	Kě kǒu kě lè
Sprite	雪碧	Xuě bì
Mineral Water	矿泉水	Kuàng quán shuǐ
Hot Water	开水	Kāi shuǐ

Condiments

Salt	盐	Yán
Pepper	胡椒	Hú jiāo
Chilli	辣椒	Là jiāo
Soy Sauce	酱油	Jiāng yóu
Vinegar	醋	Cù

BRIEF CHINESE PHRASE LIST

Greetings

Hello	你好!	nǐ hǎo
How are you	你好吗?	nǐ hǎo ma?
I'm fine	我很好	wǒ hěn hǎo
May I ask your name	您贵姓?	nín guì xìng?
My surname is	我姓 …	wǒ xìng …
Goodbye	再见	zài jiàn
Thankyou	谢谢	xièxie
You're welcome	不客气	bù kè qì
I'm sorry	对不起	dùi bù qǐ
No, not so	不	bù
No, don't have	没有	méi yǒu
I come from	我是 … 人	wǒ shì … rén
It doesn't matter.	没关系	méi gūan xì
I want ...	我要	wǒ yào
No, I don't want	我不要	wǒ bù yào
I don't understand	听不懂	tīng bù dǒng
Do you understand?	你听懂吗	nǐ tīng dǒng ma?
Pleased to meet you	认识您很高兴	rèn shì nǐn hěn gāo xing

Money

How much is it?	多少钱?	dūo shǎo qián
Is there anything cheaper?	有没有便宜的?	yǒu piányi yidian de ma?
That's too expensive!	太贵了!	tài guì le!
RMB (people's money)	人民币	rénmínbì
Bank of China	中国银行	Zhōngguó Yínháng
Traveller's Cheque	旅行支票	lüxíng zhípiào
Change Money	钱换	huàn qián
I need the bill	请买单	qǐng mǎi dān
I want to buy …	我要买 …	wǒ yào mǎi …
Train ticket	火车票	hǔochē piào
Hard sleeper	硬卧票	yìngwò piào
Soft Sleeper	软卧票	rǔanwò piào
Hard Seat	硬座票	yìngzuo piào
Boat ticket	船票	chúan piào
Plane ticket	飞机票	fēijī piào

Toilets

Toilet	厕所/卫生间	cèsǔo/wèishēngjiàn
Men's/Women's	男/女	nán/nü
Toilet Paper	卫生纸	wèishēngzhǐ
Where is the toilet?	厕所在哪?	cèsǔo zài nǎ?

Post & Telecommunications

Post Office	邮局	yóujú
Letter	信	xìn
Envelope	信封	xìnfēng
Package	包裹	bāogǔo
Air Mail	航空	hángkōng
Stamps	邮票	yóu piào
Fax	传真	chuánzhēn
Internet Café	网吧	wǎngba

Time

When?	什么时候?	shénme shíhòu
Now	现在	xìanzài
Today	今天	jīntīan
Tomorrow	明天	míngtīan
Yesterday	昨天	zùotīan
Morning	上午	shàngwǔ
Afternoon	下午	xìawǔ
Wait a moment	等一会儿	děng yīhui'r

Useful Phrases

I want to go to the ...	我要去...	wǒ yào qù
Where is the ...	... 在哪儿?	... zài nǎr?
Train	火车	huǒchē
Train Station	火车站	huǒchē zhàn
Bus	公共汽车	gōnggòng qì chē
Bus Station	长途汽车	chángtú qì chē
Taxi	出租汽车	chū zū qì chē
Airport	机场	jī chǎng
Police	公安局	gōng ān jú
Bank	银行	yínháng
Hospital/Doctor	医院/医生	yī yuàn/yī shēng
University	大学	dàxúe
Hotel	宾馆/饭店	bīn guǎn/fàn diàn
Boat Wharf	码头	mǎ tóu
I am unwell and need a doctor	我不舒服，请送我去医院	wǒ bù shū fu, qǐng sòng wǒ qù yī yuàn

Counting

1	一	yī
2	二	èr
3	三	sān
4	四	sì
5	五	wǔ
6	六	liù
7	七	qī
8	八	bā
9	九	jiǔ
10	十	shí
11	十一	shí yī
12	一二	shí èr
20	二十	èr shí
21	二十一	èr shí yī
22	二十二	èr shí èr
30	三十	sān shí
100	一百	yī bǎi
101	一百零一	yī bǎi líng yī
150	一百五十	yī bǎi wǔ shí
1,000	一千	yī qiān
10,000	一	yī wàn
23,400	二万三千四	èr wàn sān qiān sì bǎi

FIVE

Setting Up in Beijing

Setting Up in Beijing

EMBASSY REGISTRATION

If you move to Beijing long-term, make it a priority to register yourself and your family at your home country's embassy. This will help you in the event of replacing lost passports, evacuation in a civil emergency, assistance in a family crisis, etc. If your family is made up of more than one nationality,

then register at all relevant embassies. Many embassies now offer registration online through a secure website. See the *Directories* section of this book for Beijing's embassies.

PERSONAL SECURITY CHECKLIST

1. Make copies of all your important documents, including:
   - Passports
   - Current visa/Foreign Expert's Certificate/ Student ID
   - Birth and Marriage Certificates
   - Insurance Policy Numbers
   - Current prescriptions — including eyeglasses
   - House Contract
   - Social Security Numbers (if applicable)
   - Bank Account Numbers
   - Credit Card Numbers
   - Contents and location of safe repository/name of

power of attorney
- Names and addresses of important contacts
- Important financial information

Keep one set of copies with you in a safe place and other sets with a trusted family member or friend. The above documents should be in a sealed packet to be opened only in the event of death, extreme emergency or by permission of the owner.

2. File a current will detailing the care and custody of your children, the distribution of your personal effects and power of attorney for all bank accounts at home and in Beijing. Put the original will in a safe repository and leave additional copies with your lawyer, a family member, or the executor of your estate.

3. Create a telephone directory detailing local emergency contact numbers, embassy contacts, hospital clinics and other important numbers. Put it in a place where all family members with you know where to find it.

4. Prepare an information sheet listing personal details for use in an emergency situation: full name, date of birth, passport info, visa details, blood type, health details, next of kin contact information, first contact information, and insurance company emergency assistance numbers. Keep this information in a safe place and swap sheets with a trusted friend or colleague in Beijing.

5. Develop a crisis plan detailing emergency contacts, where to go in the event of a crisis, and establish how you will access monetary funds in case of emergency.

6. Make an extra set of house keys and leave these with a trusted friend in Beijing.

RENTING LOCAL HOUSING

In the past few years, foreigners have been permitted to rent local housing in Beijing. Guidelines, including those regarding Public Security Bureau (PSB) registration and contract laws, are as follows:

Locating an Apartment
Most people find local housing through Internet sites, real estate agents or privately through friends. Agents will assist you in contract negotiations and signing. An agent or your landlord should also help you with PSB registration and offer

ongoing support throughout the duration of the contract. One website with extensive listings on available housing is www.wuwoo.com

Signing a Contract

It is important to have a signed contract outlining all the conditions of rent and liability. You will often be required to put down a deposit equal to two months rent and pay the first two months in advance. Do not be shy about negotiating the price. Clarify whether the rent includes any management fees and winter heating fees. Prior to signing the contract (usually in Chinese) make sure you understand all conditions

of rental and ask to view the landlord's ownership papers (房产证) and ID card (身份证). It is your right to ask the landlord to register the apartment as a rental and ask for locks on the main door to be changed. A list of furnishings and contents of the house should be checked and signed by both parties. Initial water, gas and electricity metre readings should also be recorded.

Utilities

You will be required to pay for all water, electricity, gas, telephone and Internet bills. Find out when and where bills are to be paid, and understand the billing systems. It is

becoming increasingly common for electronic cards to be used for prepayment of electricity and gas.

Moving Out

Many contracts require that you notify the landlord up to two months in advance of your intentions for either renewing or moving out. Deposits should be returned at the time of vacating the apartment, provided all conditions of contract have been met. Landlords will sometimes ask to keep a portion of the deposit to cover any potential outstanding bills. Make sure you have a clear agreement on when any remaining money is to be returned.

PUBLIC SECURITY BUREAU (PSB) REGISTRATION

All foreigners residing in Beijing are required by law to register with the local PSB within 24 hours of moving to a new place. Bring each resident's passport, work permit, foreign expert certificate or other relevant documentation, and a copy of your rental contract to the PSB office. Most offices require the landlord to be present with their house ownership papers and ID card. Students staying on campus or foreigners staying

in a hotel are registered at the point of check in and need not go to the local PSB office unless directed to do so.

A Registration Form of Temporary Residency will be issued, valid until the expiry of your current visa.

注意 Note:

You are required to show a Registration Form of Temporary Residency when making changes to, extending or renewing your visa at the Aliens Exit and Entry Bureau. You will not be able to submit any visa application without having first registered with the PSB.

It is not uncommon in Beijing for PSB officers to make spot checks on foreigners, to check registration details. It is important to have the stamped copy of the Registration Form of Temporary Residency available with your passport. Failure to register may result in a fine, or being accompanied to the local PSB office to complete registration.

It is also necessary that you re-register if there is any change to the type of visa, renewal of a visa or if moving into a new place of residency.

HEALTH CHECK

A health check is required for all foreigners applying to work or study in China for more than six months. This includes blood tests for AIDS, a chest X-ray and a consultation with a doctor. The Beijing International Travel Health Centre (中华人民共和国北京卫生检疫局/国际旅行卫生保健中心) handles all immigration related health checks. Forms and fee schedules are available at the centre. Address: 20 Hepingli Beijie, Dongcheng District (东城区, 和平里北街20号). Telephone: 6512-4222 or 6421-6273.

TAXES

All foreigners working in Beijing are required to register with the Tax Bureau and pay tax. A deduction applies with the first ¥800 of the monthly income tax-free. Other deductions and reimbursements can be applied for, but only with official government-issued receipts. For more information, visit the website: http//:english.tax861.gov.cn.

BANKING

Receiving funds from overseas can be done in a number of ways.

- **ATMs** — Credit, debit or bank cards are the fastest and most convenient way to draw money from overseas. Look for an ATM with the Visa, MasterCard, Cirrus and Plus logos. Most ATMs allow withdrawals in amounts up to ¥2000-¥3000 per withdrawal. Banks add a surcharge on over-the-counter credit card cash advance withdrawals.
- **Telegraphic Transfers (TTs)** can sometimes take up to one week to clear. They do, however, offer a convenient way for receiving large sums or funds in foreign currencies. Funds can be received in most major currencies.

- **International Bank Drafts** are a safe form of sending money through the post, but they can take up to one month to clear, depending on the currency, and will incur a service fee.
- **Personal overseas cheques** require one to two weeks to clear and will incur a service fee.

The Bank of China is the main bank through which foreigners may change money and hold accounts. This bank offers *Renminbi* (RMB) accounts, and multi-currency accounts containing up to 13 additional currencies including US Dollars, British Pounds, Euros, Hong Kong Dollars, Japanese Yen, Singapore Dollars, Deutsche Marks and Swiss Francs. *Renminbi* accounts can also be opened with other local banks including CITIC.

Opening a local bank account requires presentation of a passport and a minimum deposit of ¥10 or sum of foreign currencies equivalent in value to ¥20. A Bank of China Great Wall Debit Card can be applied for when you set up a bank account.

MONEY TRANSFER SERVICES

International Money Transfers can be sent and received through Western Union and Moneygram.

Western Union services are available at some China Post service centres and Agricultural Bank of China outlets in Beijing. Forms and information are available in English. Be sure to carry a valid ID with you when sending or receiving funds. A list of Western Union agents can be found on their website at www.westernunion.com or by calling 800-820-8668

MoneyGram services are available through the Bank of Communications, CITIC Bank and ICBC Bank. A list of MoneyGram agents in Beijing can be found by visiting the website at www.moneygram. com.

INTERNET AND BROADBAND SERVICES

Dial-up access is available by either using 'pay-as-you-go' which charges directly to your telephone bill, prepaid Internet cards or by setting up an account with CNC (China Netcom). While convenient, dial-up access has its limitations. With a vast number of users using dial-up, access speed can at times be very slow or even very difficult to get online. Telephone charges can also add up if you are frequently accessing the net. Setting up an ADSL or LAN connection is the recommended option.

ADSL and LAN offer high-speed access and are affordable to use. Many new buildings have pre-installed Broadband lines and may only require setting up an account before connecting your LAN port using PPPOE. ADSL requires setting up an account and installation of cables in your apartment. You will also need an ADSL modem which may be purchased from the service provider. Fixed rates for ADSL and LAN services are ¥120 per month for 500M or ¥150 per month for 1G with unlimited access. Visit a China Netcom (CNC) service centre or their website at www. chinanetcom.com.cn/en/ for further information.

Cable and Wireless are also available. Increasing numbers of cafés and restaurants offer wireless services for customers. Cable internet is available in Beijing through Gehua Cable TV (歌华有线电视有限公司). Details are available directly by telephone 96196 or website at www.bgctv.com.cn (Chinese only).

APPLYING FOR A CHINESE DRIVER'S LICENCE

Foreigners holding a residence permit and valid overseas driver's licence can apply for a Chinese driver's licence.

Applicants will need to submit a completed driver's licence application form (in Chinese), current health check, a passport with resident's permit, three passport photos and an overseas driver's licence with a certified translation in Chinese. You must pass a computer-based road theory exam which comprised 100 questions with a passing score of 90% or above. The cost is ¥50 for the exam and ¥5 for the driver's licence. An exam preparation book can be purchased from Beijing FESCO Chenguang Labour Service Co., Ltd. Obtain and submit application forms at the Beijing Traffic and Vehicle Department, No. 18 South Fourth Ring East Road, Chaoyang District 朝阳区南四环东路18号 (南四环外环十八里店南桥西南侧).

STUDYING IN BEIJING

There are currently over 40,000 overseas students studying in either Chinese language programmes or pursuing degrees in a number of fields. Beijing University, Qinghua University, Beijing Culture and Languages University, and Beijing Normal University all have well over 1,000 foreign students each.

Many universities offer quality Chinese language programmes for both short-term and long-term study. Separate courses can also be arranged for short-term studies in Chinese culture, calligraphy, music, tai'qi (太极拳), cooking, Peking Opera or sports.

It is possible to complete Bachelor's, Master's and PhD degrees in a number of fields. A level 6 pass or more in the HSK Chinese Language Proficiency Test is a prerequisite to pursuing a degree.

The more well-known universities are more expensive, and gaining acceptance to study may also be difficult. While many other universities have fewer foreign students, many do offer good Chinese language acquisition programmes. These tend to be cheaper and are less pressured. Most offer students preparatory classes and coaching for sitting the HSK Chinese Language Proficiency Test.

A list of universities accepting foreign students is found in the *Directories* section of this book.

Accommodation

Foreign students in Beijing now have the option of either staying on campus in an International Students' dormitory or renting local housing. Some universities require students to live on-campus for a period of time. It may be required by the Foreign Affairs Office to submit copies of your rental contract, PSB temporary registration form, or have their prior consent to live off-campus.

A shared room without a private bathroom can cost from US$5 per day up to US$15 per day or more for a single room with a private bathroom and full facilities. Most rooms have beds, bedding, TV, telephone, desks and a bookshelf. Very few rooms offer kitchen facilities. Some dormitories have communal kitchens. Most students usually eat at campus dining halls or at local restaurants.

Insurance

Universities in Beijing require self-paying foreign students to have medical insurance. You are encouraged to arrange this before leaving for China. Local medical insurance programmes are available for foreign students in Beijing on group rates through universities, e.g. Ping An Life Insurance of China offers accident and medical emergency insurance for six months to one year. Contact your school or insurance provider directly for details.

Private Language Schools

In addition to the many universities and institutes receiving foreign students of Chinese, there are many private language schools operating throughout the city. Prices and services vary widely. Some offer both standard scheduled classes and private classes.

Several affordable private language schools located in Wudaokou offer a range of weekday and weekend classes for all levels. Specific part-time Chinese language courses for foreign business personnel living in Beijing are available in both Haidian and Chaoyang Districts. For a short listing of schools offering Chinese language courses, check out English magazines such as *That's Beijing Magazine, Beijing Insider's Guide, or City Weekend,* or their related websites. Private language schools do not usually offer a student visa, even for full-time students.

SIX

Key Sites in Beijing

Key Sites in Beijing

Beijing has been an important centre in education, innovation and cultural development throughout much of China's history, and is therefore rich with historical and cultural sites. Information on some key sites is provided here to help you gain deeper insights and understanding into the city of Beijing.

注意 Note:
While every effort has been made to provide accurate information, please note that prices and opening hours are subject to change.

TIANANMEN SQUARE
天安门广场
Tiananmen Square, located in

Tiananmen Square.

the heart of Beijing, is the largest city centre square in the world. Measuring 880 metres long and 500 metres wide, it has the capacity to hold up to one million people. Gatherings in this square marked significant events in China's past such as the May 4th Movement in 1919, the March 18th Massacre in 1926, the December 9th Students' Movement in 1935 and the declaration marking the founding of the People's Republic of China on October 1st, 1949.

Prior to 1949, the area was an imperial access way leading to the Forbidden City and used only for the emperor and high-ranking court officials. The area formed a 'T' shape with an open area at the top of the 'T' in front of the Tiananmen rostrum. Government bureaus were on either side of the access way. After 1949, the area was cleared and made into a square.

At the north end of the square is the National Flagpole. At sunrise, the national flag is raised with great pomp and ceremony. Every evening at sundown, the flag is lowered ceremoniously as well. Qianmen Gate lies to the south of the square.

Tiananmen Gate and the Forbidden City are to the north of Tiananmen Square. On the west side of Square is the Great Hall of the People. To the east is the National Museum. The Monument to the People's Heroes and Chairman Mao's Mausoleum are in the centre of the Square. Qianmen Gate lies to the south.

How to get there: Subway Line 1, Tiananmen East (天安门东) or Subway Line 2, Qianmen (前门).

> **Entrance fee** : Free
> **Hours**   : 05:00 - 22:00
> **Official website:**
> http://www.tiananmen.org.cn/index.asp
> *(in Chinese only)*

TIANANMEN GATE
天安门城楼

Tiananmen Gate, known as the 'Gate of Heavenly Peace', sits at the north end of Tiananmen Square and marks the main entrance to the Forbidden City. This gate was built in 1417 and served as a rostrum for announcing the enthronement of new emperors and issuing edicts to assembled officials. Top candidates in the imperial exams were also honoured here and prisoners were sentenced to death at the foot of the gate. From atop Tiananmen Gate, Mao Zedong made the historic proclamation marking the founding of the People's Republic of China in 1949. It is for this reason that the gate is featured on the national emblem.

One of the distinguishing features of this landmark is the giant portrait of Mao hanging over the central entranceway. To the left of the portrait is a slogan (中华人民共和国万岁), 'Long live the People's Republic of China'. To the right of Mao's portrait is another slogan (世界人民大团结万岁), 'Long live the great unity of the peoples of the world'.

Tiananmen Gate has five passageways/gates; the middle gate was reserved for the emperor alone. In front of the gate are the Seven Stone Bridges over the stream. Historically, each bridge was used by different ranks of officials with the centre bridge being reserved for the emperor.

By the gate are two pairs of stone lions. These served as 'guardians' for the emperor's

walkway in times past. The lions are popular today especially as background for tourists' photographs.

Another feature at Tiananmen Gate is two ornamental columns, 'huabiao', which have a 4,000-year history. In the period of Yao, one of the sage kings set up wooden pillars on which commoners could post their comments, advice, or complaints for the king. Over time, the pillars stopped serving this purpose and became purely ornamental. The wooden pillars were replaced with white marble, as seen today.

In 1988, Tiananmen Gate was opened to the public. Visitors can pay an admission fee, stand on top of the Gate and see the enormity of Tiananmen Square. When you go up onto the gate, take your camera only. All other belongings must be left at the baggage check area. Security is tight and guards are on duty at all times to protect this important national site.

How to get there: Subway Line 1, Tiananmen East (天安门东).

Entrance fee : ¥15
Hours   : 08:30 - 16:30
Official website: http://www. tiananmen.org.cn/index.asp
(in Chinese only)

The National Museum.

THE NATIONAL MUSEUM OF CHINA 中国国家博物馆

Located on the east side of Tiananmen Square is the National Museum of China, formerly called The Museum of Chinese History and the Revolution. The museum chronicles Chinese history and culture. Some of the relics include ancient stoneware, bronze ware and money. There are also more than 200,000 books housed here.

The former Museum of Chinese History was divided into four display areas: Primitive Society (2.5 million to 4,000 years ago), the Slave Society (21st century BC to 476BC), Feudal Society (457 to 1840AD) and Semi-Colonial/Semi-Feudal Society (1840 to 1919).

The new National Museum (reopening in 2009) will feature both permanent and temporary exhibits in a comprehensive, state-of-the-art complex. The renovated buildings will house more than 620,000 collections. With a floor space area of 192,000 square metres, it will be one of the largest museums in the world. One of the features of the museum will be the Supreme Hall of Culture and Art for the Chinese Nation, showcasing the best of Chinese arts.

The National Museum will provide a variety of services

for guests including volunteer guides, lectures, acoustic/audio guides/tours in various languages, as well as assistance for the disabled.

How to get there: Subway: Line 1, Tiananmen East (天安门东) or Line 2, Qianmen (前门). Bus: 1, 4, 10, 20, 22, 120, 726, 826区间.

Entrance fee : ¥30
Hours (Daily): 08:30 - 16:30 (08:00 - 18:00 during May First, National Day and summer holidays)
Official website: www.nmch.gov.cn

GREAT HALL OF THE PEOPLE 人民大会堂

The Great Hall of the People, built in only 10 months in 1959, was constructed as one of 10 major projects commemorating

Great Hall of the People Ceiling.

the 10th anniversary of the founding of the People's Republic of China (1949). Located on the west side of Tiananmen Square, it has a total floor area of 170,000 square metres. The complex consists of three main parts: the Grand Auditorium, the Banquet Hall, and the offices for the National People's Congress.

The Grand Auditorium has a seating capacity of 10,000 and is able to provide simultaneous translation in 12 languages. Many top-level government meetings are held here as well as concerts, shows, operas, and other performing arts galas. One distinguishing feature of the auditorium is the giant red star in the centre of the ceiling. This star symbolizes China's Communist Party and has 500 smaller stars around it symbolizing the Chinese people united around the Party.

The Banquet Hall has a seating capacity of 5,000. State leaders use this hall to host banquets for distinguished guests from around the world.

Every year, the National People's Congress (NPC), the Central Committee of the Communist Party of China (CCCPC), the State Council, and other government agencies hold meetings in the Great Hall of the People. There are thirty-four reception halls for various functions. Each of these reflects something about the area for which it is named — a province, municipality, or autonomous region under the Central Government. The building is open for tours, but it is inaccessible when government functions are being held.

How to get there: Subway: Line 1, Tiananmen West (天安门西) or Line 2, Qianmen (前门). Bus: 1, 2, 4, 7, 20, 44, 48, 120, 309支, 特1, 特2, 特4, 特7, 729, 808, 821

Entrance fee : ¥30
Hours : 08:00 - 16:00 (depending on time of year)
Official website: http://www.tiananmen.org.cn/index.asp *(in Chinese only)*

The Mao Zedong Mausoleum.

MAO ZEDONG MAUSOLEUM
毛主席纪念堂

The Mausoleum, located in Tiananmen Square, pays tribute to Chairman Mao Zedong, who served in the Communist Party, 1943-1976, and led the Party to found the People's Republic of China in 1949. Mao is a significant political and historical figure, still revered by many in China today. Construction on the mausoleum began soon after Mao's death on September 9, 1976, and was completed in May 1977.

The mausoleum is made up of three main halls. The North Hall features a white marble statue of Mao Zedong. The Central Hall, known as the Hall for Paying Respects to the Remains of Chairman Mao, is where his body lies in state in a crystal coffin. An inscription in white marble reads, "Eternal glory to the Great Leader and Teacher, Chairman Mao Zedong." The South Hall contains memorial rooms which pay tribute to other figures of China's historical and political past such as Zhou Enlai, Zhu De and Deng Xiaoping.

How to get there: Subway: Line 1, Tiananmen East (天安门东); Subway Line 2, Qianmen (前门).

Entrance fee : Free
Hours:
Tues to Sun   08:30 - 11:30
Tues & Thurs 14:00 - 16:00
Website:
http://www.tiananmen.org.cn/index.asp *(in Chinese only)*

QIANMEN 前门/正阳门

Qianmen, meaning 'front gate' at the south end of Tiananmen Square, was previously called Zhengyangmen, meaning 'south facing gate'. This gate/tower was built in 1420 during the early Ming Dynasty and was one of the nine inner city gates in the old city of Beijing. Connecting the inner and outer city areas, it served as the exclusive entry and exit point for the emperor and his family.

How to get there: Subway: Line 2, Qianmen (前门) or Line 1, Tiananmen East (天安门东).

Entrance fee : ¥10
Hours   : 08:30 - 16:00
Official website:
http://www.tiananmen.org.cn/index.asp
(in Chinese only)

FORBIDDEN CITY 故宫

The Forbidden City, located in the centre of Beijing, stands as a grand monument to China's imperial history and culture. Also known as the Purple Forbidden City, this complex served as the Imperial Palace for 24 Ming and Qing emperors over 491 years. Commoners and lower officials were denied access to the palace, thus the name 'Forbidden City'. The last emperor resided in the palace up until 1924. In 1925, the whole complex was opened to the public and officially renamed as the Palace Museum. With a total of 9,999 rooms, it covers 72 hectares (178 acres), stretching 960 metres from north to south and 750 metres from east to west.

Construction on the Forbidden City began in 1406

Qianmen   south end of Tiananmen.

The Forbidden City.

and took 14 years to complete. Most of the structures are made of wood, white marble, stone or brick from different areas of China. A total of 100,000 artisans and more than one million civilian labourers helped to construct it.

The Meridian Gate (south gate) is the main access point to the Forbidden City. Facing south, the gate took its name from the meridian line running through the palace from north to south. It was also believed that the emperor, as the son of heaven, was at the centre of the cosmos. The emperor had exclusive use of this gate and significant announcements were made from here. Captives, criminals, and anyone who

displeased the emperor were also taken out through this gate where they received beatings or were killed in the courtyard.

The Gate of Supreme Harmony is the front gate of the three main halls in the outer court of the Forbidden City. This was the place where the emperor met with officials, accepted documents, and made decisions. Past this gate is the Hall of Supreme Harmony (the 'Throne Hall'), the largest and most important building in the Forbidden City. From here, the emperor ruled the nation, received high-ranking officials and generals and held grand ceremonies.

The emperor, empress and concubines lived in the northern

most inner section of the Forbidden City. Following these private palaces is an Imperial Garden containing grand pavilions, rockeries, ponds, and ancient trees.

The Nine Dragon Screen is another of the grand sights in the Forbidden City. The first, fifth and ninth dragons are yellow (representing the emperor) and the others are different colours. The number nine is significant as the symbol of supremacy.

The Forbidden City/Palace Museum is open for visitors. Audio tours in a number of languages are available for rent. Tour guides may be helpful in pointing out the symbolism throughout the palace.

How to get there: Subway: Line 1, Tiananmen East (天安门东).

Entrance fee:
Winter   : ¥40
Summer   : ¥60
Hours:
October 15 - March 31: 08:30 - 16:30 (last tickets sold at 15:30);
April 1 - October 14: 08:30 - 17:00 (last tickets sold at 16:00)
Official website: http://www.dpm.com.cn

JINGSHAN (COAL HILL) PARK 景山公园

Located to the north of the Forbidden City, this hill was once the highest point in old Beijing. Originally built on principles of geomancy to protect the Forbidden City and used as a private imperial garden, Jingshan Park today offers visitors breathtaking views overlooking the Forbidden City. Five pavilions were built on each of the five peaks in 1758. Each pavilion housed a Buddhist image, all of which were later looted by the Allied Forces at the end of the Boxer Rebellion. A replacement Buddhist statue today sits in the pavilion at the highest peak.

The park is also identified as the place that the last Ming Emperor, Chongzhen, hanged

Coal Hill.

himself in the face of defeat from a peasant uprising in 1644.

Jingshan Park is sometimes known as Coal Hill possibly due to the fact that coal was once heaped around the foot of the hill. In some guides, it is also referred to as Prospect Hill. Many visitors combine a visit to Jingshan Park with their visit to the Forbidden City, due to their close proximity.

Address: 北京市西城区景山西街44号 44 Jingshan West Rd (Opposite Forbidden City North Gate)

How to get there: Bus: 5 (景山西街), 58, 60, 111 (景山东街), 111, 819 (景山), 101, 103, 103快, 109, 812, 814 (故宫)

Entrance fee : ¥2
Hours   : 06:00 - 21:30

SUMMER PALACE 颐和园

With a history of over 850 years, the Summer Palace is a must-see site in Beijing. Located 20 kilometres northwest of the city centre, the Summer Palace consists of Longevity Hill, Kunming Lake, and their surrounding gardens, pavilions, palaces and temples. It served as one of several summer retreats for China's emperors. Access to the Summer Palace for the royal family was primarily by

Summer Palace.

boat along the imperial canals. While the canals no longer reach the Forbidden City, it is still possible to take a boat from Yuyuantan Park to the palace along the former imperial waterways.

Originally built as an imperial garden during the Jin Dynasty, the Summer Palace was rebuilt in 1750 as a birthday gift from the emperor Qianlong for his mother.

The palace was later attacked, looted and destroyed by the Anglo-French forces in 1860 and rebuilt again in 1888 by the Empress Dowager Cixi. Funds designated for the building of a modern navy for China were diverted for the construction of the private imperial gardens. The only boat built from those funds was the Marble Boat which we still see today at the Summer Palace.

After the last Qing Emperor was dethroned in 1924, the Summer Palace was turned into a park, which is visited by six million visitors and locals throughout the year. Some of the key structures in the Summer Palace include:

- The Hall of Benevolence and Longevity was where Empress Dowager Cixi and Emperor Guangxu handled state affairs and received officials.
- The Marble Boat was first built in 1750 and rebuilt in 1893. The boat was used by the royal family as a vantage point from which to enjoy the lake and surrounding scenery.
- Emperor's Shopping Street (or Suzhou Street) was modelled after what Suzhou would have looked like in the Qing Dynasty. The street was only restored in 1986. It includes 60 shops, six bridges, a temple, and 30 archways.
- The Long Corridor is a covered walkway which stands between Longevity Hill and Kunming Lake. It is 728 metres long with 273 sections, and described as the 'longest painted corridor in the world'. The beams feature over 8,000 exquisite paintings depicting landscapes, stories, characters, or scenes from Chinese literature.
- The 17-Arch Bridge provides access to the Temple of the Dragon King which stands on an island in Kunming Lake and was the site from which Emperor Qianlong oversaw the training of his navy. The bridge is 150 metres long, and mimics the design of the Lugou Bridge (Marco Polo Bridge). There are 544 carved lions on the pillars of the bridge.

How to get there: Subway Line 4, Summer Palace (颐和园). Bus: 375 from Xizhimen (西直门), 332 from Beijing Zoo, 808 from Qianmen (前门). Boat from Yuyuantan Park (玉渊潭公园), directly behind the Millennium Monument.

Entrance fee:
November 1 - March 31, ¥20;
April 1 - October 31, ¥30;
Through ticket: ¥50, ¥60
Hours:
Summer : 06:00 - 18:00
Winter : 07:00 - 17:00
Official Website:
http://www.en.summerpalace-china.com

TEMPLE OF HEAVEN 天坛

The Temple of Heaven is one of the must-see tourist destinations in Beijing. First built in 1420, it was reconstructed during the late Ming and then Qing dynasties. It was here that the emperor would come to worship *Shangdi* — the God of Heaven, and pray for good harvest.

Temple of Heaven.

Altogether nine emperors (also known as 'Sons of Heaven') made sacrifices and worshipped at the Temple of Heaven. The emperor would visit the temple twice a year, once to pray for good harvest and once to offer sacrifices to heaven. For many Chinese, the Temple of Heaven was a place where their wishes could be conveyed to Heaven by the emperor. The emperor was believed to be the 'Son of Heaven', and as such stood as a mediator between Heaven and earth.

The complex and park cover an area of 273 hectares (674 acres), three times larger than the Forbidden City!

The Temple of Heaven is designed thematically. For example, the round-shaped walls of the main buildings represent heaven and the square-shaped walls at the base represent earth. The complex is also symbolically laid out on a north-south axis.

The main sites include the Hall of the Heavenly Emperor, the Circular Mound, the Imperial Vault of Heaven, the Abstinence Hall, the Beamless Hall and the Echo Wall. The most significant building at the Temple of Heaven is the Hall of Prayer for Good Harvests — the ultimate destination of the emperor when he came to pray. The hall was constructed of wooden interlocking beams, without any nails, and its roof has three conical roofs made of blue glazed tiles. Symbolism abounds, with colours and numbers of objects representing everything from the four seasons, to the terms in the Chinese calendar, to constellations. Images of the Hall of Prayer for Good

Harvests are today commonly used as a symbol of Beijing. Signs with descriptions of the various structures and their purposes are posted throughout the complex.

How to get there: Subway Line 5, Tiantan East (天坛东门). Bus: 6, 15, 17, 20, 35, 39, 54, 106, 120, 122, 803, 特8

Entrance fee:
Park Entrance ¥10 (November 1 - March 31); ¥15 (April 1 - October 31); Through ticket ¥30 (November 1 - March 31); ¥35 (April 1 - October 31)
Hours (Daily) : 08:30 - 18:30
Official website:
http://www.tiantanpark.com

WANGFUJING 王府井大街

Wangfujing, Beijing's number one shopping street, has over 200 grand shopping centres,

department stores, restaurants, bookshops and entertainment venues. Each day, over 400,000 tourists and locals enjoy shopping and sightseeing along this street.

Wangfujing, named after the 'Well of the Prince's Mansion', was a busy commercial area of the Yuan Dynasty. In the pre-1949 era, the street was called Morrison Street. In 1998, the street underwent extensive renovation when it was developed into a pedestrian mall.

Saint Joseph's Cathedral ('Dongtang') is situated in a prime location at the north end of Wangfujing.

Food is another popular draw. Visitors can get a taste of old Beijing by sampling all sorts of local delicacies and snacks on a stick from a snack street (小吃街), just off the main pedestrian mall. At night, food stalls are also set up along Donganmen Street (东安门大街) at the north end of Wangfujing.

How to get there: Wangfujing has a subway stop. It is also within walking distance of Tiananmen Square and the Forbidden City. Subway: Line 1, Wangfujing Station (王府井).

XIDAN 西单
Xidan is often referred to as Beijing's number two shopping street. Popular with young

Xidan.

people, especially on the weekends, Xidan has developed into a key shopping area for fashion and electronics. Both high-end shopping complexes and small shops with more of a local flavour can be found here.

How to get there: Subway: Line 1 and Line 4; Xidan (西单).

QIANMEN DAJIE 前门大街/DASHILAR 大栅栏

Qianmen Dajie has a long history as a key commercial district in old Beijing. As such, many famous restaurants and shops known as 'Laozihao' can trace their origins to this area. Most famous of the many lanes

and streets stemming from the main thoroughfare is Dashilar (大栅栏). This small street is home to renowned guildhalls, which provided accommodation for imperial examination candidates, shops, banks and business associations. During the late Qing Dynasty, the area was also home to numerous brothels and other entertainment venues for officials and royal family members. Recent restorations have sought to recreate Qianmen as it appeared during its heyday in the 1920's.

How to get there: Subway Line 2, Qianmen (前门)

HUTONGS 胡同

Hutongs are an important part of Beijing's heritage. First appearing in the Yuan Dynasty, these alleys and lanes are formed by closely arranged quadrangle houses known as *siheyuan*. Arranged around a central courtyard, or successive courtyards, *siheyuans* were the traditional dwellings in old Beijing. Some of these were made up of four houses built around a shared courtyard, with one family in each house. *Siheyuan* varied in size and design depending on the status of the residents.

Most of the *hutongs* are found near the Forbidden City. They have their roots in the Yuan, Ming and Qing dynasties in which emperors planned the city and arranged residential areas by ranking people in order of their status. Overcrowding in the 1950s affected the *hutongs'* grandeur. In the 1990s, many *hutongs* were torn down indiscriminately and replaced with modern buildings. Some efforts are now being made to preserve those *hutongs* with historical significance.

How to get there: *Hutongs* are found around Houhai, the Bell Tower and areas south of Qianmen Gate.

ZHONGNANHAI 中南海

Zhongnanhai is sometimes referred to as the 'New Forbidden City'. Originally palace grounds, the complex today serves as the residence and offices of China's highest government leaders. Meetings between Chinese and foreign heads of state are sometimes conducted here. As such, Zhongnanhai is today inaccessible to visitors.

This compound was built between the 10th and 13th centuries as a retreat for emperors, royal family members and high-ranking imperial officials. After the overthrow of imperial rule and the establishment of the People's Republic of China, Zhongnanhai has served as the site of the presidential compound.

How to get there: Located west of the Forbidden

City. Metro: Subway Line 1, Tiananmen Xi (天安门西).

SHICHAHAI SCENIC ZONE 什刹海 (THREE REAR LAKES 后三海)

The Shichahai Lakes District originally dates back to the Yuan Dynasty. Three connected lakes, Xihai (West Lake西海), Houhai (Rear Lake后海) and Qianhai (Front Lake前海), sit surrounded by winding *hutong*s, classical *siheyuan* courtyard houses and former imperial gardens. Today a pleasant area for taking a leisurely stroll and for enjoying the city's most characteristic *hutong*s, the lakes were originally important for the imperial city's water supply.

Several historically significant sites are located around the lakes. These include the Prince Gong's Palace (恭王府), one of the grandest existing courtyard complexes from the Qing Dynasty; the former residence of Soong Ching Ling (宋庆龄故居), who was honorary president of the People's Republic of China; the

Guo Moruo Museum (郭沫若故居), that is devoted to the life and works of one of China's most famous writers and poets, Guo Moruo; and the Guanghua Temple (广化寺).

How to get there: Subway: Line 2, Jishuitan (积水潭), Line 4 Xinjiekou (新街口). Located opposite the north gate of Beihai Park (北海公园).

CAPITAL MUSEUM
首都博物馆

The Capital Museum features both traditional Chinese and modern architectural styles. Opened in 2005, the museum houses comprehensive exhibitions detailing Beijing's history and cultural heritage.

The museum has a number of regular exhibitions including displays on ancient Beijing's history and culture, urban development and old stories of Beijing. Over 5,600 items are on display, most unearthed or originating from Beijing Municipality. The Fine Arts exhibitions include displays of chinaware, bronze art, calligraphy, paintings, jade and Buddhist statues. Temporary exhibitions highlight Beijing's relationships with other cities and countries around the world.

How to get there: Located on the western end of Chang'an Avenue (长安西街). Subway: Line 1, Muxidi (木樨地). Bus: 1, 4, 52, 37, 937, 727, 717, 650, 708, 26, and 319.

> **Hours :** 09:00 - 17:00 Tuesdays through Sundays (closed on Mondays)
> **Entrance fee :** ¥30
> **Official website:** www.capitalmuseum.org.cn

BEIHAI PARK 北海公园

Beihai Park is considered one of the best preserved imperial gardens in China and is the oldest in the world. Located to the northwest of the Forbidden City, it was used as a pleasure garden by China's imperial rulers. The 68.2 hectare park has two main parts: the Jade Flowery Islet and the lake.

Beihai Park was first built during the Liao Dynasty (10th

Strolling through Beihai Park.

century). When the Jin Dynasty overthrew the Liao in 1115 and established Beijing as their capital city, orders were given to expand the city. The lake was dug, creating the central Jade Flowery Islet. Palaces and halls were also built during this time and Taihu rocks placed on the island as decoration. Following the Mongolian invasion and sacking of the former Jin city, Kublai Khan built his imperial palaces adjacent to the park in 1268. Significant construction took place during the Ming Dynasty. This included construction of the Five Dragon Pavilion, the Nine Dragon Screen and other pavilions, galleries and halls. A white marble bridge crossing the lake was also built. In 1651, the present Tibetan-style pagoda was erected, supposedly holding a relic of Buddha.

How to get there: Bus 107, 118 or 701 from Ping'anli Subway Station, Line 4 (平安里); Bus 109, 101, 103, or 104 from Xisi Subway Station, Line 4 (西四). Also within walking distance from the north gate of the Forbidden City.

Entrance fee : ¥10
Hours : 06:30 - 20:00
Official website:
www.beihaipark.com.cn

OLD CITY GATES

Beijing is a city of gates. During the Ming and Qing Dynasties, there were nine inner city gates and seven outer city gates. Each gate served a specific purpose. Today, many place and street names have taken on the names of the gates of times past. Five of these gates still stand today and are testimonies to Beijing's strength and organization. Former inner city gates still standing include Qianmen (前门) and Deshengmen (德胜门). Former outer city gates still standing include Dongbianmen (东便门), Xibianmen (西便门) and the newly-rebuilt Yongdingmen (永定门).

NIUJIE MOSQUE 牛街礼拜寺 AND DONGSI MOSQUE 东四清真寺

More than 66 mosques serve more than 250,000 Muslims in Beijing. Of these, the Niujie

Mosque and the Dongsi Mosque
are two of the most well-known.

The **Niujie Mosque** dates
back to the Liao Dynasty
(996AD) and is the oldest
mosque in Beijing. Still active
today, it features Arabian
architecture combined with
Chinese symmetrical design.
The mosque houses important
cultural relics and the tombs
of Arabian elders who came to
China to lecture on Islam during
the Yuan dynasty. An inscribed
stele written in Arabic script
stands by the Tombs. There is
an imperial edict by the emperor
Kangxi (1664) on site, as well
as a handwritten copy of the
Qur'an, preserved for more
than 300 years. Ming Dynasty
porcelain and copper and iron
vessels from the Qing dynasty
are also housed in the mosque.

Address: Niu Jie, Xuanwu
District (宣武区，牛街).

How to get there: Bus
10, or 626 from Changchun Jie
Subway Station, Line 2 (长椿街);
or within walking distance of
Caishikou Subway Station, Line
4 (菜市口).

Entrance fee	: ¥10
Hours	: 08:10 - 17:00

The **Dongsi Mosque** was
first constructed during the
Ming Dynasty (1368-1644).
The Prayer Hall is the structure
remaining from that period;
other structures being built
during the Qing Dynasty.
Much of its design reflects
Arabian courtyard-style. The
complex includes ablution
rooms, an impressive library
(with a 700-year-old copy of
the Qur'an) and a prayer hall.
The Dongsi Mosque is the
headquarters for the Beijing
branch of the Chinese Islamic
Association.

Address: 13 Dongsi
Nandajie, Dongcheng District
(东城区，东四南大街13号).

How to get there: Dongsi
Subway Station, Line 5 (东四).

LUGOU BRIDGE 卢沟桥

Lugou Bridge, also known as
the Marco Polo Bridge, was first
built during the Jin Dynasty

(1115-1234). The bridge served as a vital link connecting Beijing to the rest of the nation in the south, and was a gateway to the city. Marco Polo saw the bridge in 1279 and described its beauty and grandeur in his travel journals, making it famous internationally.

In 1751, Emperor Qianlong personally inscribed poetic stele tablets and named the Lugou Bridge as one of eight scenic spots of Beijing at the time. He gave it the title 'Lugou Xiaoyue' (卢沟晓月), the Morning Moon over Lugou Bridge.

The Lugou Bridge is in southwest Beijing, 15 kilometres from the city centre. This marble bridge is 260 metres in length, and has 10 piers and 11 arches. Atop the balustrades on both sides of the bridge are 485 stone lions which add to its appeal. It is the only multi-arch stone bridge which spans the Yongding River.

Address: Fengtai District, Wanping, Lugou Bridge (丰台区, 宛平城, 卢沟桥).

How to get there: Bus 309 from Qianmen (前门). Bus 624 from Gongzhufen Station, Line 1 (公主坟站) or Bus 748 from Wukesong Station, Line 1 (五棵松站).

> **Hours :** 08:30 - 16:30
> **Entrance fee:**
> Lugou Bridge ¥20

Lugou Bridge.

THE MUSEUM OF THE CHINESE PEOPLE'S ANTI-JAPANESE WAR
中国人民抗日战争博物馆

On July 7th, 1937, the first shots of the Japan-China War were fired at Lugou Bridge. Chinese history books refer to the resulting war as the 'War of Resistance against Japan' (1937-1945). The Museum of the Chinese People's Anti-Japanese War was built in 1987 to commemorate China's fallen heroes. Over 35 million Chinese people were either wounded or killed during this conflict.

The museum's three exhibition halls display photographs, documents, and artefacts and the garden features bronze sculptures and monuments depicting various stages of the war. Most of the explanations are in Chinese only. A commemoration ceremony is held each year on July 7th to remember this historic period in modern Chinese history.

Address: Located in the centre of the walled town of Wanping (宛平城).

How to get there: See Lugou Bridge above.

> **Hours :** 08:30 - 16:30 Tuesday to Sunday (Closed Monday)
> **Entrance fee:** Lugou Bridge: ¥20; The Museum of the Chinese People's Anti-Japanese War: ¥15
> **Official website:** http://www.1937china.org.cn/

TEMPLES

Temples are significant in Beijing's history and development. At one time, old Beijing was said to have over

The Anti-Japanese War Memorial.

Temples in Beijing.

2,500 temples! A number have been destroyed but many still stand today. Some temples are active places of worship, while others have been turned into museums housing cultural relics and items of interest. Some of the larger temples are active around traditional festivals and are the sites of annual temple fairs at Chinese New Year.

Buddhism

Buddhism was introduced in 2 BC and has had a strong influence in China over the centuries. It was most widespread in the Sui and Tang Dynasties. Buddhist images are fairly commonplace, and the religion affects many people's worldview. Most people have gone to a temple on occasions to pray for something significant in their lives.

Tibetan Buddhist Temples

Yonghegong 雍和宫 (Lama Temple) was constructed in 1694 by Emperor Kangxi for his fourth son, Yongzheng, as a palace residence. Upon becoming emperor, Yongzheng turned part of his palace residence into a temple for monks of the Yellow Sect. In 1744, the temple was upgraded in status with the addition of yellow glazed tiles, traditionally reserved only for imperial residences and sites.

The complex consists of seven courtyards and six main buildings, located on a north to south axis. The main hall of the temple is the Hall of Harmony and Peace which houses three Buddha statues made of bronze. The Hall of the Dharma Wheel is the largest hall and is used by the resident lamas for rituals and rites. The elaborate Pavilion of Ten Thousand Happiness is the most elaborate building featuring a 26-metre-high Buddha carved from a single tree trunk of white sandalwood. Under special government protection for its history, Yonghegong houses Tibetan paintings, frescoes, scriptures, calligraphy and steles. There are currently about 100 lamas in residence at the temple.

How to get there: Subway: Line 2 or Line 5, Yonghegong Station (雍和宫站).

> **Entrance fee** : ¥25
> **Hours**   : 09:00 - 16:00
> **Official website:**
> http://www.yonghegong.cn/

Huang Si 黄寺 **(Yellow Temple)** was first built during the Ming Dynasty as one of two yellow temples in Beijing. Destroyed by fire at the end of the Ming Dynasty, it was rebuilt in 1651 as a temporary residence for the 5th Dalai Lama. In the 1730s, Mongol dignitaries helped with the temple's reconstruction efforts. In 1780, the visiting Panchen Lama died at the temple and his clothes were buried under the white marble pagoda. Tibetan Buddhists believe that these clothes give the temple a connection with the deceased. Another feature of the temple complex is the three white stone dormitories for housing Tibetan students. The temple is currently closed to the public.

How to get there: Bus 123 from Dongzhimen Station, Line 2 (东直门).

Buddhist Temples

Dajue Temple 大觉寺 **(Temple of Enlightenment)** is in Haidian District, at the foot of Yangtai Hill. Smaller temples sit on hills to the east and west of the temple. The Dajue Temple was built in the Liao Dynasty (1068) and it has basically remained unchanged in structure since that time. It was revered by emperors as a holy place of worship. Both Emperor Qianlong and Empress Dowager Cixi worshipped in the temple.

There are several halls and structures. The main hall is the Mahavira Hall which features a statue of Sakyamuni, the founder of Buddhism. This central statue is flanked by 20 standing Zuntian statues.

Another hall features a statue of Amitabha and a relief sculpture of Guanyin, Goddess of Mercy. Guanyin is one of the top sculptures from ancient China due to its artistic detail and design.

How to get there: Bus 903 from Shandi Station, Line 13 (上地站).

> **Entrance fee:**
> ¥10 (low season)
> ¥20 (high season)

Dazhongsi Temple 大钟寺 **(Great Bell Temple),** not far from Zhongguancun, was built in 1733 to house China's largest bell, the Yongle Bell. The bell, cast in 1403, was commissioned by the third Ming Emperor, Yongle, to atone for his sins.

China's 46-ton 'King of Bells' is inscribed with Buddhist sutras (scriptures) both inside and out, consisting of more than 230,000 Chinese characters. The unmuted bell could potentially be heard 50 kilometres away on a quiet night. Dazhongsi Temple has been converted into a bell museum. Besides the Yongle Bell, there is a collection of more than 500 bells from China and around the world. Many people visit this temple on New Year's Eve and Chinese New Year's Eve to ring the Yongle Bell for good luck in the coming year.

How to get there: Subway: Line 13, Dazhongsi Station (大钟寺).

> **Entrance fee : ¥10**
> **Hours   : 09:00 - 16:00**

Fahai Temple 法海寺 is located in Shijingshan District at the foot of Cuiwei Mountain, and is famous for its large number of Buddhist murals (frescos) dating from the Ming Dynasty. Painted more than half a century before Michelangelo began his work on the Sistine Chapel, they are regarded as important masterpieces in the religious art world. A total of 77 unique, brightly-coloured figures which include guardians of Buddhist scripture, Bodhisattvas, animals, and heavenly beings are depicted.

How to get there: Bus 311 from Pingguoyuan Station (苹果园站).

> **Entrance fee : ¥20**

Dazhongsi Temple (Great Bell Temple).

Fayuan Temple 法源寺 is one of the oldest existing temples within the city area and is a key site for Buddhism. Located in Xuanwu District, it was originally built during the Tang Dynasty. Fayuan temple has been destroyed by fire, earthquake and social upheaval, but has been rebuilt repeatedly on the original site keeping its initial design. The College of Buddhism is here as well as the Buddhist Relics Library. In recent years, the government-appointed Panchen Lama has studied Buddhist teachings here.

How to get there: Within walking distance of Caishikou Station, Line 4 (菜市口站).

Guangji Temple 广济寺 has a history of more than 800 years. One of the most well-known temples in Beijing, Guangji Temple was particularly important to the Qing rulers. Emperor Qianlong and Kangxi both left inscriptions here. It is currently the headquarters for the Buddhist Association of China.

How to get there: Located at Fuchengmen, east of the Imperial Temple. Subway: Xisi Station, Line 4 (西四站).

Hongluo Temple 红螺寺 **(Red Snail Temple)** is on Hongluo Mountain, 7 km north of Huairou town. It covers an area of 16.6 acres and is the largest temple in northern Beijing. It was originally built during the Tang Dynasty and named Daming Temple (Great Brightness). Its current name 'Hongluo' comes from the legend that two glowing red snails were seen in the temple. It is a protected site due to its historical significance and ancient cultural relics. Many monks from China, Japan, and other countries have been trained here.

How to get there: Bus 916 or 936 from Dongzhimen (东直门) to Huairou (怀柔) — then Hongluosi (红螺寺) mini bus.

Entrance fee : ¥30

Jietaisi 戒台寺 **(Ordination Terrace Temple)** was originally built in the Tang Dynasty in 622 and is located in the Western Hills. An altar was built during the Liao Dynasty for ordaining new monks into the Buddhist priesthood. Jietaisi is also famous for its ancient pine trees which date back to the Liao and Jin Dynasties. Each tree has a name which reflects something of its 'character or appearance'. These include the Reclining Dragon Pine, Unrestrained Pine, and Sensitive Pine.

How to get there: 931 from Pingguoyuan Station, Line 1 (苹果园站).

Entrance fee : ¥30

Tanzhe Temple 谭柘寺, 45 kilometres west of the city in Mentougou District, is the oldest existing temple in Beijing Municipality dating back to over 1,600 years. A local saying goes, "Before there was Beijing, there was the Tanzhe Temple" ("先有谭柘寺, 后有北京城"). Tanzhe Temple is also well-known due to the group of 72 small pagodas and the room where Kublai Khan's daughter lived as a nun.

How to get there: Bus 931 from Pingguoyuan Station, Line 1 (苹果园站) or Tour Bus

Line 7 from Qianmen (前门) or Fuchengmen (阜成门).

Entrance fee : ¥35

Temple of Azure Clouds 碧云寺 **(Biyun)** is located in Fragrant Hills Park. First built during the Yuan Dynasty, the temple consists of six courtyards rising one after the other up a forested mountain slope.

In the Hall of Arhats, there are 508 statues which represent the disciples of Buddha and the 'Heavenly Kings', four colourful statues representing the 'protectors of the universe and the seasons'. One of the halls is dedicated to Dr. Sun Yatsen, as this was where his body was placed until his final resting place (in Nanjing) was completed. Probably the most recognizable feature of the Temple of Azure Clouds is the Diamond Throne Pagoda at the northern end of the temple complex. Buried within the pagodas are the graves of Chinese monks, a Buddha tooth relic, and the hat and clothes of the late Dr. Sun Yatsen.

How to get there: Bus 904 from Xizhimen Station, Line 2 and Line 4 (西直门站) or Mini-bus 23 from Pingguoyuan Station, Line 1 (苹果园站).

Entrance fee : ¥10

Temple of the Reclining Buddha 十方普觉寺或卧佛寺 is located inside the Beijing Botanical Gardens, close to the Fragrant Hills Park. Built in the 7th century, it was later expanded to accommodate the 5.2 metre long, 54 ton (25,000 kg) bronze statue of a reclining Buddha in 1321.

In recent years, graduating university students flock to the temple because the Chinese name 'wofosi' sounds similar to the English word 'office'. They believe prayers offered here will guarantee them a desirable office job.

How to get there: Bus 904 from Xizhimen Station, Line 2 and Line 4 (西直门站), Bus 360 from Beijing Zoo (动物园), or Bus 331 from Wudaokou Station, Line 13 (五道口站).

> **Entrance fee** : ¥15
> **Hours** : 08:00 - 17:00

White Dagoba (Stupa)
Temple 白塔寺 Its namesake (at the back of the temple) is identical to the one in Beihai Park. The dagoba is the biggest of its kind in China with a base measuring more than 30 metres in circumference. Built in a Tibetan style, the upper part of the dagoba has 13 rings and is topped by a round, engraved copper plate with a small bronze pagoda on top of the plate. Under state protection today, this temple is significant as it was included in Kublai Khan's construction plans for the capital in the early Yuan Dynasty.

How to get there: Within walking distance of Fuchengmen Station, Line 2 (阜成门站), Bus 13 or 101 from Xisi Station, Line 4 (西四站).

Tianningsi 天宁寺 (Temple of Heavenly Peace) dates back to the 5th century. Of particular interest is the 13-storey pagoda. Originally built during the Sui Dynasty and rebuilt during the Liao Dynasty, the pagoda is one of Beijing's oldest structures.

How to get there: Bus 703 from Xuanwumen Station, Line 2 and Line 4 (宣武门站) or Bus 47 from Xidan Station, Line 1 and Line 4 (西单站).

DAOIST TEMPLES
Daoism (or Taoism)
Daoism (or Taoism) has a history of over 1,800 years. It is a religion based on the 6th century BC philosopher, Laozi, who advocated living in harmony with nature and the universe. Over time, Daoism has incorporated many shamanistic practices and superstitious beliefs, numerous gods and goddesses, along with many sacred texts.

Beijing has 29 Daoist temples or monasteries including Wudaomiao (五道庙), Sangongmiao (三官庙), Xiufengmiao (秀峰寺), Luzuge (吕祖阁), Luzugong (吕祖宫), Pantiaogong (蟠桃宫), Guandimiao (关帝庙),

Yaowangmiao (药王庙), Xuanrenmiao (宣仁庙), Ninghemiao (凝和庙) and Huoshenmiao (火神庙). The two most significant in Beijing are the Dongyue Temple and White Cloud Temple.

Dongyue Temple 东岳庙 was first built in 1319. Featuring Yuan, Ming and Qing characteristics, its three courtyards and 600 rooms cover 4.73 hectares (11 acres). In 1995, the temple became a folklore museum featuring traditional handicrafts. In recent years, the Chaoyang District Government has taken steps to restore the temple to its former grandeur. One of the largest temple fairs is held here during Chinese New Year.

How to get there: Subway: 600 metres to the east of Chaoyangmen Station, Line 2 (潮阳门站).

> **Hours**   : 08:30 - 16:30
> Tuesday to Sunday
> (closed Monday)

White Cloud Temple 白云观 **(Baiyunguan)** was first built in the Tang Dynasty to house a stone statue of Laozi. Its current name was given in the Ming Dynasty and its structure today is much the same as it

was after renovations in 1706. The temple features a grand archway entrance and a number of buildings, shrine halls, and courtyards. One shrine hall is named after the late Qiu Changchun, founder of the Longmen sub-sect of Daoism. Another shrine hall is Laolu, which houses seven statues of Daoist saints. The White Cloud Temple is significant today as it serves as the headquarters for the China Daoist Association. It is under government protection as a national key relic site.

How to get there: Bus 727 from Muxidi Station, Line 1 (木樨地站).

OTHER TEMPLES
Temple of Successive Emperors 历代帝王庙. Built in 1531 during the Ming Dynasty, the Temple of Successive Emperors was one of Beijing's imperial temples where Ming and Qing rulers offered sacrifices to their predecessors, 188 successive emperors, 79 persons who had rendered outstanding service, heroes, and the forefathers of the Chinese people. Used as a school from 1949 until recently, the temple was renovated and reopened to the public in 2003.

How to get there: Within walking distance of Xisi Station, Line 4 (西四站).

A statue of Confucius.

The Temple of Confucius
孔庙. Located on Guozijian
Street, this temple was first
built in 1302 (Yuan Dynasty)
to honour Confucius. The
teachings of Confucius (Kong
Fu Zi 孔夫子), the 'Great
Sage', were not necessarily
well-received during his
lifetime (551-479 BC), but later
generations recognized his
wisdom. In particular, beliefs in
the family as the basic unit of
society, the concept of filial piety
and the maintenance of a stable
social order are philosophies
which still influence Asian
thinking today. Confucius was
also a proponent of the need
for academic study. One of his
proverbs states, "All walks of
life are lowly, only the scholar
stands high." Value placed on
education is part of the Chinese
worldview today.

The Temple of Confucius
covers an area of 22,000 square
metres, with four courtyards
and numerous structures. The
Hall of Great Accomplishment
was where Confucius was
worshipped.

How to get there: Subway:
Yonghegong Station (雍和宫站),
Line 2 and Line 5.

ZHALAN CEMETERY AND MATTEO RICCI'S TOMB
栅栏墓地
Behind the French church at
12 Maweigou Road (west of
Chegongzhuang metro stop)
is the Zhalan Cemetery. This
is the final resting place for a
number of foreign missionaries
who committed themselves
to reaching China, spanning a
history of 400 years. Famous
missionaries such as the Italian,
Matteo Ricci; the German,

Matteo Ricci Tomb.

Adam Schall von Bell; and the Belgian, Ferdinand Verbiest, are located here. Tombstones marking the graves of many of their successors are also found in this cemetery. A small chapel also stands here.

In addition to sharing their faith, many of these missionaries made contributions to the nation in the areas of science, art, music, medicine and Sino-Western cultural exchange. They were honoured and respected by emperors and the royal families as well as the Chinese people in general, and shared in China's progress.

In 1610, the Italian Jesuit Matteo Ricci was the first to be buried here on land given by the Ming emperor, Wanli. By regulation, foreigners had to be buried in Macao, but upon a request from the Jesuits, the emperor made an exception for Ricci in light of his contributions to the nation such as those in the areas of geometry and astronomy. His excellent mastery of Chinese language and culture earned him great respect and inroads into the hearts of the royal family and ordinary Chinese people. Ricci is remembered today as a foreigner who honoured and embraced China as a nation.

By 1949, the tombs of several hundred Western missionaries had been moved to Zhalan Cemetery. At present, tombstones mark the grave sites of missionaries from different countries: 14 Chinese or Macanese, 14 Portuguese, 10 Italians, 10 Germans, nine French, three Czechs, two Belgians and one Slovene.

How to get there: Located within the grounds of the Beijing Communist Party Cadres Institute (北京市委党校 — 三塔寺). Bus 19 from Chegongzhuan Station, Line 2 (车公庄站), or Bus 107 from Ping'anli Station, Line 4 (平安里站).

MONASTERY OF THE CROSS RUINS 十字寺

Located in the Fangshan District, the Monastery of the Cross is one of only a few existing ruins of a Nestorian church site remaining in China. Originally built during the Jin Dynasty (265 - 420), it became a Nestorian monastery during the Tang Dynasty (618 - 907) when Nestorian Christianity was first introduced to China. The site became a Buddhist temple during the Liao Dynasty, before reverting back to a Nestorian monastery during the Yuan Dynasty. This was the site where the Nestorian priests, Raban Bar Sauma and Bar Marcus lived before embarking on their epic journey to Baghdad and Europe during the early Yuan Dynasty (1268 - 1368).

Getting there: Bus 917 from Liuliqiao to Fangshan (方山站), then a mini-bus to Chechang Village 车厂村西北 鹿门峪, 十字寺.

GREAT WALL 长城

An old Chinese saying goes: "You aren't a real man (or a hero) if you haven't climbed the Great Wall." Whether this is true or not, most visitors to Beijing make climbing the Great Wall one of their highest priorities. Far more than just a tourist site, it holds much significance for China. The Great Wall is listed as one of the world's cultural heritage sites and is regarded by many as one of the modern wonders of the world.

The Great Wall's various sections have a combined length of more than 6,700 kilometres. Starting in Hebei Province at Shanhai Pass, it stretches across China's Northern provinces before ending at the Jiayu Pass in Gansu Province. Much of the wall follows the natural line of mountains.

Originally, the Great Wall was built to defend against various neighbouring inner-Asian tribal groups invading from the north. It therefore marked the northern-most limits of what was considered China proper at the time. Construction first began in the 7th and 8th Centuries BC

and continued until the Ming Dynasty in the 17th century when much of it was reinforced with brick. In 221 BC, the Emperor Qinshihuang first gave the order to connect and extend existing walls to form one continuous line of defence. This construction project over exceedingly difficult terrain and without modern machinery makes it a truly amazing architectural wonder.

More than 13 accessible sections of the Great Wall lie in the mountains north of Beijing within the municipality. Several sections remain unrestored and may be off-limits in efforts to protect against further erosion. The most well-known are the sections at Badaling, Mutianyu, Simatai, Juyongguan, Gubeikou, Huanghua and Jinlinshan.

Badaling (八达岭长城), in Yanqing County, is the closest and most famous of all the sections of the wall within reach of Beijing. Built during the Ming Dynasty, this section served as a defensive layer protecting Juyong Pass to the south. A visit to the Great Wall at Badaling is often combined with a trip to the Ming Tombs.

Getting there: Bus: 919 from Deshengmen (德胜门) ¥12; Tour bus from Tiananmen Tour Dispatch Centre ¥90 or

Badaling .

¥160 including visit to the Ming Tombs; **Train** ¥5: Beijing North Station, Xizhimen (西直门, 北京北站); Train# 6427 departing Beijing North 08:29 arriving Badaling 11:07. Return: Train# 6428 departing Badaling 14:34 arriving Beijing North 17:07.

Entrance fee:
¥80 (peak season)
¥60 (low season).
Hours:
06:00 - 22:00 (summer)
07:00 - 16:00 (winter)
Official website:
www.badaling.gov.cn

Mutianyu (慕田峪长城) has fewer crowds than Badaling, interesting watchtowers and spectacular views of surrounding mountains and valleys. Constructed during the Northern Dynasties Period (386-581), this site was restored during the Ming Dynasty. It is steep in parts, but there is access by cable car. The luge ride down from the wall is also popular.

Getting there: Bus 916 from Dongzhimen (东直门) to Huairou (怀柔) and then minibus from across the road; Tour Bus 6 from Xuanwumen (宣武门) or Dongsishitiao (东四十条). Private car hire with driver can be arranged for the day.

> **Entrance fee** : ¥40
> Cable Car: ¥35 one way;
> ¥50 return.
> **Official website:**
> www.mutianyugreatwall.com

Simatai (司马台长城), located in Miyun County, is 110 kilometres northeast of Beijing (about 3-4 hours' journey). This site is one of the most spectacular sections of the Great Wall with steep and rugged sections and a sharp peak at the

Mutianyu.

top, also making it a dangerous section. Simatai, built during the Ming Dynasty, is known for having maintained much of the original appearance of the Great Wall.

Getting there: Bus 970 or 980 from Dongzhimen (东直门) to Miyun (密云) and then minibus to Simatai; Tour Bus 12 from Xuanwumen (宣武门) or Dongsishitiao (东四十条). Private car hire with driver can be arranged for the day. Several youth hostels also offer bus trips to the Simatai section of the Great Wall.

> **Entrance fee** : ¥40
> Cable Car: ¥30 one way;
> ¥50 return.
> **Hours** : 08:00 - 17:00
> **Official website:**
> http://www.simatai-greatwall.net/

Juyongguan (居庸关长城) in Changping District is on the way to the Badaling

Juyongguan.

section of the Great Wall. This site was a former military fort and command post guarding the pass into Beijing. It was first built during the Northern and Southern Dynasties period (420 - 589) and rebuilt as a defensive fort during the early Ming Dynasty (1368 - 1644). To the north of the main gates lies a smaller marble tower dating from the late Yuan Dynasty (1279 - 1368). The archway which has unique relief sculptures of numerous Buddhist images was originally the foundation of a Lama temple. The walls are also engraved with Tibetan, Sanskrit, Chinese, Uyghur, Mongolian and Tangut languages. This section of the wall rises steeply up the side of the mountain.

Getting there: Tour Bus 1 from Qianmen (前门), 2 from Beijing Station (北京站), 3 from Dongdaqiao (东大桥), 4 Beijing Zoo (动物园), and 5 Qianmen West (前门西). Private car hire with driver can be arranged for the day.

Entrance fee : ¥30
Official website:
http://www.juyongguan.com/

Gubeikou (古北口长城) is 128 kilometres northeast of Beijing in Miyun County and was once known as Beijing's gateway. Every year the emperor would pass through this entrance on his journey to his summer resort at Chengde. Also seen as the road to Inner Mongolia, much of this section remains unrestored. It might be possible to walk from here to the Simatai section.

Getting there: Bus 970 or 980 from Dongzhimen (东直门) to Miyun (密云) and then minibus to Gubeikou. Private car hire with driver can be arranged for the day.

Entrance fee : ¥25.
Official website:
http://www.gubeikou.com.cn/

Huanghua (黄花长城), also known as Jintang, is located in Huairou District. Built in the Ming Dynasty, it is named Huanghua after the yellow flowers which cover the hills and mountains around Jintang Lake in summer. Much of the section has until recently remained unrestored.

Getting there: Bus 916 from Dongzhimen to Huairou then minibus across the street (¥8). Private car hire with driver can be arranged for the day.

Entrance fee : ¥25

Jinshanlin (金山岭长城), 140 kilometres from Beijing in Miyun County, remains one of the best preserved and least visited sections of the Great Wall. Built on the Yan Shan ranges during the Ming Dynasty, Jinshanlin is linked to the Simatai and Gubeikou sections to its west.

Getting there: Bus 970 or 980 from Dongzhimen to Miyun then minibus to Jinlingshan Great Wall. Private car hire with driver can be arranged for the day.

Entrance fee : ¥30

XIANGSHAN (FRAGRANT HILLS PARK) 香山公园

Xiangshan is located 30 kilometres northwest of Beijing. These 'hills' of 160 hectares (395.36 acres) originally served as a resort area and hunting grounds for the emperors and are now popular with local tourists.

The first structure to be built in the park was the Fragrant Hills Temple during the Jin Dynasty (1186). The Park was completely destroyed in 1860 and 1900. Although efforts have been made to restore the park, Xiangshan today cannot compare to the original scale and grandeur of the park in ancient times.

This site is significant as it was the seat of government after 1949 until officials moved into Zhongnanhai.

A main attraction today is its natural beauty in autumn, with the changing colours of the leaves. Visitors can stay overnight at the Xiangshan Hotel. Other sites that are of particular interest include: Spectacles Lake consisting of two ponds separated by a stone bridge, making it look like a pair of glasses; the Studio of Tranquil Heart, featuring a heart-shaped pool; a seven-storey-high pagoda covered in yellow and green tiles; the Lacebark Pine

Xiangshan Park.

Pavilion; the Ruins of the Fragrant Hills Temple; the Lofty Wind Pavilion and Incense Burner Peak at the summit.

How to get there: Bus 360 Beijing Zoo, 634 or 714 from Xizhimen (西直门) (West of Xizhimen Station, Line 1 and Line 4).

Entrance Fee : ¥10
Hours   : 07:00 - 18:00
Official website:
http://www.xiangshanpark.com.cn

RUINS OF YUANMINGYUAN 圆明园

Yuanmingyuan, also known as the Garden of Perfection and Brightness, was one of five famous gardens built in the Qing Dynasty. The construction of the garden began in 1723 and lasted for 150 years. Originally made up of three separate gardens, Yuanmingyuan was immaculately landscaped accentuating the natural beauty of the area. Impressive fountains were built to give the gardens a special touch.

The buildings and structures on this property once totalled 160,000 square metres. Yuanmingyuan was built primarily in the style of a classical Chinese garden, but Western artists and missionaries added their creative contributions, so both Eastern and Western designs featured in the garden. Ancient Yuanmingyuan had an impressive collection of paintings, ceramics, porcelain, glassware and bronze ware.

During the Second Opium War of 1860, and again in 1900 with the invasion of the Allied Forces, relics were looted and the structures of the grand Yuanmingyuan were brought to ruin. Over time, attempts have been made to restore the

Yuanmingyuan.

gardens and to protect the ruins. A museum on site shows the history of Yuanmingyuan and plans for its future development.

How to get there: Subway: Yuanmingyuan Station, Line 4 (圆明园站); Bus 特4 (from Qianmen 前门), 330, 332, 333, 346, 362, 394, 801, 808.

Entrance Fee: ¥20 (low season), ¥30 (high season)
Official website: http://www.yuanmingyuanpark.com/

BEIJING'S CENTRAL BUSINESS DISTRICT (CBD) 北京商务中心区

Beijing's CBD, located in Chaoyang District, comprises office buildings, residential blocks, commercial services, multi-national companies and 136 foreign embassies. Beijing's tallest buildings are located in this area as well as the now famous CCTV tower with its unique 'Z' shape. There are several markets and shopping areas in the CBD such as Xiushuijie, a multi-storey market for garments and gifts; Panjiayuan, a market area for Chinese antiques; and Sanlitun, an area popular for its restaurants, bars, coffee houses and entertainment venues.

The CBD is being developed as the capital's showcase for business, enterprise, trade, economic development, foreign relations, ingenuity in architecture and for the beauty of urbanization.

Beijing's CBD area in Chaoyang District.

How to get there: Subway: Guomao Station, Line 1 and Line 10 (国贸站).

CHINA WORLD TRADE CENTRE 中国国际贸易中心

The China World Trade Centre.

The China World Trade Centre is a massive complex of four state-of-the-art office buildings in the heart of Beijing's CBD. The China World Trade Centre Tower 3 is the tallest building in Beijing at 330m (1,083ft) and with 74 floors. The complex, which was first built in 1988, and later expanded in 2007, is significant for what it represents — the height of business, commerce and trade in China. Other features of the World Trade Centre include an exhibition hall, two apartment blocks, Chinese gardens, an indoor ice-skating rink, restaurants, a shopping mall and an underground atrium.

New York's World Trade Centre was once the largest in the world. Following the destruction of the twin towers by terrorist attacks on September 11th, 2001, the China World Trade Centre took its place as the largest Trade Centre in the world.

How to get there: Subway: Guomao Station, Line 1 and Line 10 (国贸站).

BEIJING SIGHTSEEING TOWER/CHINA CENTRAL TELEVISION TOWER 北京观光塔/中央电视塔

This Tower is a significant landmark for the west side of Beijing. Standing 405 metres, it overlooks Haidian District and offers great aerial views of the city on a clear day. Built in 1989, it features a three-storey structure at 240 metres which houses a rotating restaurant, lounge, observation decks, balconies and other facilities. It was originally designed as a TV tower by China Central Television.

How to get there: Third Ring Road West. Bus: 323, 724, 854, 901, 944

Entrance fee : ¥50
Official website:
http://www.ctvt.com.cn/

CCTV Tower.

OLYMPICS PARK
奥运公园

The 2008 Olympics Park and Games Village are situated north of the Fourth Ring Road, near the Asian Games Village. The Olympics Park lies on the north-south axis running through Beijing in line with the Forbidden City and Tiananmen Square. Upon its completion in mid-2008, it will be the largest park in Beijing.

The main attraction at the site is the Olympic Stadium. Built with a capacity for 100,000, it will be the site for the Games' opening and closing ceremonies. Covering an area of 204,100 square metres, this bowl-shaped structure has been nicknamed the 'Bird's Nest' due to its design. The stadium is largely made of steel covered with a transparent membrane.

To the west of the Olympic Stadium is the National Swimming Centre, also known as 'The Water Cube'. The translucent, bubble-like geometric patterns on the outside of the building are designed to facilitate solar energy for heating the pools. The Swimming Centre has the capacity to hold 17,000 spectators.

In addition to these major sites, the Olympics Park is the location of the Olympic Village, the Olympic Forest Park, and other venues and services for athletes and spectators during the games.

How to get there:
Subway: Olympic Branch Line, Olympic Sports Centre Station (奥体中心站), Olympic Green Station (奥林匹克公园站), and Forest Park (森林公园站).

The 'Bird's Nest' Olympics stadium.

MING TOMBS 十三陵

Ming Tombs.

Prior to 1911, Chinese history is divided into periods of dynastic rule. Emperors ruled over the land, only to be succeeded by a son or close male family member. Each dynasty has its own legacy. The Ming Dynasty was one with strong influence and staying power, spanning from 1368 to 1644.

The Ming Dynasty was first established with Nanjing as its capital. The third Ming emperor, Yongle, wrestled power from his nephew and later moved the capital to Beijing in the early 15th century. With Mongol armies still posing a threat to China, it was strategic to have a capital in the north.

The site of the Ming Tombs was first chosen by the emperor Yongle as his final resting place according to the principles of geomancy. Located 44 kilometres north of Beijing, the site is today the burial grounds of 13 Ming emperors and their empresses and concubines. The tombs are scattered over approximately 40 kilometres, hemmed in by mountains on the three sides to the west, north and east.

The valley was considered sacred ground and was formerly guarded by imperial troops. The road leading to the tombs is considered auspicious, with Tiger Hill on the left and Dragon Hill to the right. Known as the 'Spirit Way', it was the route along which the bodies of the dead rulers were carried to their final resting places. Key sites along the road include the Memorial Arch, a white marble carved structure featuring carvings of lions, dragons, and lotus flowers; the Big Red Gate with three wooden doors (the centre door being reserved for the emperor); the Tablet House; and the avenue of stone animals and statues of military and civilian officials, symbols of power and protection meant to serve the emperor in the next world.

Only three of the tombs are open to the public. These are the tombs of Yongle (Changling), Wanli (Dingling) and Longqing (Zhaoling). The Changling Tomb was the first and largest tomb. Today, its above-ground structure is basically intact. The Dingling Tomb is the only one that has been excavated and opened to the public. During this excavation, numerous treasures and artefacts were discovered, some of which are on display in the accompanying exhibition rooms. The Zhaoling Tomb has undergone extensive renovations. The other tombs remain unexcavated and closed to the public. Many have been looted or destroyed by fire.

Most of the above-ground structures have been destroyed or remain in a state of disrepair.

A 20th century addition to the area was the building of the Ming Tombs Reservoir. This reservoir powers a hydro-electric station and is a source of water for Beijing.

In the chart below are the names of Ming tombs, the Ming emperor buried there, and the period of each emperor's reign.

注意 Note:

Emperors prior to Yongle and Emperor Jingtai who reigned from 1457-1464 are not among the emperors buried in the Ming Tombs Valley.

Name of Tomb	Emperor's Reign Title	Reign Period
Changling	Yongle	1403-1424
Xianling	Hongxi	1425
Jingling	Xuande	1426-1435
Yuling	Zhengtong	1436-1449
Maoling	Chenghua	1465-1487
Tailing	Hongzhi	1488-1505
Kangling	Zhengde	1506-1521
Yongling	Jiajing	1522-1566
Zhaoling	Longqing	1567-1572
Dingling	Wanli	1573-1620
Qingling	Taichang	1620 (reigned for 29 days)
Deling	Tianqi	1621-1627
Siling	Chongzhen	1628-1644

How to get there: Bus 345 from Deshengmen to Changping Bei or Bus 345支 to Changping Dongguan. Then change to Bus 314 to the Imperial Way, Dingling Tomb and Changling Tomb. Tour Bus: 1 Qianmen (前门), 2 Beijing Station (北京站), 3 Dongdaqiao (东大桥), 4 Beijing Zoo (动物园).

Entrance fee :
¥50 (Peak season),
¥30 (low season)
Hours   : 07:00 - 18:00
Official website:
http://www.mingtombs.com/

EASTERN AND WESTERN QING TOMBS

Note on the Qing Tombs:
While the Qing Tombs are not in the Beijing Municipality, they are worth mentioning as they are the final resting place for Qing emperors. The tombs are the most complete group of imperial tombs in China. First built in 1663, the Eastern Qing Tombs are located in nearby Hebei Province in Zunhua County, 125 kilometres east of Beijing. The Eastern Qing Tombs are a grouping of 15 tombs including those for five Qing emperors, 14 empresses and 136 concubines. Among those buried in the Eastern Qing Tombs is the infamous Empress Dowager Cixi. Her tomb is a particularly ornate structure. Also in Hebei Province are the Western Qing Tombs which are located in Yixian County, 130 kilometres to the southwest of Beijing. These tombs are the final resting place for four emperors, three empresses and 69 imperial family members and concubines.

Official websites:
Eastern Tombs
http://www.qingdongling.com/
Western Tombs
http://www.qingxiling.com/

PEKING MAN SITE
周口店北京人

The Peking Man.

In December 1929, paleoanthropologist Pei Wenzhong discovered a complete skull of a primitive caveman at Dragon Bone Hill near the town of Zhoukoudian (about 50 kilometres southwest of Beijing). This skull later became known as the 'Peking Man'. Some archaeologists believe that the skull could date back 500,000 to 700,000 years. Note: The original skull found by Pei Wenzhong cannot be viewed on site, however, as it disappeared during the Second World War.

Near the site of the discovery of Peking Man, the fossils of the 'Upper Cave Man' were also found, which date back 18,000 years. These sites have historical, anthropological and archaeological significance, giving credence to China's claim to being an ancient civilization.

A museum at the site chronicles the history and findings.

How to get there: Bus 917 from Tianqiao (天桥).

| Entrance fee : ¥30 |

CHINESE ETHNIC CULTURE PARK
中华民族园

This Chinese Ethnic Culture Park, also known as the China Nationalities Museum, is a unique display of the diversity of culture in China. The museum/park features the landscapes, cultures, architecture, cultural relics, art,

Naxi woman.

handicrafts, native dress, folk music, dance, games, food and festivals of the 56 recognized minority groups of China, each with its own pavilion. Located in Chaoyang District on Minzuyuan Road, this park is divided into two large areas, the northern part and the southern part. Some pavilions feature photograph displays from their native areas. Throughout the day, there are shows featuring songs and dances from different minority groups, and some art and handicraft displays. Others demonstrate special festival activities unique to their minority group. In July and August, evening shows are held on weekends and visiting hours are extended.

How to get there: Subway: Xiongmao Huandao Station (Panda Roundabout), Line 10

(熊猫环岛站); Bus 407 from Andingmen Station, Line 2 (安定门站).

Entrance Fee : ¥90
Official website:
www.emuseum.org.cn

NATIONAL GRAND THEATRE 国家大剧院

The National Grand Theatre, often referred to as 'The Eggshell', is situated on the west side of the Great Hall of the People in Xicheng District. Designed by French architect, Paul Andreu, this dome-like structure, covering an area of 118,900 square metres, can accommodate 2,416 people in the Opera Hall and 2,017 in the Music Hall. The shell of the theatre is made of titanium and glass so the sky can be seen through its translucent dome. This structure is in striking contrast to more traditional Chinese architecture and reflects a modern, international style. The National Grand Theatre, which serves as a venue for national and international arts performances and exhibitions, is a showcase for various art forms.

How to get there: Subway: Tiananmen West, Line 1 (天安门西站).

Official website:
http://www.
nationalgrandtheater.com

The National Grand Theatre.

DASHANZI ARTS DISTRICT
大山子798艺术区

The Dashanzi Arts District began when the Central Academy of Fine Arts rented space in an old factory to form a sculpture workshop in 2001. Soon after, a speciality art bookshop, Timezone 8, was opened nearby. Artists and trendsetters in the art world were then drawn to the area and an arts district was born.

A popular destination for visitors here is the 798 Cultural Complex, home to art studios, galleries, clubs, restaurants and shops. Young artists and those on the cutting edge are given a place to cultivate their gifts and display their creations including new forms of art expression. The Dashanzi Arts Festival, held in recent years, draws crowds to experience art exhibitions and various musical and theatrical performances.

How to get there: Bus 403 from Sanyuanqiao Station, Line 10 (三元桥站) or Beijing Station, Line 2 (北京站站), Bus 402 from Liangmahe Station, Line 10 (亮马河站). **Website:** www.798.net.cn

IMPERIAL OBSERVATORY
北京古观象台

The Imperial Observatory, first built in the Ming Dynasty, played an important role in imperial China. Imperial rites were required to be performed at precise times during the earth's orbit around the sun. The observatory was established to help ensure the rites were carried out at the correct times. The platform, originally part of the 'Inner City' walls, features large bronze astronomical instruments including an artillery sphere and a celestial globe.

The observatory was renovated and reopened to the public in 1983. One of the current telescopes on display has an impressive 2.2 metre reflector made of a special type of ultra-low expansion glass, built for enhanced viewing accuracy. The observatory is located on the corner of the Second Ring Road and Jianguomen Avenue.

How to get there: Subway: Jianguomen Station, Line 1 and Line 2 (建国门站).

Entrance Fee : ¥15
Hours:
09:30 - 11:30,
13:00 - 16:30
Wednesday to Sunday

WESTERN ZHOU YAN STATE CAPITAL SITE MUSEUM — LIULIHE SITE 西周燕都遗址博物馆

Liulihe Bronze.

This museum is located in Fangshan District, 1.5 kilometres north of Liulihe Town. The site is significant as it contains the ruins of the Yan State Capital from the early Western Zhou Period (1100-771 BC). Extensive archaeological digs have unearthed the tombs of more than 200 Yan nobles, remnants of a city wall, evidence of a moat, foundations for homes and buildings and numerous cultural relics such as bronze ware, lacquer ware, pottery, stone ware, bone ware and jade. The research, which was mostly carried out in the 1970s, provides evidence that what is today's Beijing was a civilized city more than 3,000 years ago!

The Western Zhou Yan State Capital Museum was opened to the public in 1995. The public can view two of the Yan tombs, several chariot pits, and many of the excavated relics found on the site. One of the extremely precious and rare relics is a tripod cauldron (the largest bronze vessel discovered here). Significant findings among the lacquer ware include a 'gu', a type of goblet; and a 'dou', a type of standing cup. Archaeologists believe the advanced nature of these items reveal a high level of civilization in the Yan State Capital at the time.

How to get there: Bus 917 Hancunhe line (韩村河支线) to Dongjialin Village (董家林村口).

IMPERIAL COLLEGE 国子监

West of the Confucian Temple is the Imperial College site, or Guozijian. First built in 1279 as a small school, this was the highest institute of learning during the Yuan, Ming and Qing Dynasties. Students who attended the Imperial College at this time mostly came from noble families. Upon completing their studies, they became government ministers and high-ranking officials.

The Imperial College was the place where Qing emperors would come to lecture students on subjects like Confucianism,

Chinese classical literature, or Chinese thought. Tradition had it that a newly-enthroned emperor would first visit the Confucian Temple to pay his respects. After this, he would go to the Imperial College to give a lecture which would be attended by court scholars and officials.

The Imperial College site was opened to the public in 1998. The main building, the Biyong Hall, was built in 1784. Apparently, Emperor Qianlong was not satisfied with the standard of education at the time and felt a new, grand hall needed to be constructed to provide a place of learning fitting for the best of the best. The Biyong Hall is unique, with a vaulted roof, round on the outside and square on the inside, and four bridges that lead to four gates facing north, south, east and west. These bridges and gates represented the dissemination of information and education in every direction. In addition, the Biyong Hall features inscriptions by Emperor Qianlong and a throne with a screen behind it. Emperor Qianlong gave a speech in this hall to an audience of more than 4,000 people in 1784.

How to get there: Subway: Yonghegong Station, Line 2 and Line 5 (雍和宫站), in the lane opposite Yonghegong Lamasery entrance.

Entrance Fee :	¥10
Hours	: 08:30 - 17:00

MUSEUMS

As the capital of China, Beijing is a centre for culture and education, as seen by the number of museums across the city. Several of the major museums have been described in detail in this section: Forbidden City (Palace Museum), the Capital Museum, the National Museum and the Chinese People's Anti-Japanese War Museum.

Other museums feature a variety of exhibitions and

Military Museum.

displays. Information about these museums can be found on the internet, in city guides or on Beijing maps. These include the following: the Archaeology and Art Museum, the Beijing Aviation Museum, the China Arts and Crafts Museum, the China Science and Technology Museum, the Constabulary Museum, the Military Museum of the Chinese People's Revolution, the Museum of Ancient Architecture, the National Museum of Modern Chinese Literature, the Natural History Museum, the Stone Carving Art Museum, the Urban Planning Museum and the Waxworks Palace.

PARKS AND GARDENS

Located amongst the skyscrapers and elevated highways are green spaces designated for leisure and enjoyment. Many residential areas have small parks for the locals to walk, practise music, meet friends and conduct their morning exercises. There are 135 parks in the city, some with historical significance. The Summer Palace, the Temple of Heaven Park, Yuanmingyuan, Jingshan (Coal Hill), Beihai, Fragrant Hills and the China Ethnic Culture Park have already been described in detail.

Other major parks and gardens in Beijing include:

Chaoyang Park 朝阳公园 — Located near the embassy area, Chaoyang is the city's second largest park (320 hectares) after the Olympic Forest Park. Chaoyang Park was opened in 1999 to commemorate the 50th anniversary of the founding of the People's Republic of China. Apart from the gardens, it features a water park, a movie theatre complex, an amusement park and a beach resort. Chaoyang Park is often used a venue for cultural performances, fairs, concerts, and exhibitions. Construction is underway on the world's largest Ferris wheel (slated to be bigger than the London Eye), due for completion in 2010.

How to Get There: Bus 117, 302, 703, 710, 815, 985 to Chaoyang Park (朝阳公园); 419,

852, 985 to Chaoyang Park West Gate (朝阳公园西门).

> **Entrance Fee : ¥5**
> **Official website:**
> www.sun-park.com

Ditan Park 地坛公园 — This park has both historical and religious significance. It was here that Ming and Qing emperors worshipped the god of earth on a sacred altar.

More than 100 years prior to the park's construction, Ming Emperor Yongle built the Temple of Heaven and Earth (1420) where he offered sacrifices to heaven on the winter solstice and sacrifices to earth on the summer solstice. Later Emperor Jiajing received advice that the gods of heaven and earth should be worshipped separately and so two places of worship were built: the Altar of the Earth and the Temple of Heaven. On important imperial occasions, a representative from the imperial court would visit the altar to report events to the god of earth.

The largest structure in the park is the altar itself, a two-tiered terrace surrounded by two square enclosures and surrounded by a moat. The surfaces of the altar are made of flagstone and the walls are topped with yellow tiles. Adorning the terraces are 23 sculptures, which represent mountains, rivers and seas.

By 1911, the park and altar were no longer used for their original purposes. Ditan Park was opened to the public in 1925, and has since undergone extensive renovation and expansion. The park is the site for a large temple fair during Chinese New Year.

How to get there: Subway: Yonghegong Station, Line 2 and Line 5 (雍和宫站).

> **Entrance Fee : ¥2**
> **Official website:**
> http://www.dtpark.com/
> (*Chinese only*)

Grand View Garden 大观园 — Located in Xuanwu District, this garden is a replica of Daguanyuan, described in the famous Chinese novel, *A*

Dream of Red Mansions, by Cao Xueqin. Originally built in 1988 as a temporary backdrop for the garden scenes for a television series based on the novel, it was subsequently transformed into a permanent garden park. Experts were consulted during the design process to ensure that the layout and design of Grand View Garden remained faithful to Cao's description of the imperial garden in his book.

Grand View Garden covers 12.5 hectares (31 acres) and features 40 scenic spots such as rockeries, flower gardens, lakes, canals, courtyards, bridges, and pavilions. The homes and courtyards of the main characters in the novel are also featured.

How to get there: Bus: 59, 819, 717, 122, 721, 806, 939, 816 (大观园站).

Entrance Fee : ¥40
Official website:
www.bjdgy.com
(Chinese only)

Imperial City Wall Relics Park/Imperial Wall Ruins Park 皇城根遗址公园 —

During the Ming and Qing Dynasties, the area immediately outside the Forbidden City walls was reserved exclusively for the court's highest-ranking officials. This area, known as the Imperial City, was located within the northern 'Inner City' area and enclosed by a nine-kilometre wall with seven gates. Most of the wall was torn down in the 1920s. The remaining section has been turned into the Imperial City Wall Relics Park (or Huangchenggen Relics Park). Stretching from East Chang'an Avenue to Di'anmen Dongdajie, this narrow, 2.4-kilometre park features paths lined with excavation sites, information plaques, murals and statues which depict city life during the Ming and Qing Dynasties. Near the entrance, there is a granite block which is engraved with a map of the Imperial City and the area during the Qing Dynasty.

How to get there: Ruins run from north to south along Beiheyan Dajie (北河沿大街). Accessible by walking from subway: Tiananmendong Station, Line 1 (天安门东站) or Wangfujing Station, Line 1 (王府井站).

Entrance Fee : Free

Ming City Walls Relics Park 明城墙遗址公园 —

Kite flying.

Construction of the Ming Dynasty city walls began in 1414. Reinforced with brick, these walls originally stretched 40 kilometres around the city area. While most of the original sections were destroyed during 1960s and 1970s to make way for roads and subway lines, a one-kilometre long portion of the original walls is preserved within the Ming City Walls Relics Park. Stretching from Chongwenmen to Dongbianmen Arrow tower, this section was restored in 2001 - 2002 using 120,000 original bricks. The Dongbianmen

Arrow Tower, built in 1436, is the largest and oldest city wall tower in China. Recognizable by the 144 arrow holes from which archers protected the city, it today houses an art gallery and other displays about the wall's history.

How to get there: Dongbianmen (东便门) — Within walking distance of Chongwenmen Station, Line 2 and Line 5 (崇文门站) and Jianguomen Station, Line 1 and Line 2 (建国门站).

Entrance Fee : ¥10

Old Beijing Mini Landscape Park 老北京微缩景园 — Located in Nankou, Changping District, 40 kilometres from the city, this park gives insight into what Beijing might have looked like

during the Ming and Qing Dynasties. It features more than 100 miniature replicas and models of living quarters, traditions, folk life and more. Eight performance areas are located throughout the park where imperial and folk art demonstrations are given. Other features include a bird market, a children's play area, a teahouse, puppet shows, and film areas.

How to get there: Bus 919 from Deshengmen (德胜门) to Longhutai (龙虎台), then change to the minibus for Old Beijing Mini Landscape Park 老北京微缩景园.

Entrance Fee : ¥45

Purple Bamboo Park 紫竹院公园 — Located on Baishiqiao Road, south of the National Library, the park is centred around three conjoined lakes. These lakes served as a water reservoir for the city during the Yuan Dynasty (13th century). The park is today popular for its lush green gardens, bridges, lakes and hills.

How to get there: Subway: Guojiatushuguan Station (National Library 国家图书馆站), Line 4; or Bus 334 from Xizhimen Station, Line 1 and Line 4 (西直门站).

Couple dancing.

Ritan Park 日坛公园 — Ritan Park was originally built as an altar where Ming and Qing Dynasty emperors made sacrifices to the god of the sun. Formerly known as the Altar of the Sun Park, the area was turned into a public park in 1949. Located in the heart of the embassy district, the park is popular with both locals and foreigners.

How to get there: Within walking distance of Jianguomen Station (建国门站), Line 1 and Line 2.

Entrance Fee : ¥2

Taoranting Park 陶然亭公园 — Located in Xuanwu District (south Beijing), Taoranting is also referred to as the Joyful Pavilion Park. Known for both its beauty and historical significance, Taoranting is a popular scenic spot in Beijing today. The man-made lake and hills were first constructed in the Liao Dynasty. The hills were popular as the tallest points in old Beijing accessible to common people.

During the Yuan Dynasty, a temple called Cibei'an (Temple of Mercy) stood on the highest point of the Taoranting Park site. Later during the Qing Dynasty, the park was a place where scholars and poets gathered to drink wine and write poems during the autumn months. A scholar, Jiang Zao, is recorded to have constructed a pavilion overlooking the lake in 1695. He named this structure, Taoranting, or Joyful Pavilion, after a poem written by Bai Juyi, a famous Tang Dynasty poet.

This name was later adopted for the entire park area. Today's Taoranting Park features seven hills, 36 pavilions, halls and miniature models of famous Chinese structures.

How to get there: Subway: Taoranting Subway, Line 4 (陶 然亭站), Bus: 59路 40路 613路 819路.

> **Entrance Fee :** ¥2
> **Hours**   : 06:30 - 21:00
> **Official website:**
> www.trtpark.com

World Park in Beijing 北 京世界公园 — Built to display miniature replicas of famous structures and sites from around the world, this park is worth a visit for its attention to detail. A total of 106 miniature replicas and models are laid out like a map in this park to give visitors a quick trip 'around the world'. Well-known sites include the Eiffel Tower, the Pyramids, the Leaning Tower of Pisa, Red Square and the Statue of Liberty. Many of the replicas have been created using the same materials as the actual structures. International parades with performances from countries around the world are sometimes held. The park also features a garden maze, a musical laser fountain and a children's play area. The park is located in Fengtai District in the south of the city.

How to get there: Bus 744, 905, 特7, 944支线.

Entrance Fee : ¥65
Hours   : 08:00 - 17:00
Official website:
www.beijingworldpark.cn

Yuan Dynasty Capital City Wall Site Park 元大都土城遗址公园 — Stretching from east to west in the north of Beijing, this park preserves the remaining sections of the Yuan Dynasty capital's original city walls. The park runs between the northern Third and Fourth Ring Roads and is divided into seven blocks and nine scenic areas spanning both Chaoyang and Haidian Districts.

These rammed earth walls were built in the period from 1267 - 1276 to protect Kublai Khan's imperial capital, Dadu. The park was built to protect this historic site. Initially opened to the public in 1988, the park was further developed in 2003.

In addition to the remains of the Yuan Dynasty wall, the park features giant statues of 19 historical figures, including Kublai Khan, the Imperial Concubine and Italian explorer, Marco Polo. Well laid-out gardens, walkways and pavilions make the park a pleasant and popular site to enjoy a leisurely stroll. Signs in English and Chinese explain the history of the wall and its significance.

How to get there:
Subway: Line 10, Huayuan Donglu Station (花园东路站), Xueyuanlu Station (学院路站), Xiongmao Huandao Station (熊猫环岛站), Huixin Xijie Nankou Station (惠新西街南口站) Line 5 and 10 intersection; Bus: 21, 104, 387, 719, 748, 833, 932.

Entrance Fee : Free
Hours   : 06:00 - 22:00

Zhongshan Park 中山公园 — Centrally located, to the west of Tiananmen Gate, this park was formerly the site of Xingguosi Temple (the Temple

Yuan Dynasty capital's City Wall Park.

of National Revival) during the Liao and Jin Dynasties (916 - 1234). The Taimiao Temple (Imperial Ancestral Temple) and Altar of Land and Grain were built on this site in 1420 and 1421 respectively, as important sites where the Ming and Qing emperors performed important rituals.

Following the 1911 revolution, the park was first opened to the public in 1914 as Central Park before being renamed Zhongshan Park in 1928, in honour of the revolutionary leader Dr. Sun Yat-sen.

A grove of ancient cypress trees, estimated to be more than 1,000 years old, stand as testimony to the park's earlier history. Statues, halls, courtyards, rockeries and an altar all make the park a popular site for locals and visitors to the city. The marble Altar of Land and Grain is at the north end of the park and was used by Ming and Qing emperors for offering sacrifices to the gods of land and grain.

Adjacent to the park is the Zhongshan Concert Hall. A pipe organ with more than 3,000 pipes was installed in 1999, the largest in China.

How to get there: Subway: Tiananmen Xi (天安门西站), Line 1.

Entrance Fee :	¥3
Hours	: 06:00 - 21:00

SEVEN

Directories/Resources

Directories/Resources

USEFUL TELEPHONE NUMBERS

Ambulance	120
Fire	110
Police	119
General Emergency	999 (English available)
Public Security Bureau Foreigner Section	8401-5300
Tourist Hotline (24 Hour)	6153-0828
Entry/Exit Bureau (Visa Office)	8401-5300
Beijing International Travel Health Centre	6421-4222
Telephone Repair	112
Directory Assistance	114 (Chinese), 2689-0114 (English)
International Directory Service/Operator	116
Time Report	117
Weather Forecast	121
Road Accident	122
EMS Inquiries	185
Tourist Hotline	6513-0828 (English available)
Bus Inquiries	96166

Train Inquiries	6512-9525
C-trip Hotel/Travel Reservations	800-820-6666
E-long Hotel/Travel Reservations	800-810-1010 (010-6588-1999)
Legal Hotline for Foreigners	1600148 (press 4 for English)
Beijing Mayor's Office	12345
Taxi Booking Service	96103

USEFUL WEBSITES RELATED TO BEIJING

Beijing Government	www.ebeijing.gov.cn
Beijing Muncipal Public Security Bureau	www.bjgaj.gov.cn/epolice/index.htm
Beijing Capital International Airport	http://www.en.bcia.com.cn
Project Beijing	www.projectbeijing.com
The Beijinger	www.thebeijinger.com
Map of Beijing	http://www.mapmatrix.com/asia/02101.pdf
Beijing this month	www.btmbeijing.com
Beijing Review	www.bjreview.com.cn
Beijing Today	http://bjtoday.ynet.com/
That's Beijing	www.thatsbj.com
China Briefing — Business	www.china-briefing.com
China Daily	www.chinadaily.com.cn
News Around China	http://chinanews.bfn.org
China News	www.china.org.cn
China Development	www.chinagate.com.cn/english
C-trip — Hotel booking	http://english.ctrip.com
E-long — Hotel booking	http://www.elong.com
Weather Forecast	www.wunderground.com (enter PEK)
Wuwoo Apartment Search	www.wuwoo.com
Zhaopin Job Recruitment	www.zhaopin.com

INTERNATIONAL CHURCHES IN BEIJING

Beijing International Christian Fellowship (21st Century)
北京国际基督教联会 (二十一世纪)
Sunday 09:30am and 11:30am
21st Century Theatre,
21st Century Hotel, 40 Liangmaqiao
Lu, Chaoyang
朝阳区, 亮马桥路40号,
二十一世纪饭店
Tel: 8454-3468
www.bicf.org
For Foreign Passport holders only

Beijing International Christian Fellowship (Zhongguancun)
北京国际基督教联会 (中关村)
Sunday 09:00am, 11:00am
Raycom Building C, B1, Kexueyuan
Nan Lu, Haidian District
海淀区, 科学院南路, 融科咨询中心
C座B1
Tel: 8286-2813
www.bicf.org
For Foreign Passport holders only

Beijing Baptist Church
北京浮信会教堂
Sunday 11am, 5:30pm
3rd Floor, CTS Plaza, 2 Beisanhuan
Dong Lu
北三环东路2号, 中旅大厦3层
Tel: 6474-1869,   13521427124
For Foreign Passport holders only

River of Grace Church
河恩到教堂
Sunday 10am
Great Hotel, 2nd Floor, 1
Zuojiazhuang Road
左家庄路1号, 北京贵国酒店2层
www.theriverofgrace.com
For Foreign Passport holders only

The Congregation of the Good Shepherd
Capital Mansion Athletic Center 3F,
No, 6 Xinyuan Nan Lu,
Chaoyang District
朝阳区, 新源南路6号,
京城首都俱乐部3层
Tel: 13522001229
www.goodshepherdcongregation.com
For Foreign Passport holders only

Redeemed Christian Fellowship
Bible Study: Wednesdays 6pm - 8pm.
Hour of Miracle: 3rd Saturday of
every month 6pm - 8pm
北三环东路2号, 中旅大厦3层
Tel: 1336681574
E-mail: rcf_kingscourtparishbj@
yahoo.com
For Foreign Passport holders only

Capital Community Church
首都社会教堂
Bible Study: Wednesdays 6pm - 8pm.
Shunyi, Yosemite Club House
Tel: 8046-3880
www.capitalcommunitychurch.org
For Foreign Passport holders only

PROTESTANT CHURCHES IN BEIJING

Chongwenmen Church
崇文门堂
Sunday 09:30
2 Ding Hutong, Hou Gou,
Chongwenmen Nei
北京, 崇文门内, 后沟胡同丁2号
Tel: 6524-2193
www.chwmch.com

Kuanjie Church
宽街堂
Sunday 09:00
50 Di An Men Street East,
Dongcheng District
北京, 东城区, 地安门东街50号
Tel: 8403-9432

Haidian Church
海淀堂
Sunday 08:00, 10:30, 14:00
39 Haidian West Street,
Haidian District
北京, 海淀区, 海淀西大街39号
Tel: 6257-2902 or 8261-3773
www.hdchurch.org

Zhushikou Church
珠市口堂
Sunday 07:30 and 10:00
129 Qianmen Street, Beijing
北京, 前门大街129号
Tel: 6301-6678

Gangwashi Church
缸瓦市堂
Sunday 07:30, 09:30, 13:00, and 19:00
57 Xisi Street South, Beijing
北京, 西四南大街57号
Tel: 6617-6181
E-mail: tangxuan_gwsh@sohu.com

Nanyuan Church
南苑堂
22 Nanyuan North Street,
Daxing, Beijing
北京, 大兴区, 南苑北街22号
Tel: 6796-4963

Fengtai Church
丰台教堂
Fengtai, Majialou
北京, 丰台区, 马家楼

Chaoyang Church
朝阳教堂
Sunday 08:00, 10:00
Fourth Ring Road North,
Dongfeng Qiao
东四环北路东风桥
Tel: 6433-0511

Tongzhou Church
通州教堂
Yangzhuang Xiguoyuan
杨庄西果园
Tel: 6053-2124

Xibeiwa Church
西北旺教堂
北旺付家窑7号
Tel: 6289-8779

Qinghe Church
清河教堂
Tel: 62572902

Daxing Church
大兴教堂
Tel: 8924-1641

Fangshan Church
房山教堂

Nankou Church
南口教堂

Shunyi Church
顺义礼拜堂

Theological Seminary Church
神学院教堂
海淀区清河镇清河路181号
Tel: 6290-4272-8005

Yanjing Theological Seminary
燕京神学院
181 Qinghe Road, Qinghe Township,
Haidian District, Beijing
Tel: 6290-4272 ext 8005 or 8015
海淀区清河镇清河路181号

**Chinese Christian Council
Beijing Headquarters**
181 Dongdanbei Jie
东单北街181号

CATHOLIC CHURCHES
IN BEIJING

**Dongtang Cathedral,
Church of St. Joseph**
王府井天主堂
(Services in Chinese and Latin)
Sunday 6am and 8am
74 Wangfujing Dajie, Dongcheng
东城区王府井大街74号
Tel: 6521-2162 or 6521-2161

**Xitang Cathedral
(Our Lady of Mt. Carmel)**
西直门天主堂
Sunday 8am, Friday 6:30pm
130 Xizhimen Dajie, Xicheng
西城区西直门内大街130号
Tel: 6615-6619

**Nantang Cathedral, St. Mary
Church**
宣武门天主堂
(Latin, Chinese, English)
前门西大街141号
Tel: 6608-7238

**Beitang Cathedral, St. Resurrection
Jesus Church**
西什库天主堂 (北堂)
西城区西什库大街33号
Tel: 6617-5198 or 6613-2259

**Dongjiaominxiang Cathedral,
St. Michael's Church**
东交民巷天主堂
(Services in Korean, Latin, Chinese)
东城区东交民巷13号
Tel: 6513-5170

Nangangzi Church
南岗子天主堂
崇文区幸福大街永生巷6号 (天主堂)
(service in Chinese)
Tel: 6714-3341

Mentougou Church
后桑峪天主堂
Tel: 6181-7545

Niufang Church
牛坊天主堂举行新堂祝圣典礼
Tel: 8026-9103

Niuniutun Church
牛牧屯天主堂
Tel: 6157-6404

Tongzhou Church
贾后疃天主堂
Tel: 6152-1366

Daxing Church
西胡林堂
Tel: 8921-3450

Qiufu Church
求贤堂
Tel: 8921-3064

Longzhuang Church
龙庄堂
Tel: 8056-6204

Dongguantou Church
东管头堂
Tel: 6349-3436

**Yongning Church,
Yanqing District**
永宁天主堂
Tel: 6017-2693

Caogezhuang Church
曹各庄堂
Tel: 6980-2445

HOSPITALS/MEDICAL CLINICS

Amcare Women's & Children's Hospital
北美中宜和妇儿医院
地址: 北京朝阳区劳园西路9号
Add: 9 Laoyuan West Rd,
Chaoyang District
www.amcare.com.cn
Tel: 6434-2399

American-Sino OB/GYN Service
美华妇产服务
地址: 北京朝阳区安外小关北里218号
Add: 218 Xiaoguan Beili,
Anwai, Chaoyang District
www.asog-beijing.com
Tel: 6496-8888

Bayley & Jackson Medical Center
庇利积臣医疗中心
地址: 北京朝阳区日坛东路7号
Add: 7 Ritan Dong Lu,
Chaoyang District
www.bjhealthcare.com
Tel: 8562-9998 (24 hours)

Beijing Children's Hospital
北京儿童医院
地址: 北京西城区南礼士路56号
Add: 56 Nanlishi Rd.,
Xicheng District
Tel: 6802-8401

Beijing Friendship Hospital
北京友谊医院
地址: 北京宣武区永安路95号
Add: 95 Yong An Lu,
Xuan Wu District
Medivac Center in Bangkok:
66-2-236-8444
Email: gdbjing@163bj.com
Tel: 8456-9191 or 8315-1915

Beijing Hospital
北京医院
地址: 北京东单大华路1号
Add: 1 Da Hua Lu, Dong Dan
Tel: 6513-2266

Beijing International Medical Center (IMC)
北京国际医疗中心
地址: 北京朝阳区亮马桥路50号燕莎中心办公楼S106室
Add: Lufthansa Center,
Office Building, Suite 110,
50 Liang Ma Qiao Rd.,
Chao Yang District
www.imcclinics.com
Tel: 6465-1561/2/3 (24-hour number)

Beijing New Century International Children's Hospital
北京新世纪国际儿童医院
地址: 北京西城区西二环路复兴门月坛南桥
Add: Yuetan Nanqiao, Fuxingmen,
Xi er huan lu, Xicheng District
Tel: 6802-5588

Beijing Red Cross Chaoyang Hospital Affiliated to Capital Medical University
首都医科大学附属北京红十字朝阳医院
地址: 北京朝阳区白家庄路8号
Add: 8 Bai Jia Zhuang Lu,
Chao Yang District
Tel: 6500-7755 Ext. 2380
6502-4704

Beijing SOS International (Medical Emergency and Evacuation Service)
北京亚洲国际紧急救援医疗服务中心
地址：北京朝阳区三里屯西五街5号北信租赁中心C座
Add: Building C,
BITIC Leasing Center,
5 Sanlitun Xiwujie,
Chao Yang District
www.internationalsos.com
Tel: 6462-9100
　　　(24-hour Alarm Centre)
　　　6462-9112

Beijing United Family Clinic — Shunyi
北京和睦家诊所顺义
地址：北京顺义区天竺房地产开发区日祥社区818号
Add: Pinnacle Plaza, Unit # 818,
Tian Zhu Real Estate
Development Zone,
Shunyi District
www.unitedfamilyhospitals.com
Tel: 8046-5432

Beijing United Family Health and Wellness Centre
北京和睦家医院健康中心
地址：北京朝阳区建国门外大街21号
Add: 21 Jianguomen wai da jie,
Chao Yang District
www.unitedfamilyhospitals.com
Tel: 8532-1221
Emergency Hotline: 6433-2345

Beijing United Family Hospital
北京和睦家医院
地址：北京朝阳区将台路2号
Add: 2 Jiang Tai Lu,
Chao Yang District
www.unitedfamilyhospitals.com
Tel: 6433-3960 (24-hour number)
Emergency Hotline: 6433-2345

Hong Kong International Medical Clinic
北京香港国际医务诊所
地址：北京东四十条立交桥港澳中心9层
Add: Swissotel 9 Fl., Beijing Hong
Kong Macau Center,
Dong Si Shi Tiao Li Jiao Qiao
Tel: 6501-4206

Intech Eye Hospital
英智眼科医院
地址：北京朝阳区潘家园南里12号潘家园大厦1,4,5层
Add: 12 Pan Jia Yuan Nan Li,
Chao Yang District
www.intecheye.com
Tel: 6771-5558

James Charles Optometrist
北京朝阳区三里屯西五街5号北信租赁中心C座
Add: Building C,
BITIC Leasing Center,
5 Sanlitun Xiwujie,
Chao Yang District
www.bjhealthcare.com
Tel: 6529-5284

MEDEX Assistance Corporation (Medical Evacuation Service)
Email: medexasst@aol.com;
medexws@sina.com
Add: No. 871 Poly Plaza,
14 South Dongzhimen
Tel: 6595-8510

No. 3 Hospital of Beijing Medical University
北京医科大学第三医院
地址：北京海淀区花园北路49号
Add: 49 Hua Yuan Bei Lu,
Hai Dian District
Tel: 6201-6925 or 6201-7691

Peking Union Medical College Hospital
北京协和医院
地 址： 北京东城区帅府园1号
Add: 1 Shui Fu Yuan,
Dong Cheng District
www.pumch.ac.cn
Tel: 6529-5120; 6529-5284

Sino-Japanese Friendship Hospital
中日友好医院
地 址： 北京和平里樱花东路
Add: Ying Hua Dong Lu,
He Ping Li
Tel: 6422-2965 or 6422-1122

Smart Health Medical Clinic
北京维健医疗中心
北京朝阳区将台路6号,
丽都广场102/215室
Add: Room 102/215, Lido Place, 6
Jiangtai Rd., Chao Yang District
www.smarthealth.cn
Tel: 6437-6898

Vista Clinic
维世达诊
地 址: 北京朝阳区光华路1号
嘉里购物中心B29B
Add: Kerry Center
Shopping Mall B29
No.1 Guanghua Road,
Chao Yang District
www.vista-china.net
Tel: 8529-6618

Yanhuang Traditional Chinese Medicine Clinic
北京炎黄医馆
北京东城区三金宝街1号
Add: 1 Jinbao Jie,
Dongcheng District
Tel: 8542-4435

DENTISTS

Arrail Dental
瑞尔齿科
Room 208, CITIC Bldg.,
19 Jianguomenwai Dajie,
Chaoyang District
北京建国门外大街19号
Tel: (86 10) 6500-6472/3, 8526-3235/6

Arrail Dental
瑞尔齿科
Room 308, Raycom Infotech Park,
Tower A, Haidian District
海淀区, 科学院南路2号
科资讯中心A座308室
Tel: (86 10) 8286-1956, 13911001367

SDM Dental — 21ˢᵗ Century Hotel
固瑞齿科固瑞诊所
21ˢᵗ Century Hotel, 40 Liangmaqiao
Road, Chaoyang District
北京朝阳区亮马桥40号
二十一世纪饭店二层FC222
www.sdmdental.com
Tel: (86 10) 6466-4814, 6461-2745

SDM Dental China World Shopping Mall
固瑞齿科国瑞诊所
China World Trade Shopping Mall,
NB210
北京建国门外大街小1号国贸商城地下二
层NB210 (商城西门, 冰场对面)
www.sdmdental.com
Tel: 6505-9439

SDM Dental — Sunshine Plaza
固瑞齿科美科口腔
Sunshine Plaza, 68 Anli Road,
F-D186B, Chaoyang District
北京朝阳区安立路68号阳光广场
F-D186B (阳光广场东侧)
www.sdmdental.com
Tel: 6498-5887

Oceanwide Dental Clinic
欧威齿科
R1509 Jingtai Tower, Jianguomenwai
Dajie, Chaoyang District
北京朝阳区建国门外大街24号
京泰大厦1509室
Tel: 6515-6489

Dean Dental Clinic
迪恩齿科诊所
11-1-2 Liulitun, Chaoyang Gongyuan
Nanlu, Chaoyang District
北京朝阳区朝阳公园南路
六里屯11号楼一层二号
Tel: 6592-8258

IMC Dental and Orthodontics Clinic
Suite 111, Lufthansa Center,
50 Liangmaqiao Lu,
Chaoyang District
Tel: 6465-1384

King's Dental
京典口腔
Shop 118, 1/F, Beijing Towercrest
Plaza, No. 3 Maizidian West Street,
Chaoyang District
北京朝阳区菜太花卉新恒基
国际大厦一层118室
Tel: 8458-0388

INTERNATIONAL SCHOOLS AND KINDERGARTENS

3e International School
国际幼儿园
Ages 3 to 6
18 Jiangtai Xilu, Chaoyang District
朝阳区将台西路18号
Tel: (86 10) 6437-3344
Website: www.3eik.com

**Asia Pacific Experimental
School of Beijing Normal University**
Dongsan Qi, Changping District
Tel: (86 10) 6975-9602
www.asia-pacificschool.net

**Attached Middle School of Capital
Normal University**
33 Beiwa Lu, Haidian District
Tel: (86 10) 6890-3410
E-mail: jiaoliubu@cunschool.org.cn

**Australian International
School of Beijing**
北京澳大利亚国际学校
Grades K to 6
7 Louzizhuang Lu,
Chaoyang District
朝阳区楼梓庄路7号
Tel.: (86 10) 84394315-6
Website: www.aisb.cn

**Beanstalk International Bilingual
School and Kindergarten (BIBS)**
青豆国际双语学校
Grades K to 7
Location: East side of Beijing,
near the Lido
Tel: (86 10) 8456-6019, Ext. 200/202
Email: office@bibs.com.cn
Website: www.bibs.com.cn

**Beanstalk International
Kindergarten (BIK)**
青豆国际幼儿园
1/F, Building B,
40 Liangmaqiao Lu, Chaoyang
at the 21st Century Hotel)
朝阳区亮马桥路40号21世纪饭店院内
B座1层
Tel: 6466-9255
Website: www.bibs.com.cn

Beijing BISS International School
北京BISS国际学校
Grades K to 12
No. 17, Area 4, Anzhen Xi Li
(just off North 3rd Ring Road),
Chaoyang 朝阳区安贞西里四区17号楼
Tel: (86 10) 6443-3151
Website: www.biss.com.cn

Beijing City International School
北京乐成国际学校
Grades Pre-K to 11
77 Baiziwan Nan Er Lu,
Chaoyang District
朝阳区百子湾南二路77号
Tel: (86 10) 8771-7171
Website: www.bcis.cn

Beijing Huijia Kindergarten
北京汇佳幼儿园
Ages 1.5 to 5
Address for Head Office: 33C,
Building B, Huating Jiayuan,
6 Beisanhuan Zhonglu,
Chaoyang District
朝阳区北四环中路6号华亭嘉园B座33C
Tel: (86 10) 5165-2252 Ext. 605
Website: www.hjkids.com

Beijing Huijia Private College
北京汇佳私立学校
Grades 1 to 12
Zhongguancun Kejiyuan,
Changping Yuan, Huijia Kejiaoyuan,
Changping District
昌平区中关村科技园昌平园汇佳科教园
Tel: 6078-5555/1
Website: www.huijia2000.com

Beijing Huiwen High School
6 Peixin Jie, Chongwen District
崇文区
Tel: 6712-4120

Beijing New Century Kindergarten
北京新世纪幼儿园
Ages 2 to 6
Location #1: Jiayuyuan Bieshu,
Xiangjiang Beilu, Chaoyang District
朝阳区香江北路家育苑别墅区
Tel: (86 10) 8430-2547
Location #2: Kangcheng Huayuan,
9 Shuangqiao Donglu,
Chaoyang District
朝阳区双桥东路康城花园
Tel: (86 10) 8537-1225

Beijing No. 1 Kindergarten Experimental Sister School
北京第一幼儿园附属实验园
Ages 3 to 6
Building 117, Xiaohuangzhuang
Xiaoqu, Qingniangou Lu,
Dongcheng District
东城区青年沟路小黄庄小区117号楼
Tel: (86 10) 8428-8913 or
(86 10) 8427-5713
Website: http://yiyou.sch.dcjy.net

Beijing No. 39 Middle School
北京第三十九中学
No 6 Xihuangchenggen North Jie,
Xicheng
西城区 北街6号
Tel: 6617-5807
www.bj39zhx.org

Beijing No. 4 Middle School
北京第四中学
Tel: 6611-2896
E-mail: guojb@bj4hs.edu.cn

**Beijing No. 55 Middle School
and High School**
北京第五十五中学
Ages 11-17
12 Xin Zhong Jie,
Dongcheng District
东城区新中街12号
Tel: (86 10) 6416-4252 or
        (86 10) 6416-9531
Website: www.bj55z.net
E-mail: bj55@vip.163.com

Beijing No. 65 Middle School
北京第六十五中学
115 Beiheyan Jie,
Dongcheng District
东城区
Tel: (86 10) 6525-1920
Website: www.bj65z.com

Beijing No. 80 Middle School
北京第八十中学
Tel: (86 10) 6478-3450
Website: www.bj80.com

Beijing Ritan High School
北京日坛中学
4 Guanghua Xili,
Chaoyang District
朝阳区
Tel: (86 10) 6503-1815
Website: www.bjrtedu.cn

**Beijing Star River Telford
International Preschool**
北京星河湾德福双语幼儿园
Ages 8 months to 6
Sijixinghe Lu, Chaoyang Beilu,
Chaoyang District
朝阳区四季星河路 (星河湾内)
Tel: (86 10) 8551-6666 Ext. 0
Website: www.telfordeducation.cn/
beijingeng

**Beijing World Youth
Academy (WYA)**
北京市世青中学
Ages 10-18
40 Liangmaqiao Lu,
Chaoyang District
朝阳区亮马桥路40号
Tel: (86 10) 6461-7787
Website: www.ibwya.net
Email: admissions@ibwya.net

Beijing Xiyi Elementary School
北京西颐小学
Ages 6-12
49 Beisanhuan Xilu, Haidian District
海淀区北三环西路49号
Tel: (86 10) 8263-2789
Website: www.hdxyxx.bjedu.cn

Beijing Yucai School
Tel: (86 10) 8310-1298
Website: www.bjyucai.com

**Beijing Zhonguancun
International School**
北京中关村国际学校
14 Taiyangyuan,
Dazhongsi, Haidian District
海淀区大钟寺太阳园14号
Tel: (86 10) 8213-9966
Website: www.bzis2002.com

British School of Beijing
北京英国学校
Ages 2 to 16
Location #1: Linyin Lu,
Tianzhu Zhen, Shunyi District
顺义区天竺镇林荫路
Tel: (86 10) 6458-0884
Location #2: 5 Sanlitun Xiliu Jie,
Chaoyang District
朝阳区三里屯西六街5号
Tel: (86 10) 8532-3088
Website: www.british-school.org.cn

Canadian International School of Beijing

加拿大国际学校
Grades Preschool to Grade 11
38 Liangmaqiao Lu,
Chaoyang District
朝阳区亮马桥路38号
Tel: (86 10) 6465-7788
Website: www.cisb.com.cn

Children's House Montessori Kindergarten

北京巧智博仁国际幼儿园
Ages 0 to 6
Location #1: Level 1, North Lodge,
China World Trade Center,
1 Jianguomenwai Dajie,
Chaoyang District
朝阳区建国门外大街1号
中国世界贸易中心北公寓1层
Tel: (86 10) 6505-3869
Location #2: Unit 114, Lufthansa
Center Tower, 50 Liangmaqiao Lu,
Chaoyang District
朝阳区亮马桥路50号写字楼114室
Tel: (86 10) 6465-1305
Location #3: Yosemite Villas,
4 Yuyang Lu, Houshayu Zhen,
Shunyi District
顺义区后沙峪镇榆杨路4号
优山美地别墅区
Tel: (86 10) 6505-3869
Website: www.montessoribeijing.com

Children's Learning Center of Beijing (CLCB)

爱嘉励儿童双语学校
Ages 1 to 5
Unit 6811, Capital Paradise,
Baixinzhuang, Houshayu,
Shunyi District
顺义区后沙峪白辛庄名都园6811
Tel: (86 10) 8046-1840 or 13502101368
(English) or 13611334043 (Chinese)
Website: www.clcbkids.com

Der Kindergarten

北京德国幼儿园
Ages 2 to 6
Merlin Champagne Town,
6 Liyuan Lu, Tianzhu,
Shunyi District
顺义区天竺镇丽苑路6号美林香槟小镇
Tel: 13718615812 (English) or
      13522069836 (German)
Website: www.derkindergarten.com

Dulwich College Beijing

Ages 1 to 18
Location #1: River Garden
Villas Kindergarten, Houshayu,
Baixinzhuang, Shunyi District
顺义区后沙峪白辛庄 裕京花园别墅
Tel: (86 10) 8046-5132
Location #2: 7 Sanlitun Beixiao Jie,
Chaoyang District
朝阳区三里屯北小街7号
Tel: (86 10) 6532-6713 or 6532-4518
Location #3: Legend Garden Villas,
89 Jichang Lu, Shunyi District
顺义区机场路89号丽京花园
Tel: (86 10) 6454-9000
Location #4: Beijing Riviera,
1 Xiangjiang Beilu, Jingshun Lu,
Chaoyang District
朝阳区京顺路香江北路香江花园
Tel: (86 10) 8450-7676
Website: www.dcbeijing.cn

**Eton International
Bilingual Academy**
伊顿国际双语幼儿园
Ages 1.5 to 6
Location #1: Palm Springs
International Apartments, 8
Chaoyang Gongyuan Nanlu,
Chaoyang District
朝阳区朝阳公园南路8号
Tel: (86 10) 6539-8967
Email: psadmin@etonkids.com
Location #2: Block D, 3/F, Global
Trade Mansion, Guanghua Lu,
Chaoyang District
朝阳区光华路世贸国际公寓D座3层
Tel: (86 10) 6506-4805
Email: gtadmin@etonkids.com
Location #3: Pinnacle Plaza, Tianzhu
Real Estate Development Zone,
Shunyi District
顺义区天竺房地产开发区荣样广场
Tel: (86 10) 8046-5338
Email: pinnacleadmin@etonkids.com
Website: www.etonkids.com

Eton International School
伊顿国际学校
Ages 1.5 to 9
Location #1: Palm Springs
International Apartments,
8 Chaoyang Gongyuan Nanlu,
Chaoyang District
朝阳区朝阳公园南路8号
Tel: (86 10) 6539-8967
Email: psadmin@etonkids.com
Location #2: Lido Country Club,
Lido Place, Jichang Lu, Chaoyang
District
朝阳区北京首都机场路丽都广场俱乐部
C103室
Tel: (86 10) 6436-7368
Email: lidoadmin@etonkids.com

Location #3: Pinnacle Plaza,
Tianzhu Real Estate Development
Zone, Shunyi District
顺义区天竺房地产开发区荣样广场
Tel: (86 10) 8046-5338
Email: pinnacleadmin@etonkids.com
Location #4: Block D, 3/F, Global
Trade Mansion, Guanghua Lu,
Chaoyang District
朝阳区光华路世贸国际公寓D座3层
Tel: (86 10) 6506-4805
Email: gtadmin@etonkids.com
Website: www.etonkids.com

Family Learning House
家育苑
Ages 1.5 to 6
B7 Liyuan Xiaoqu,
Xiangjiang Beilu,
Chaoyang District
朝阳区香江北路育苑小区
Tel: (86 10) 8430-2547
Website: thefamilylearninghouse.com

Fang Cao Di Primary School
Grades 1 to 6
1 Ritan Bei Lu,
Chaoyang District
朝阳区日坛北路1号
Tel: (86 10) 8563-5120 ext. 2005
Website: www.fcd.com.cn

**German Embassy School
(Deutsche Botschaftsschule Peking)**
北京德国使馆学校
Kindergarten to Klasse 13
49A Liangmaqiao Lu,
Chaoyang District
朝阳区亮马桥路49A
Tel: (86 10) 6532-2535
Website: www.dspeking.net.cn

Happy Baby Kindergarten
至尊宝宝幼儿园
Ages 1.5 to 6
Location #1: 22 Zhongli Xibahe,
Chaoyang District
朝阳区西坝河中里22号楼
Tel: (86 10) 6462-0449 Ext. 806
Location #2: 23 Yiyan, Anhui Beili,
Yayuncun, Chaoyang District
朝阳区亚运村安慧北里逸园23号楼
Tel: (86 10) 6498-1518
Website: www.zzbaby.com

Harrow International School Beijing
北京哈罗英国学校
Ages: 11-19
5 Anzhenxili, Block 4,
Chaoyang District
朝阳区安贞西里四区5号
Phone: (86 10) 6444-8900
Website: www.harrowbeijing.cn

International Academy of Beijing (IAB)
IAB国际学校
Grades K to 9
Lido Office Tower 3, Lido Place,
Jichang Lu, Jiangtai Lu,
Chaoyang District
朝阳区将台路机场路丽都广场
丽都写字楼3座
Tel. (86 10) 6430-1600 or 6430-1142
Website: www.iabchina.net
Note: IAB is a member of the
Association of Christian Schools
International.

International Montessori School of Beijing (MSB)
北京蒙台梭利国际学校
Near River Garden Villas, Houshayu
Baixinzhuang, Shunyi District
顺义区后沙峪白辛庄裕京花园别墅
Tel: (86 10) 8046-3935
Websitie: www.msb.edu.cn

Indian Embassy School
1 Ritan Dong Lu,
Chaoyang District
朝阳区日坛东路1号
Tel: (86 10) 6532-1827

International School of Collaborative Learning (ISCL)
北京协力国际学校
Grades K to 12
Naidong Gongyequ,
Shunbai Lu,
Chaoyang District
朝阳区顺白路奶东工业区 (在白楼内)
Tel: (86 10) 6431-2607 or 6422-7366
Website: www.iscl-beijing.org

Ivy Academy Beijing
艾毅幼儿园
Ages 2 to 6
East Lake Villas No. 35
Dongzhimenwai Dajie, Suite C101,
Dongcheng District
东城区东直门外大街35号
Tel: (86 10) 8451-1380
Website: www.ivyacademy.cn

Ivy Bilingual Preschool
艾毅童真双语幼儿园
Ages 2 to 6
Location #1: Ocean Express,
Bldg. E, 2 Dongsanhuan Lu,
Chaoyang District
朝阳区东三环北路
远洋新干线E座
Tel: (86 10) 8453-0366
Location #2: Seasons Park, 36B
Dongzhimenwai Dajie,
Dongcheng District
东城区东直门外大街36B号

Japanese School
6 Jiangtai Xi Lu,
Chaoyang District
朝阳区将台西路6号
Tel.: 64636-3250

**Kinstar Bilingual
International School**
海嘉双语国际学校
Grades Pre-K to 7
Location #1: Elementary School
at 5 Yumin Road, Houshayu,
Shunyi District
顺义区后沙峪裕民路5号
Tel: (86 10) 8041-0390
Location #2: Kindergarten at Merlin
Champagne Town Clubhouse,
6 Liyuan Jie, Tianzhu Zhen,
Shunyi District
顺义区天竺镇丽苑路6号
美林香槟小镇会所
Tel: (86 10) 6450-8259
Website: www.kinstarschool.org

**Korea International School
in Beijing**
531 Qiliqu, Changping District
Tel: (86 10) 8072-4526
Website: www.kisb.net

Limai School (Chinese language)
北京市力迈学校
Grades K-12
Tianzhu Real Estate Development
Zone, Shunyi District
顺义区天竺开发区
Tel: (86 10) 8046-3653 or 8046-7470
Website: www.limai.com.cn

**Lycée Français de Pekin
(French School of Beijing)**
Ages 2 to 18
Location #1: Primary and Secondary
School at 13 Sanlitun Dongsijie,
Chaoyang District
朝阳区三里屯东四街13号
Tel: (86 10) 6532-3498

Location #2: Kindergarten
at 4 Sanlitun Dongsijie,
Chaoyang District
朝阳区三里屯东四街4号
Tel: (86 10) 6532-7881
Website: www.lfp.com.cn

Mammolina Children's Home
三为园幼儿园
Ages 2.5 to 6
36 Maquanying Siqu, Liyuan Xiaoqu,
Xiangjiang Beilu,
Chaoyang District
朝阳区香江北路马泉营四区
丽苑小区36号
Tel: (86 10) 8470-5128
Website: www.montessori.ws

Muffy's Place
儿童英语之家
Ages 3 to 6
1/F, Wanli Xinxinjiayuan Club,
Haidian District
海淀区万柳新新家园俱乐部1层
Tel: (86 10) 8889-2378 or 8889-2029
Website: www.muffys.com.cn

**New Garden International
Kindergarten**
爱博阳光国际幼儿园
Ages 1.5 to 6
Area 2, Upper East Side, 6
Dongsanhuan Beilu,
Chaoyang District
朝阳区东四环北路6号阳光上东二区
Tel: (86 10) 8610-5130 or 8610-3861

**New School of Collaborative
Learning (NSCL)**
Anning Zhuang, Haidian District
Tel: (86 10) 6298-5758
Website: www.nscl-beijing.org

NIT International School Beijing

7 Louzizhuang Road,
Chaoyang District
朝阳区楼梓庄路7号
Tel: (86 10) 8439-4315
Website: www.nitbj.edu.cn

Oxford Baby Bilingual Kindergarten

北京小牛双语幼儿园
Ages 1.5 to 6
Location #1: 6 Nanxinyuan,
Chaoyang District
朝阳区南新园6号
Tel: (86 10) 8731-1098
Location #2: 10 Anhuili, Section 4,
Yayuncun, Chaoyang District
朝阳区亚运村安慧里4区10号
Tel: (86 10) 6489-5533
Location #3: 308 Huizhongli,
Yayuncun, Chaoyang District
朝阳区亚运村慧忠里308号
Tel: (86 10) 6493-6636
Location #4: 88 Jianguo Lu, Soho
New Town, Chaoyang District
朝阳区建国路88号Soho现代城
Tel: (86 10) 8589-7363
Website: www.oxfordbaby.org

Pakistan Embassy College

Ages 4 to 18
1 Dongzhimenwai Dajie, Sanlitun,
Chaoyang District
朝阳区三里屯东直门外大街1号
Tel: (86 10) 6532-1905

Potter's Wheel International School

匠心之轮国际学校
Grades Pre-K to 5
1 Chajia Donglu, Lanxinzhuang,
Chaoyang District
朝阳区郎辛庄茶家东路1号
Phone: (86 10) 8538-2803
Website: www.potters-wheel.cn

Renda Middle School and High School (Chinese language)

人大附中
Ages 12 to 16
37 Zhongguancun Dajie,
Haidian District
海淀区中关村大街37号
Phone: (86 10) 6251-3962 or 6251-2094
Website: www.rdfz.cn/English

Ritan School (Chinese language)

北京日坛中学
Grades 1 to 12
Address (Elementary School and
Middle School): 38 Nanshiliju,
Chaoyang District
朝阳区南十里居38号
Address (Middle School): Inside
Bajiazhuang No. 80 Middle School,
2 Bajiazhuang Xili,
Chaoyang District
朝阳区白家庄第八十中学
里白家庄西里2号
Address (High School—senior
year only): 36 Dongsanhuan Beilu,
Chaoyang District
朝阳区东三环北路36号
Address (High School):
A7 Daojiayuan, Chaoyang District
朝阳区道家园甲7号
Phone: (86 10) 8595-1513
Website: http://211.153.152.41/

Sanlitun Kindergarten

三里屯幼儿园
Ages 1 to 5
3 Jiqingli, Chaowai Dajie,
Chaoyang District
朝阳区朝外大街吉庆里3号
Tel: (86 10) 6551-0877

Sino Bright School
中加高中学校
Grades 7-12
55 Dengshikou Dajie at Beijing
No. 25 Middle School,
Dongcheng District
东城区灯市口大街55号
(在北京第二十五中学内)
Tel: (86 10) 6527-8189
Website: www.schoolbj.com

Sunshine Learning Center
北京顺义阳康复培训中心
Grades 7 to 12
2066 Gahood Villa, Houshayu,
Baixinzhuang, Shunyi District
顺义区后沙峪白辛庄嘉活别墅城2066
Tel: (86 10) 8046-1606
Website: www.sunshine.org.cn

Swedish School Beijing
瑞典小学
Ages 2 to 12
Legend Garden Villas,
89 Capital Airport Road,
Chaoyang District
朝阳区机场路89号丽京花园别墅
Tel: (86 10) 6456-0824
www.swedishschool.org.cn

**The High School Affiliated with
Beijing Normal University**
Tel: (86 10) 6304-0392

Western Academy of Beijing (WAB)
北京京西学校
Age 3 to Grade 12
10 Laiguangying Donglu,
Chaoyang District
朝阳区来广营东路10号
Tel: (86 10) 8456-4155
Website: www.wab.edu

**Yew Chung International
School of Beijing (YCIS)**
北京耀中国际学校
Grades K2 to Year 13
Honglingjin Gongyuan Ximen,
5 Houbali Zhuang,
Chaoyang District
朝阳区后八里庄5号红领巾公园西门
Tel: (86 10) 8583-3731
Website: www.ycis-bj.com

AIRLINE OFFICES
IN BEIJING

Aeroflot
Ground Fl, Jinglun Hotel,
3 Jiangguomenwai
Tel: 6585-0511
www.aeroflot.ru/eng/

Aerosvit Ukrainian Airlines
922, Towercrest Plaza
Tel: 8458-0909
www.aerosvit.ua/eng

Air Canada
Rm. C201 Lufthansa Center,
50 Liangmaqiao Rd.,
Tel: 6463-0576
www.aircanada.com

Air China
Civil Aviation Mansion,
15 Chang'an Ave.
Tel: 800-810-1111; 6605-0875(Night)
www.airchina.com.cn

Air Europa
CITS Building, 1 Dongdan Beida
Ave, Dongcheng
Tel: 6527-5188
www.aireuropa.com

Air France
5/F Full Link Plaza,
18 Chaoyangmen wai jie,
Tel: 6588-4266, 6588-1388
    or 4008-808-808
www.airfrance.com.cn

Air Koryo
8th Floor, Hong Kong Macau Center,
2 Chaoyangmen bei dajie.
Tel: 6501-1557

Air Macau
8/F 22 Scitech Tower,
22 Jianguomenwai dajie
Tel: 6515-8988
www.airmacau.com.mo

Air Zimbabwe
Beijing Capital International Airport
(Terminal 2, Room S32083)
www.airzimbabwe.com

Alitalia
Rm. 139 Jianguo Hotel,
Jianguomenwai
Tel: 65079297
www.alitalia.com

ANA
N200 Beijing Fortune Building,
#5 Dongsanhuan Bei lu, Chaoyang
Tel: 6590-9191 or 800-820-1122
www.ana.co.jp

Asiana Airlines
12th Floor, A/F Tower
Gateway, Chaoyang
Tel: 400-650-8000
www.cn.flyasiana.com

Austrian Airlines
Rm. C215, Lufthansa Center,
50 Liangmaqiao Rd., Chaoyang
Tel: 6462-2161/4
www.austrianairways.com.cn

British Airways
Rm. 210, Scitech Tower,
22 Jianguomenwai
Tel: 8511-5599 or 6512-3637
www.britishairways.com

Cathay Pacific
28/F, East Tower, Twin Towers,
12 Jianguomenwai
Tel: 800-852-1888
www.cathaypacific.com

China Eastern Airlines
1/F 12 Xinyuan Xi Li Lu
Tel: 800-820-3883 or 6468-1166
www.ce-air.com

China Southern Airlines
2 Dongsanhuan Nan Lu
Tel: 6459-0539 or 6567-2208
www.cs-air.com

Continental Airlines
Suite 500, Beijing Sunflower Tower,
37 Maizidian Jie,
Tel: 8527-6686 or 800-810-0088
www.continental.com

Dragon Air
28/F, East Tower, Twin Towers,
12 Jianguomenwai
Tel: 800-852-1888
www.dragonair.com

Egypt Air
Rm. 2260 Beijing Sunflower Tower,
37 Maizidian St.
Tel: 8527-5944
www.egyptair.com

El Al
Rm. 2906 Jing Guan Center,
Hujia Lu, Chaoyang
Tel: 6597-4515
www.elal.co.il

Emirates
www.emirates.com
Tel: 5108-8696

Ethiopian Airlines
Rm. 203 Tower 2,
China World Trade Center
Tel: 6505-0314 or 6505-0315
www.ethiopianairlines.com

Etihad Airways
www.etihadairways.com
Tel: 8523-3065

Finnair
Scitech Tower 203,
22 Jianguomenwai
Tel: 6512-7180
www.finnair.com.cn

Garuda Indonesia
1902 Kuntai Int. Mansion
12 Chao Wai Ave
Tel: 5879-7699
www.garuda-indonesia.com

Hainan Airlines
1 Jingsong nan lu, Chaoyang
Tel: 800 876-8999 or 950718
www.chinaxinhuair.com

Iran Air
Rm. 701, CITIC Plaza,
19 Jianguomenwai
Tel: 6512-4940
www.iranair.com

Japan Airlines
1/F Changfugong Office,
26 Jianguomenwai
Tel: 6513-0888 or 800-8105-553
www.cn.jal.com/en

JAT
Rm. 440 Kunlun Hotel,
2 Xinyuan nan lu, Chaoyang
Tel: 6590-3166 or 6590-3388
www.jat.com

KLM
1609 Kun Tai Int. Plaza,
12 Chao Wai
Tel: 4008-808-222
www.klm.com.cn

Korean Air
901 #3 Hyundai Motors Towers
China World Trade Center
Tel: 40065-88888
www.koreanair.com

Kras Air
Room 32087, Terminal Two,
Beijing Capital International Airport
www.krasair.ru

LTU International Airways
17F, Avic Building,
10B Dongsanhuan Zhong lu
Tel: 6566-6160
www.ltu.com

Lufthansa
Rm. 101, Lufthansa Center,
50 Liangmaqiao Rd.
Tel: 40088-68868
www.lufthansa.com.cn

MIAT Mongolian Airlines
705 Sunjoy Mansion,
6 Ritan Lu
Tel: 6507-9297
www.miat.com

Malaysia Airlines
Rm. 115A
China World Trade Center
Tel: 6505-2681 or 6505-2683
www.malaysiaairlines.com

Northwest Airlines
Rm. W501
China World Trade Center
Tel: 40081-40081
www.nwa.com

Philippine Airlines
Tel: 6510-2991
www.philippineairlines.com

**Pakistan International Airlines
(PIA)**
Rm. 617 China World Trade Center
Tel: 6505-1681, 6505-1682
    or 6505-1683
www.piac.com.pk

Qantas
10/F West Towers, Twin Towers,
12 Jianguomenwai
Tel: 6567-9006
www.qantas.com

Qatar Airways
16F/A Gateway Plaza,
18 Xiaguangli
Tel: 5923-5100
www.qatarairways.com

Royal Brunei
Lufthansa Center,
50 Liangmaqiao Lu
Tel: 6465-1625
www.bruneiair.com

S7 Airlines
Kuntai International
Building East 10,
12 Yi Chaowai Da Jie
Tel: 5879-0741
www.s7.ru

SAS Scandinavian Airlines
1830 Beijing Sunflower Tower,
37 Maizidian St., Chaoyang
Tel: 8527-6100
www.flysas.com

Shandong Airlines
Tel: 6459-0777

Shanghai Airlines
Civil Aviation Mansion,
15 Chang'an Ave.
Tel: 6459-9091 or 800-820-1018
www.shanghai-air.com

Shenzhen Airlines
Tel: 96737 or 6459-4874
www.shenzhenair.com

Sichuan Airlines
Tel: 6522-2258 or 6459-0362

Singapore Airlines
Rm. 8-1-8, Tower 2,
China World Trade Center
Tel: 6505-2233
www.singaporeair.com

Spanair
www.spanair.com

SriLankan Airlines
Unit S119, Lufthansa Center,
50 Liangmaqiao Lu
Tel: 6461-7208
www.srilankan.aero

Swiss Airlines
5101 Lufthansa Center,
50 Liangmaqiao Lu
Tel: 8454-0180
www.swiss.com

Thai Airways
Units 303-304, Level 3,
Office Tower W3, Oriental Plaza
Tel: 8515-0088
www.thaiairways.com

Turkish Airlines
Rm. 103 Lufthansa Center,
50 Liangmaqiao Rd.
Tel: 6465-1867
www.turkishairlineschina.com

United Airlines
1. Lufthansa Center,
2. 204 Scitech Tower
Tel: 8468-6666 or 800-810-8282
www.cn.united.com

Uzbekistan Airways
Rm. 2-01B CITIC Building
Tel: 6500-6442
www.uzairways.com.

Vietnam Airlines
Lufthansa Center,
50 Liangmaqiao Lu
Tel: 8454-1289
www.vietnamairlines.com

Xiamen Airlines
Tel: 800-858-2666
　　or 6459-6899

EMBASSIES

**Embassy of the Islamic
State of Afghanistan**
8 Dongzhimenwai Dajie
东直门外大街8号
Tel: 6532-1582 or 6532-2269

**Embassy of the Republic
of Albania**
28 Guanghua Road
光华路28号
Tel: 6532-1120

**Embassy of the Democratic
People's Republic of Algeria**
7 Sanlitun Road
三里屯路7号
Tel: 6532-1231, 6532-1496
　　or 6532-1220

Embassy of the Republic of Angola
1-8-1 Tayuan Diplomatic Office
Building
塔园外交人员办公楼1-13-1
Tel: 6532-6968 or 6532-6839

Embassy of Antigua and Barbuda
朝阳门南大街2号
Tel: 6596-1114

Embassy of the Argentine Republic
11 Dongwujie, Sanlitun
三里屯, 东五街11号
Tel: 6532-1406, 6532-2090
　　or 6532-2142

**Embassy of the Republic
of Armenia**
9-2-62 Tayuan Diplomatic
Compound
塔园外交办公寓9-2-62
Tel: 6532-5677

Embassy of Australia
21 Dongzhimenwai Dajie
东直门外大街21号
Tel: 5140-4111

Embassy of The Republic of Austria
5 Xiushuinanjie, Jianguomenwai
建国门外,秀水南街5号
Tel: 6532-2061 or 6532-2062

**Embassy of the Republic
of Azerbaijan**
Qijiayuan Diplomatic Compound
Villa No B-3
齐家园外交公寓B-3号别墅
Tel: 6532-4614

**Embassy of the Commonwealth
of The Bahamas**
2-4, Ta Yuan Diplomatic Office
Building, 14 Liangmahe Nan Lu,
亮马河南路14号塔园外交公寓2-4
Tel: 6532-2922 or 6532-2422

**Embassy of the Kingdom
of Bahrain**
10-06, Liangmaqiao Diplomatic
Residence Compound,
No. 22, Dong Fang Dong Lu,
东方东路22号亮马桥外交公寓 10-06
Tel: 6532-6483, 6532-6485
　　or 6532-6486

Embassy of the People's Republic of Bangladesh
42 Guanghua Road
光华路42号
Tel: 6532-2521 or 6532-3706

Embassy of the Republic of Belarus
1 Dongyijie Road, Ritan
日坛，东一街1号
Tel: 6532-1691 or 6532-6427

Embassy of Belgium
6 Sanlitun Road
三里屯6号
Tel: 6532-1736, 6532-1737
    or 6532-1738

Embassy of Republic of Benin
38 Guanghua Road
光华路38号
Tel: 6532-2741 or 6532-2302

Embassy of the Republic of Bolivia
2-3-2 Tayuan Diplomatic Office Building
塔园外交人员办公楼2-3-2
Tel: 6532-3074

Embassy of Bosnia and Herzegovina
1-5-1 Tayuan Diplomatic Office Building
塔园外交人员办公楼1-5-1
Tel: 6532-6587 or 6532-0185

Embassy of the Republic of Botswana
Unit 811 IMB Tower,
Pacific Century Place
#2A Gongti bei lu
工体北路甲2号盈科中心，
IBM大厦811号，
Tel: 6539-1616

Embassy of the Federative Republic of Brazil
27 Guanghua Road
光华路27号
Tel: 6532-2881

Embassy of Brunei Darussalam
North Street 1, Liang Ma Qiao,
Chaoyang District亮马桥北街1号
Tel: 6532-9773, 6532-9776
    or 6532-4093

Embassy of the Republic of Bulgaria
4 Xiushuibeijie, Jianguomenwai
建国门外，秀水北街4号
Tel: 6532-1946 or 6532-1916

Embassy of the Republic of Burundi
25 Guanghua Road
光华路25号
Tel: 6532-1801 or 6532-2328

Royal Embassy of Cambodia
9 Dongzhimenwai Dajie
东直门外大街9号
Tel: 6532-1889

Embassy of the Republic of Cameroon
7 Dongwujie, Sanlitun
三里屯，东五街7号
Tel: 6532-1771 or 6532-1114

Embassy of Canada
19 Dongzhimenwai Dajie
东直门外大街19号
Tel: 6532-3536

Embassy of the Republic of Cape Verde
6-2-121, Ta Yuan Diplomatic Compound
塔园外交人员办公楼6-2-121
Tel: 6532-7547

Embassy of the Republic of Central Africa
1-1-132 Ta Yuan Diplomatic Compound
塔园外交人员办公楼1-1-132
Tel: 6532-7353

Embassy of the Republic of Chad
No.1, Xin Dong Lu
新东路1号塔园外交公寓2号楼
2单元10层2号
Tel: 8532-3822

Embassy of the Republic of Chile
1 Dongsijie, Sanlitun
三里屯, 东四街1号
Tel: 6532-1591

Embassy of the Republic of Colombia
34 Guanghua Road
光华路34号
Tel: 6532-3377

Embassy of the Republic of the Congo
7 Dongsijie, Sanlitun
三里屯, 东四街7号
Tel: 6532-1658/6532-1417

Embassy of the Democratic Republic of Congo
6 Dongwujie, Sanlitun
三里屯, 东五街6号
Tel: 6532-3224

Embassy of the Republic of Cote d'Ivoire
9 Beixiaojie, Sanlitun
三里屯, 北小街9号
Tel: 6532-1482 or 6532-3572

Embassy of the Republic of Croatia
2-7-2 Sanlitun Diplomatic Apartments
三里屯外交人员公楼2-7-2
Tel: 6532-6241 or 6532-6256

Embassy of the Republic of Cuba
1 Xiushuinanjie, Jianguomenwai
建国门外, 秀水南街1号
Tel: 6532-6568 or 6532-1714

Embassy of the Republic of Cyprus
2-13-2 Tayuan Diplomatic Office Building
塔园外交人员办公楼2-13-2
Tel: 6532-5057

Embassy of the Czech Republic
2 Ritan Road, Jianguomenwai
建国门外, 日坛路2号
Tel: 8532-9500

Royal Danish Embassy
1 Dongwujie, Sanlitun
三里屯, 东五街1号
Tel: 8532-9900

Embassy of the Republic of Djibouti
1-1-122 Ta Yuan Diplomatic Compound
塔园外交人员办公楼1-1-122
Tel: 6532-7857

Embassy of the Commonwealth of Dominica
LA06, Liangmaqiao Diplomatic Residence Compound,
No. 22 Dongfangdong Road,
东方东路22号亮马桥外交公寓A区
LA06号
Tel: 6532-0838

Embassy of the Republic of Ecuador
2-62 Sanlitun Office Building
三里屯外交人员办公楼2-6-2
Tel: 6532-3849 or 6532-3158

Embassy of the Arab Republic of Egypt
2 Ritan Donglu
日坛东路2号
Tel: 6532-1825 or 6532-2541

**Embassy of the Republic
of Equatorial Guinea**
2 Dongsijie, Sanlitun
三里屯, 东四街2号
Tel: 6532-3679

Embassy of the State of Eritrea
2-10-1, Ta Yuan Office Building
塔园外交人员办公楼2-10-1
Tel: 6532-6534

Embassy of the Republic of Estonia
C-617/618, Office Building, Beijing
Lufthansa Center
北京燕莎中心写字楼C-617/618
Tel: 6463-7913

**Embassy of the Federal
Democratic Republic of Ethiopia**
3 Xiushuinanjie, Jianguomenwai
建国门外, 秀水南街3号
Tel: 6532-5258 or 6532-1972

**Embassy of the Republic
of Fiji Islands**
1-15-2 Ta Yuan Diplomatic
Office Building
塔园外交人员办公楼1-15-2
Tel: 6532-7305

**Embassy of the
Republic of Finland**
Level 26, South Tower,
Beijing Kerry Center,
Guanghua Rd
光华路1号北京嘉里中心南塔楼26层
Tel: 8529-8541

Embassy of the Republic of France
3 Dongsanjie, Sanlitun
三里屯, 东三街3号
Tel: 8532-8080

Embassy of the Republic of Gabon
36 Guanghua Road
光华路36号
Tel: 6532-2810 or 6532-3580

Embassy of Georgia
亮马桥外交公寓A座3-2
LA 03-02, Section A, Liangmaqiao
Diplomatic Compound
Tel: 6532-7518 or 6532-7525

**Embassy of the Federal
Republic of Germany**
17 Dongzhimenwai Dajie
东直门外大街17号
Tel: 8532-9000

Embassy of the Republic of Ghana
8 Sanlitun Road
三里屯路8号
Tel: 6532-1319 or 6532-1544

**Embassy of the Hellenic
Republic (Greece)**
19 Guanghua Road
光华路19号
Tel: 653-21317 or 6532-1391

**Embassy of the Republic
of Guinea**
2 Xiliujie, Sanlitun
三里屯, 西六街2号
Tel: 6532-3649

**Embassy of the Republic
of Guinea-Bissau**
2-2-101 Ta Yuan
Diplomatic Compound
塔园外交人员办公楼2-2-101
Tel: 6532-7393

**Embassy of the Cooperative
Republic of Guyana**
1 Xiushuidongjie, Jianguomenwai
建国门外, 秀水东街1号
Tel: 6532-1337

**Embassy of the Republic
of Hungary**
10 Dongzhimenwai Dajie, Sanlitu
三里屯, 东直门外大街10号
Tel: 6532-1431 or 6532-1432

Embassy of the Republic of Iceland
8028 Landmark Tower 1,
8 North Dongsanhuan Road
Tel: 6590-7795 or 6590-7796

Embassy of the Republic of India
1 Ritan Donglu
日坛东路1号
Tel: 6532-1856 or 6532-1908

**Embassy of the Republic
of Indonesia**
No. 4, Dong Zhi Men Wai Da Jie
东直门外大街4号
Tel: 6532-5489 or 6532-5488

**Embassy of the Islamic
Republic of Iran**
13 Dongliujie, Sanlitun
Tel: 6532-2040 or 6532-4870

Embassy of the Republic of Iraq
25 Xiushuibeijie, Jianguomenwai
Tel: 6532-3385 or 6532-1873

Embassy of Ireland
3 Ritan Donglu
日坛东路3号
Tel: 6532-2691, 6532-2914
     or 6532-1144

Embassy of Israel
17 Tianzelu Chaoyang District
天泽路17号
Tel: 8532-0500

Embassy of the Republic of Italy
2 Dongerjie, Sanlitun
三里屯, 东二街2号
Tel: 6532-2131, 6532-2132
     or 6532-2133

Embassy of Jamaica
6-2-72, Jianguomenwai
Diplomatic Compound,
1, Xiu Shui Street
秀水街1号建国门外外交公寓6-2-72
Tel: 6532-0670, 6532-0671
     or 65320667

Embassy of Japan
7 Ritan Road, Jianguomenwai
建国门外日坛7号
Tel: 6532-2361

**Embassy of the
Hashemite Kingdom of Jordan**
5 Dongliujie, Jianguomenwai
建国门外, 东六街5号
Tel: 6532-3906

**Embassy of the
Republic of Kazakhstan**
9 Dongliujie, Sanlitun
三里屯, 东六街9号
Tel: 6532-6182 or 6532-6189

**Embassy of the
Republic of Kenya**
4 Xiliujie, Sanlitun
三里屯, 西六街4号
Tel: 6532-3381 or 6532-2473

**Embassy of the Democratic
People's Republic of Korea**
11 Ritan beilu, Jianguomenwai
建国门外日坛11号
Tel: 6532-1186

**Embassy of the
Republic of Korea**
20 Dongfangdonglu
东方东路20号
Tel: 8531-0700

**Embassy of the
State of Kuwait**
23 Guanghua Road
光华路23号
Tel: 6532-2216 or 6532-2182

Embassy of the Kyrghyz Republic
2-7-1 Tayuan Diplomatic
Office Building
塔园外交人员办公楼2-7-1
Tel: 6532-6458 or 6532-6459

Embassy of the Lao People's Democratic Republic
11 Dongsijie, Sanlitun
三里屯, 东四街11号
Tel: 6532-1224

Embassy of the Republic of Latvia
Unit 71, Greenland Garden,
No 1A Greenland Rd
嘉林路甲1号嘉林花园71号别墅
Tel: 6433-3863

Embassy of Lebanon
10 Dongliujie, Sanlitun
三里屯, 东六街10号
Tel: 65321-5606 or 6532-2197

Embassy of the Kingdom of Lesotho
302 Dongwai Office Building
东外外交办公楼302
Tel: 6532-6843 or 6532-6844

The People's Bureau of the Great Socialist People's Libyan Arab Jamahiriya
3 Dongliujie, Sanlitun
三里屯, 东六街3号
Tel: 6532-3666 or 6532-3980

Embassy of the Republic of Liberia
Room 013, Gold Island
Diplomatic Compound,
No. 1 Xi Ba He Nanlu,
西坝河南路1号, 金岛外交公寓013房
Tel: 6440-3007

Embassy of the Republic of Lithuania
E-18 King's Garden Villas,
18 Xiaoyun Lu
霄云路18号, 京润水上花园B-30
Tel: 8451-8520

Embassy of the Grand-Duchy of Luxembourg
21 Neiwubujie
内务部街21号
Tel: 6513-5937

Embassy of the Republic of Macedonia
3-2-21 Sanlitun Diplomatic
Compound
Tel: 6532-7846

Embassy of the Republic of Madagascar
3 Sanlitun Dongjie
三里屯东街3号
Tel: 6532-1353, 6532-1643
      or 6532-1616

Embassy of Malaysia
2 Liang Ma Qiao Bei Jie
亮马桥北街2号
Tel: 6532-2531

Embassy of the Republic of Mali
8 Dongsijie, Sanlitun
三里屯, 东四街8号
Tel: 6532-1704

Embassy of the Republic of Malta
1-51 Tayuan Diplomatic Apartments
塔园外交人员办公楼1-51
Tel: 6532-3114

Embassy of the Islamic Republic of Mauritania
9 Dongsanjie, Sanlitun
三里屯, 东三街9号
Tel: 6532-1346 or 6532-1703

Embassy of the Republic of Mauritius
202 Dongwai Diplomatic Office,
23 Dongzhimenwai Dajie
东直门外大街23号东外外交办公楼202
Tel: 6532-5695 or 6532-5696

**Embassy of the United
Mexican States**
5 Dongwujie, Sanlitun
三里屯, 东五街5号
Tel: 6532-2574 or 6532-2070

**Embassy of the
Republic of Moldova**
2-9-1 Tayuan Diplomatic
Office Building
塔园外交人员办公楼2-9-1
Tel: 6532-5494

Embassy of Mongolia
2 Xiushuibeijie, Jianguomenwai
建国门外, 秀水北街2号
Tel: 6532-1203

**Embassy of the
Kingdom of Morocco**
16 Sanlitun Road
三里屯路16号
Tel: 6532-1796 or 6532-1489

**Embassy of the Republic
of Mozambique**
1-7-2 Tayuan Diplomatic
Office Building
塔园外交人员办公楼1-7-2
Tel: 6532-3664 or 6532-3578

Embassy of the Union of Myanmar
6 Dongzhimenwai Dajie
东直门外大街6号
Tel: 6532-0359

**Embassy of the Republic
of Namibia**
2-9-2 Tayuan Diplomatic
Office Building
塔园外交人员办公楼2-9-2
Tel: 6532-4810 or 6532-4811

Embassy of Nepal
1 Xiliujie, Sanlitun
三里屯, 西六街1号
Tel: 6532-1795

Royal Netherlands Embassy
4 Liangmahe Nanlu
亮马河南路4号
Tel: 8532-0200

Embassy of New Zealand
1 Dongerjie, Ritan Road
日坛路, 东二街1号
Tel: 6532-2731, 6532-2732
   or 6532-2733

Embassy of the Republic of Niger
1-21 Sanlitun Apartment
Tel: 6532-4279

**Embassy of the Federal
Republic of Nigeria**
2 Dongwujie, Sanlitun
三里屯, 东五街2号
Tel: 6532-3631 or 6532-3632

Royal Norwegian Embassy
1 Dongyijie, Sanlitun
三里屯, 东一街1号
Tel: 6532-2261

Embassy of the Sultanate of Oman
6 Liangmahe Nanlu
亮马河南路6号
Tel: 6532-3692

**Embassy of the Islamic
Republic of Pakistan**
1 Dongzhimenwai Dajie
东直门外大街1号
Tel: 6532-2504 or 6532-2695

Embassy of the State of Palestine
2 Dongsanjie, Sanlitun
三里屯, 东三街2号
Tel: 6532-3327

Embassy of Papua New Guinea
2-11-2 Tayuan
Diplomatic Office Building
塔园外交人员办公楼2-11-2
Tel: 6532-4312 or 6532-4709

Embassy of the Republic of Peru
1-91 Sanlitun Diplomatic
Office Building
塔园外交人员办公楼1-91
Tel: 6532-3719 or 6532-2913

**Embassy of the Republic
of the Philippines**
23 Xiushuibeijie, Jianguomenwai
建国门外, 秀水北街23号
Tel: 6532-1872 or 6532-2518

Embassy of the Republic of Poland
1 Ritanlu, Jianguomenwai
建国门外, 日坛1号
Tel: 6532-1235, 6532-1236
      or 6532-1888

**Embassy of the Republic
of Portugal**
8 Dongwujie, Sanlitun
三里屯, 东五街2
Tel: 6532-3497

Embassy of the State of Qatar
A-7 Liang Ma Qiao Compound
亮马桥外交公寓A区7号楼
Tel: 6532-2231, 6532-2232
      or 6532-2233

Embassy of Romania
Ritanlu Dongerjie
日坛, 东二街2号
Tel: 6532-3442 or 6532-3879

Embassy of the Russian Federation
4 Dongzhimen Beizhongjie
东直门北中街4号
Tel: 6532-2051 or 6532-1381

**Embassy of the
Republic of Rwanda**
30 Xiushuibeijie
秀水北街30号
Tel: 6532-2193 or 6532-1762

Royal Embassy of Saudi Arabia
1 Beixiaojie, Sanlitun
三里屯, 北小街1号
Tel: 6532-4825 or 6532-5325

Embassy of Serbia
1 Dongliujie, Sanlitun
三里屯, 东六街1号
Tel: 6532-3516

**Embassy of the
Republic of Senegal**
305 Dong Wai Diplomatic
Office Buiding, 23,
Dong Zhi Men Wai Da Jie
东直门外大街23号东外外交办公楼305
Tel: 6532-5035 or 6532-3798

**Embassy of the
Republic of Seychelles**
Room 1105, The Spaces,
Dongdaqiao Rd. 8,
朝阳区东大桥路8号
尚都国际中心1105室
Tel: 5870-1192

**Embassy of the Republic
of Sierra Leone**
7 Dongzhimenwai Dajie
东直门外大街7号
Tel: 6532-1222 or 6532-2174

**Embassy of the Republic
of Singapore**
1 Xiu Shui Bei Jie,
Jian Guo Men Wai,
建国门外秀水北街1号
Tel: 6532-1115

**Embassy of the
Slovak Republic**
Ritanlu, Jianguomenwai
建国门外,日坛路
Tel: 6532-1531

**Embassy of the
Republic of Slovenia**
57 Block F, Yaquyuan,
King's Garden Villas, 18 Xiaoyu lu
霄云路18号京润水上花园别墅
雅趣园F区57号
Tel: 6468-1030

Embassy of the Somali Republic
2 Sanlitun Road
三里屯路2号
Tel: 6532-1651

**Embassy of Republic
of South Africa**
5 Dongzhimenwai Dajie
东直门大街5号
Tel: 6532-0171

Embassy of Spain
9 Sanlitun Road
三里屯路9号
Tel: 6532-1986, 6532-3629
    or 65323728

**Embassy of the Democratic
Socialist Republic of Sri Lanka**
3 Jianhualu, Jianguomenwai
建国门外建华路3号
Tel: 6532-1861 or 6532-1862

**Embassy of the
Republic of Sudan**
1 Dongerjie, Sanlitun
三里屯，东二街1号
Tel: 6532-3715

**Embassy of the
Republic of Suriname**
2-2-22 Jianguomenwai
Diplomatic Compound
建国门外外交公寓2-2-22
Tel: 6532-2939 or 6532-2938

Embassy of Sweden
3 Dongzhimenwai Dajie
东直门外大街3号
Tel: 6532-9790

Embassy of Switzerland
3 Dongwujie, Sanlitun
三里屯，东五街3号
Tel: 6532-2736, 6532-2737
    or 6532-2738

**Embassy of the
Syrian Arab Republic**
6 Dongsijie, Sanlitun
三里屯，东四街6号
Tel: 6532-1372 or 6532-1347

**Embassy of the
Republic of Tajikistan**
1-4, Section A, Liangmaqiao
Diplomatic Compound
亮马桥外交公寓A区1-4
Tel: 6532-2598

**Embassy of the
United Republic of Tanzania**
8 Liangmahe Nanlu, Sanlitun
三里屯，连马河南路8号
Tel: 6532-1491

Royal Thai Embassy
40 Guanghua Road
光华路40号
Tel: 6532-1749

**Embassy of the Democratic
Republic of Timor-Leste**
156 Gold Island Diplomatic
Compound, 1 Room156,
Xibahe Nanlu,
西坝河南路1号金岛外交公寓156号
Tel: 6440-3072 or 6440-3079

Embassy of the Republic of Togo
11 Dongzhimenwai Dajie
东直门大街11号
Tel: 6532-2202 or 6532-2444

Embassy of the Kingdom of Tonga
Suite 3002, Embassy House, 18
Dong Zhi Men Wai Xiao Jie
东直门外小街18号万国公寓3002号
Te: 8449-9757

Embassy of the Tunisian Republic
1 Sanlitun Dongjie
三里屯东街1号
Tel: 6532-2435 or 6532-2436

Embassy of the Republic of Turkey
9 Dongwujie, Sanlitun
三里屯, 东五街9号
Tel: 6532-1715

Embassy of Turkmenistan
Villa D-26 King's Garden Villa,
18 Xiaoyuan Lu
霄云路18号京润水上花园别墅
雅趣园D-1
Tel: 6532-6975

**Embassy of the
Republic of Uganda**
5 Sanlitun Dongjie
三里屯东街5号
Tel: 6532-1708

Embassy of Ukraine
11 Dongliujie, Sanlitun
三里屯, 东六街11号
Tel: 6532-6359 or 6532-6314

**Embassy of the
United Arab Emirates**
LA 10-04, Liangmaqiao Diplomatic
Residence Compound,
No. 22 Dongfangdong Road
东方东路22号亮马桥外交公寓
LA10-04
Tel: 6532-7650

**Embassy of the United kingdom
of Great Britain and
Northern Ireland**
11 Guanghua Road
光华路11号
Tel: 6532-1961

**Embassy of the
United States of America**
3 Xiushuibeijie, Jianguomenwai
建国门外, 秀水北路3号
Tel: 6532-3831 or 6532-3431

**Embassy of the Oriental
Republic of Uruguay**
1-11-2 Tayuan Diplomatic
Office Building
塔园外交人员办公楼1-11-21
Tel: 6532-4445 or 6532-4413

**Embassy of the
Republic of Uzbekistan**
11 Beixiaojie, Sanlitun
三里屯, 北小街11号
Tel: 6532-6305

**Embassy of the
Republic of Vanuatu**
San Li Tun Diplomatic Compound
三里屯外交公寓3号
楼1单元11号3-1-11
Tel: 6532-0337

**Embassy of the
Republic of Venezuela**
14 Sanlitun Road
三里屯路14号
Tel: 6532-1295 or 6532-2694

**Embassy of the Socialist
Republic of Viet Nam**
32 Guanghua Road,
Jianguomenwai
光华路32号
Tel: 6532-1155

Embassy of the Republic of Yemen
5 Dongsanjie, Sanlitun
三里屯, 东三街5号
Tel: 6532-1558

Embassy of the Republic of Zambia
5 Dongsijie, Sanlitun
三里屯,东四街5号
Tel: 6532-1554 or 6532-1778
    or 6532-2058

**Embassy of the Republic
of Zimbabwe**
7 Dongsanjie, Sanlitun
三里屯, 东三街
Tel: 6532-3795, 6532-3665
    or 6532-3397

**European Union, Delegation
of the European Commission**
15 Dong Zhi Men Wai Da Jie
东直门外大街15号
Tel: 8454-8000

UNIVERSITIES ACCEPTING FOREIGN STUDENTS

Peking University 北京大学
Overview:
Founded in 1898, Peking University was the first comprehensive national university established in China. As such it carries a lot of prestige as one of the top universities in China today. Departments include: Mathematics, Physics, Engineering, Applied Physics, Geophysics, Radiology, IT Science, Chemistry, Geology, Sociology, Japanese, Russian, Western Languages, Psychology, Geography, Economics, Law, International Politics, Chinese and History. There are approximately 1,500 long-term foreign students and 2,600 short-term foreign students studying here each year.

Courses:
International students can apply to study short-term or long-term Chinese Language courses as well as undergraduate and postgraduate degrees.

Contact information:
Office of International Relations, International Students Division.
Peking University, Shao Yuan Building 3, Beijing, 100871, PRC
Tel: (86 10) 6275-1230, 6275-2747 or 6275-9398
E-mail: study@pku.edu.cn
Website: http://en.pku.edu.cn

Tsinghua University 清华大学
Overview:
Tsinghua University (Qinghua) is rated as one of the top learning and intensive research institutes in China. Strong in IT, engineering and sciences, it also has disciplines in humanities, law, economics, medicine, arts, and MBA programmes. There are approximately 1,000 foreign students studying here each year.

Courses:
Foreign students can study Chinese language or pursue undergraduate and postgraduate degrees in a range of fields.

Contact information:
Foreign Students Office, Tsinghua University, Haidian District, Beijing, 100084
Tel: (86 10) 6278-4857, 6278-4621
E-mail: lxsb@tsinghua.edu.cn
Website: http://www.tsinghua.edu.cn

Beijing Normal University 北京师范大学
Overview:
Beijing Normal University is a key university in China and one of Beijing's foremost Colleges. As a comprehensive university, there are 15 colleges and 12 departments offering courses in history, education, psychology, economics, philosophy, politics, mathematics, physics, biology, chemistry and environmental protection. More than 1,000 foreign students study here each year.

Courses:
Foreign students can study both short- in and long-term Chinese language programmes as well as pursue undergraduate and postgraduate degrees in several fields.

Contact information:
The Office of International Scholars and Students' Affairs,
Beijing Normal University, 19 Xinjiekou St., Beijing, 100875, PRC
Tel: (86 10) 6220 7986, 6220 8364 or 6220 0325
E-mail: isp@bnu.edu.cn
Website: http://www.bnu.edu.cn

Beijing Language and Culture University 北京语言大学
Overview:
Beijing Language and Culture University (Beijing Foreign Languages Institute) is the only university in China whose primary task is teaching Chinese language and culture to foreign students. There are more than 7,000 foreign students and 4,000 Chinese students studying here every year. Programmes include Chinese language & culture, contemporary China studies, foreign languages, finance and literature.

Courses:
International students can study in both short- and long-term language programmes as well as pursue degrees in Chinese literature, linguistics and International studies.

Contact information:
Admission Office for Foreign Students, Beijing Language and Culture University,
15 Xueyuan Road, Haidian District, Beijing, 100083, PRC
Tel: (86 10) 8320-3026, 8320-3088 or 8230-3951
Website: http://www.blcu.edu.cn

Beijing Jiaotong University 北京交通大学
Overview:
Beijing Jiaotong University (formerly known as Northern Jiaotong University) is a key university in China. Founded in 1896, it has a strong emphasis on engineering but also offers disciplines in liberal arts, sciences, IT and management. Located close to Xizhimen Metro station, the university is close to Beijing's central districts.

Courses:
Chinese language programmes are offered for foreign students. Undergraduate and graduate degrees can also be pursued in all disciplines.

Contact information:
Foreign Affairs Office, Beijing Jiaotong University,
Xizhimenwai, Beijing 100044, PRC
Tel: (86 10) 5168-8351 or 5168-8321
Website: http://www.njtu.edu.cn/en/

Renmin University of China 中国人民大学
Overview:
Renmin University is a renowned key institute in China focusing on social sciences, humanities, economics and managerial sciences. Key disciplines include Marxist philosophy, Economics, Population Studies, Business Administration, Chinese History, Journalism, Accounting, Criminal Law and Ethics. There are approximately 700 foreign students studying here each year.

Courses:
International students can pursue both short- and long-term language programmes, BA & MA degrees in Chinese, and degrees in law, journalism & International Politics.

Contact information:
International Students' Office, Renmin University of China,
59 Zhongguancun St, Beijing 100872, PRC
Tel: (86 10) 6251-1588
Website: http://english.ruc.edu.cn/en/

Beijing Foreign Studies University 北京外国语大学
Overview:
Founded in 1941, Beijing Foreign Studies University specializes in foreign language studies. The university offers studies in 36 languages including English, Russian, Japanese, French, German, Spanish, Arabic, Slavic languages, Asian and African languages, and Chinese. There are approximately 1,000 foreign students.

Courses:
International students can study in both short- and long-term language pro-grammes, as well as pursue BA and MA degrees in Chinese or other languages.

Contact information:
Foreign Affairs Office, Beijing Foreign Studies University,
Xisanhuan Bei Lu, Haidian District, Beijing, PRC
Tel: (86 10) 6842-2277 or 6842-1166
Website: http://www.bfsu.edu.cn

Capital Normal University 首都师范大学
Overview:
Capital Normal University is key university in Beijing embracing the sciences, liberal arts, foreign languages and arts. Undergraduate programmes include Chinese, History, Mathematics, Education, Art, Music, Calligraphy and English. There are more than 1,000 foreign students studying here each year. Capital Normal University is one of the HSK examination sites in Beijing.

Courses:
International students can pursue both short- and long-term language programmes, BA degrees in Chinese, and undergraduate and postgraduate degrees in other fields.

Contact information:
Department of International Students' Affairs, College of International
Education and Exchange, Capital Normal University, Xisanhuan Bei Lu.
Beijing 100037, PRC
Tel: (86 10) 6890-2651 or 6890-0173
Website: www.cnu.edu.cn/english/intro/intro.asp

Beijing Institute of Technology 北京理工大学
Overview:
Beijing Institute of Technology (BIT) is a key university in China with emphasis on engineering, sciences, management, humanities, economics, law, IT science and education. There are approximately 350 foreign students studying at BIT each year. The International Student Centre for Chinese Language and Culture Study offers 14 classes at eight grades each year.

Courses:
International students can pursue both short- and long-term language pro-grammes, and undergraduate and postgraduate degrees in a variety of technical fields.

Contact information:
International Student Centre, (Room 1144 Central Building),
Beijing Institute of Technology, 5 Zhongguancun Nan Dajie,
Haidian District, Beijing 100081, PRC
Tel: (86 10) 6891-3294 or 6891-1438
E-mail: enlinw@bit.edu.cn rmdxlb@sohu.com
Website: http://english.bit.edu.cn

Beijing University of Aeronautics and Astronautics 北京航空航天大学
Overview:
A key university, Beijing University of Aeronautics and Astronautics is a comprehensive university of science and technology specializing in aerospace technologies and research. Fields include science, engineering, liberal arts and management.

Courses:
International students can study Chinese language, as well as pursue degree programmes in any of the main disciplines.

Contact information:
Foreign Students Administration Office, Beijing University of Aeronautics and Astronautics, 37 Xueyuan Road, Haidian District, Beijing 100083, PRC
Tel: (86 10) 8231-7685 or 8231-6488
Email: fso@buaa.edu.cn
Website: http://ev.buaa.edu.cn

Beijing International Studies University 北京第二外国语大学
Overview:
Beijing International Studies University is a key university in China specializing in foreign languages and tourism. Its main task is to train professionals proficient in foreign languages, tourism, economics, trade and finance. Languages taught include English, Japanese, German, Russian, French, Spanish, Arabic and Korean. Other studies on Chinese Language and Culture, News, International Politics, Law, Tourism Management, Journalism, Marketing and International Trade are also offered. There are approximately 900 foreign students enrolled here each year.

Courses:
International students can study Chinese Language and Culture, and pursue undergraduate and postgraduate degrees in different fields of study

Contact information:
International Exchange and Cooperative Office, Beijing International Studies University, 1 Ding Fu Zhuang Nanli, Chaoyang District, Beijing 100024, PRC
Tel: (86 10) 6577-8564 or 6577-8565
Website: http://www.bisu.edu.cn

University of Science and Technology Beijing 北京科技大学
Overview:
The University of Science and Technology Beijing is a key university renowned for its study of metallurgy and material science. A strong emphasis on engineering is complemented by programmes in basic science and humanities. A Chinese language programme is offered.

Courses:
International students can study Chinese Language in preparation for further studies in degree programmes at the university.

Contact information:
International Affairs Office, University of Science and Technology Beijing, 30 Xueyuan Road. Haidian District, Beijing 100083, PRC
Tel: (86 10) 6233-2942
Website: http://en.ustb.edu.cn

Beijing University of Chemical Technology 北京化工大学
Overview:
Beijing University of Chemical Technology is one of China's key universities in science and economic management. Specialities include International Economy and Trade, Law, Mathematics, Applied Chemistry, Non-metallic Materials Engineering, Machinery and Automation, Industrial Automation, Computer Science and Technology, Pharmaceutical Engineering, Electronic Science.

Courses:
International students can study in both short- and long-term Chinese language programmes. Undergraduate and postgraduate degrees are offered in several fields.

Contact information:
International Exchange and Cooperation Department, Beijing University of Chemical Technology, 15 Beisanhuan Lu, Beijing 100029, PRC
Tel: (86 10) 6447-5534 or 6445-1480
E-mail: faoffice@buct.edu.cn
Website: http://www.buct.edu.cn

Beijing University of Post and Telecommunications 北京邮电大学
Overview:
Beijing University of Post and Telecommunications is a key university in China with an emphasis on information and communication. Fields of study include Communication Engineering, Information Engineering, Business Administration, Information Marketing and Information Systems, Economics, Marketing.

Courses:
International students can study in both short-term and long-term Chinese language programmes, as well as pursue degree programmes in many of the main disciplines.

Contact information:
Foreign Affairs Office, Beijing University of Post and Telecommunications,
10 Xitucheng Road, Haidian District, Beijing 100876, PRC
Tel: (86 10) 6228-1949 or 6228-1945
E-mail: faoffice@bupt.edu.cn
Website: http://www.bupt.edu.cn

Beijing Union University 北京联合大学
Overview:
Beijing Union University is a comprehensive, multi-disciplinary institute of higher learning. Colleges and schools include: information engineering, mechanical engineering, automation, management, international language and culture, arts and science, tourism, education, business and biochemical engineering. There are approximately 300 foreign students studying here.

Courses:
Foreign students can study in both short-term and long-term Chinese language programmes. Additional studies in Kungfu, Taichi, Calligraphy and coaching for the HSK Chinese proficiency test are also offered.

Contact information:
International Programme Department of Beijing Union University,
Tel: (86 10) 6490-0403, 6490-0672 or 6490-0249
E-mail: admission@buu.com.cn
Website: http://www.buu.edu.cn

The Academy of Chinese Traditional Opera 中国戏曲学院
Overview:
The Academy of Chinese Traditional Opera is the only institute dedicated to training professional performers with BA and MA degree programmes. There are five departments: Department of Performing Arts, Department of Directing, Department of Music, Department of Dramatic Literature, Department of Stage Design. Professional private coaching is also available for performance students.

Courses:
Foreign students can learn both Chinese and Chinese theatrical arts and performance in both short-term and long-term programmes.

Contact information:
Office of International Exchanges, The Academy of Chinese Traditional Opera,
400 Wanquansi St., Fengtai District, Beijing, 100073
Tel: (86 10) 6344-4063 or 6343-0648
E-mail: dwb@acto.org.cn
Website: http://www.acto.org.cn

Beijing Institute of Tourism 北京联合大学旅游学院
Overview:
Beijing Institute of Tourism, of the Beijing Union University, is established to
train management and service personnel in the tourism industry. Majors include
Chinese Food and Beverage Art, Tourism English, Tourism Japanese, Tourism
Management, and Tourism Marketing. Short-term programmes in Chinese lan-
guage and Chinese cooking are offered.

Courses:
International students can study six-month to one-year Chinese language related
to the tourism industry, preparatory course for Chinese medicine, and various
fields of study related to the tourism industry.

Contact information:
99 Beisanhuan Dong Lu, Chaoyang District, Beijing 100101, PRC
Tel: (86 10) 6490-0176 or 6490-9206
E-mail: bitbj@163.com
Website: http://www.bit-univ.com

College of Arts and Sciences of Beijing Union University
北京联合大学应用文理学院
Overview:
Formerly the branch campus of Beijing University, the College of Arts and Sciences was founded as a comprehensive university in 1978. Disciplines include Information Technology, Law, Biology, International Finance, Journalism, Foreign
Language and Literature.

Courses:
Foreign students may study in Chinese language and undergraduate programmes.
Preparatory classes for the HSK Chinese proficiency test are offered.

Contact information:
West Road of Beitucheng, P.O. Box 197, Beijing 100083, PRC
Tel: (86 10) 6200-4588 or 6200-4581
Email: rqk@bjedu.gov.cn
Website: http://www.casbuu.edu.cn/gjhz/english/

China University of Political Science and Law 中国政治大学
Overview:

As a key university in China, the China University of Political Science and Law emphasizes on training high-quality legal personnel. Departments include the Law College; College of Civil, Commercial and Economic Law; International Law College; Criminal and Justice College; College of Politics and Public Management; College of Human Studies; Business College; and Foreign Languages College. There are approximately 300 foreign students studying here.

Courses:

The Chinese Training Department teaches Law-related Chinese language. A summer programme is offered for the study of Chinese Law in English.

Contact information:
25 Xitucheng Road, Haidian District, Beijing 100088, PRC
Tel: (86 10) 6222-9012 or 8221-1413
E-mail: unw@bjedu.gov.cn
Website: http://www.cupl.edu.cn

China Youth University for Political Science 中国青年政治学院
Overview:

China Youth University for Political Science is a centre for higher learning focusing on Youth issues and social sciences. Departments include: Department of Youth and Juvenile, Department of Social Work and Management, Department of Law, Department of Social Science, and Department of Chinese Language. Summer and Winter Camps are organized for Chinese Language learning.

Courses:

Foreign students can study in both short-term and long-term Chinese language programmes and pursue undergraduate courses in the main college.

Contact information:
Chinese Language Education Center, China Youth University
for Political Science
25 Xisanhuan Bei lu, Beijing 100089, PRC
Tel: (86 10) 8856-7101
E-mail: bjss@cyu.edu.cn
Website: http://www.lec.cyu.edu.cn

Beijing Youth Politics College 北京青年政治学院
Overview:

The Beijing Youth Politics College was founded in 1986 and has an emphasis on Law and Youth Education. Departments include Administration, Business Law, and Sociology. The university is situated on a new small campus located in the North East of Beijing. Foreign students are encouraged to participate in events organized by the Student Union.

Courses:
International students are able to study in short- and long-term language and culture programmes as well as pursue other courses in other departments. HSK preparatory classes are also available.

Contact information:
Chinese Teaching Department, Beijing Youth Politics College,
4 Wangjing Middle Ring, Chaoyang District, Beijing 100102, PRC
Tel: (86 10) 6472-5626
E-mail: bqylb@public.bta.net.cn
Website: http://www.bjypc.edu.cn

Central University of Finance and Economics 中央财经大学
Overview:
A multi-disciplinary university with a focus on Economics, Management, Law, Literature and Languages, Central University of Finance and Economics is a leading University in China in its field.

Courses:
International students may study Chinese Language and other courses on a short-term or long-term basis as well as part of a degree programme.

Contact information:
International Students Department, Central University
of Finance and Economics,
39 Xueyuan Nan Lu, Beijing 100081, PRC
Tel: (86 10) 6228-8336
Email: lxs@cufe.edu.cn
Website: http://www.cufe.edu.cn

Capital University of Economics and Business 首都经济贸易大学
Overview:
The Capital University of Economics and Business is a key university in Beijing with emphases on economics and management. Fields of studies include Business Administration, Marketing, Trade and Economy, Accounting, Finance Studies, Human Resource Management, Economics, Statistics, Law, Labour and Security. Foreign students are offered a Chinese Business studies programme.

Courses:
International students may study Chinese Language, Chinese Business Studies and Commerce Studies in Bachelor's, Master's and Doctorate programmes.

Contact information:
International Students Office, Capital University of Economics and Business,
2 Chaoyangmenwai, Hongmiao Jin Tai Lu, Beijing 100026, PRC
Tel: (86 10) 6506-4328 or 6597-6331
E-mail: cuebwsc@263.net.cn
Website: http://www.cueb.edu.cn

University of International Business and Economics 对外经济贸易大学
Overview:
The University of International Business and Economics is a key university that
focuses on international business management and business English. About 40
departments and schools offer a variety of Bachelor's, Master's and PhD courses
of study. Core subjects include International Trade, International Finance, Accounting, Business Management, Law, Humanities, Public Administration and
Foreign Languages. There are approximately 900 foreign students studying here
each year.

Courses:
International students are offered courses in Chinese and business studies.

Contact information:
School of International Education,
University of International Business and Economics, Beijing 100029, PRC
Tel: (86 10) 6449-2329 or 6449-2327
E-mail: dfs@uibe.edu.cn
Website: http://www.uibe.edu.cn

Beijing Institute of Economic Management 北京经济管理干部学院
Overview:
The Beijing Institute of Economic Management offers degree programmes and
certificates in various business studies. Majors include economics, administration,
science, engineering, arts and law. It also offers business administration training
for national corporate managers. Over 1,000 foreign students attend classes here
each year.

Courses:
Foreign students can study in both short-term and long-term Chinese programmes,
and pursue degree programmes.

Contact information:
19 Huajiadi Street, Chaoyang District, Beijing 100102, PRC
Tel: (86 10) 6472-2233

Beijing Technology and Business University 北京工商大学
Overview:
Beijing Technology and Business University is the result of the merger between Beijing Institute of Business and Beijing Institute of Light Industry in 1999. Its focus is on teaching and research in the fields of science, engineering, economics, business, law, literature, arts and history. Approximately 100 foreign students are enrolled here.

Courses:
Foreign students may study Chinese Language or for a number of degree programmes.

Contact information:
Beijing Technology and Business University,
33 Fucheng Road, Beijing 100037, PRC
Tel: (86 10) 6890-4692 or 6890-4669
Email: fao@btbu.edu.cn
Website: http://www.btbu.edu.cn

Beijing Forestry University 北京林业大学
Overview:
A key university of China, the Beijing Forestry University offers studies on Forestry, Biology, Landscape Gardening, Forestry Engineering, Soil and Water Conservation. Programmes include Oriental landscape gardening and architecture, economics and international trade, and environmental studies.

Courses:
International students may study Chinese Language in preparation for further studies or degree programmes at the university.

Contact information:
226#, Beijing Forestry University, Beijing 100083, PRC
Tel: (86 10) 6233-8271
Website: http://www.bjfu.edu.cn

China Agricultural University 中国农业大学
Overview:
China Agricultural University was the earliest Agricultural Sciences university in China and is a key institute of higher learning. Departments include Agronomy and Biotechnology, Animal Science and Technology, Biological Science, Food Science, Veterinary Medicine, Water Conservation, Natural Science, Economics and Management, and Natural Resources and Environment Science. There are two campuses in Beijing, both in Haidian district.

Courses:
International students may study any of the disciplines.

Contact information:
Office of International Relations, China Agricultural University
2 Yuanmingyuan Road, Haidian District, Beijing 100094, PRC
Tel: (86 10) 6289-2736 or 6289-1004
E-mail: cauie@cau.edu.cn
Website: http://www.cau.edu.cn

Communication University of China 北京广播学院
Overview:
Beijing Broadcasting University is dedicated to intensive studies and training for the media and broadcasting industries. The following colleges and schools offer a wide range of courses. College of Journalism & Communications, Television College, International Communications College, Advertising College, College of Film & Television Literature, College of Recording Technology & Art, College for Cartoon Making, College for Televised Broadcasting & Presentation, Information Engineering College, Media Management College, School of Literature and School of Social Sciences. Over 500 foreign students study here every year.

Courses:
International students have a choice of studying Chinese Language or pursuing Bachelor's, Master's or PhD programmes in the media, radio and television broadcasting industries.

Contact information:
Foreign Affairs Department of Beijing Broadcasting Institute,
1 East street, Dingfuzhuang, Chaoyang District, Beijing, 100024, PRC
Tel: (86 10) 6577-9359
Website: http://www.cuc.edu.cn

Beijing University of Chinese Medicine 北京中医药大学
Overview:
The Beijing University of Chinese Medicine was one of the earliest formal institutes of higher learning established for the teaching of traditional Chinese medicine in China. Specialities include Chinese Medicine, Acupuncture, Moxibustion, Chinese Pharmaceutical Processing, and Public Health Management.

Courses:
Foreign students can attend both short-term and long-term programmes for traditional Chinese Medicine, Acupuncture, etc, as well as Chinese Language.

Contact information:
International School, Beijing University of Chinese Medicine,
11 Beisanhuan Dong Lu, Chaoyang District, Beijing 100029, PRC
Tel: (86 10) 6428-6322, 6428-6318 or 6428-6319
E-mail: isbucm@sohu.com
Website: http://www.bjucmp.edu.cn

Beijing University of Technology 北京工业大学
Overview:
Beijing University of Technology is a comprehensive university for sciences, engineering, business management and humanities. Core courses include studies in mechanical engineering, applied electronics technology, electronic information and control engineering, architecture and engineering, computer science, economics and management, and advertising. Approximately 400 foreign students are enrolled here each year.

Courses:
International students can study in short and long-term Chinese language programmes, a Chinese business and Culture programme in English and for degrees.

Contact information:
International Exchanges, Beijing University of Technology,
100 Pingle yuan, Chaoyang District, Beijing 100022, PRC
Tel: (86 10) 6739-1858 or 6739-1465
E-mail: bpuiec@bjut.edu.cn/haoqh@bjut.edu.cn
Website: http://bjut.edu.cn

North China University of Technology 北方工业大学
Overview:
North China University of Technology is a multi-disciplinary university covering engineering, sciences, arts, management, law and economics. Programmes include computer science and technology, electronic information engineering, automation, mechanical design, business administration, accounting, law, architecture, international economics and trade, statistics, advertising, English and Japanese.

Courses:
International students can study Chinese Language as well as pursue degree programmes.

Contact information:
Foreign Affairs Office, North China University of Technology
5 Fushi Road, Shijingshan District, Beijing 100041, PRC
Tel: (86 10) 6883-9237
E-mail: fao.ncut@263.net/fao@ncut.edu.cn
Website: http://www.ncut.edu.cn

Civil Aviation Management Institute 民航管理干部学院
Overview:
As an extension of the Civil Aviation Management Institute, a Chinese Training Programme has been established offering Chinese Language and Culture courses as well as short-term programmes in Civil Aviation Services and Air Ground Management. Accommodation is in a three-star hotel on the institute grounds. Both middle school and high school students are also welcome to study here.

Contact information:
Tel: (86 10) 6472-1188 extension 6522
E-mail: ICEC.CAMIC@163.com

China University of Mining Technology 中国矿业大学
Overview:
The Beijing Campus of the China University of Mining Technology has an emphasis on engineering with science, liberal arts and management as secondary disciplines. Majors include: Mining engineering, mining safety, geological engineering, rock mechanics, environmental engineering, mineral processing, mineral investigation and exploration, land survey, map cartography and geological information, power electronics, mechanics, computer application, architecture, civil engineering, mathematics, business administration and MBA programmes.

Courses:
Foreign students can attend both short-term and long-term programmes for Chinese Language and degree programmes.

Contact information:
11 Xueyuan Road, Haidian District, Beijing 100083, PRC
Tel: (86 10) 6233-1239
E-mail: wangy@cumtb.edu.cn
Website: http://www.cumtb.edu.cn

Beijing Institute of Petrochemical Technology 北京石油化工大学
Overview:
The Beijing Institute of Petrochemical Technology is an integrated university located in the suburban district of Daxing. Few foreigners have studied here to date. A new apartment building provides students with single rooms and full amenities.

Courses:
Foreign students may study in short- and long-term Chinese programmes as well as pursue undergraduate degrees.

Contact information:
International Students Office, Beijing Institute of Petrochemical Technology,
Daxing District, Beijing 102617, PRC
Tel: (86 10) 6923-0092
E-mail: liuxue@bipt.edu.cn
Website: http://www.bipt.edu.cn

North China Electric Power University 华北电力大学
Overview:
A key university in China, the North China Electric Power University offers
degree programmes in electrical engineering, computer science and technology,
science and engineering, energy and power engineering, foreign languages,
humanities and social sciences, mathematics and physics, business administration,
mechanical engineering, and environmental science and engineering.

Courses:
International students can study Chinese Language and pursue degree programmes. HSK classes are also available. Chinese students are paired with foreign
students for language help.

Contact information:
International Education Institute, North China Electric Power University,
Zhuxinzhuang, Dewei, Beijing 100022, PRC
Tel: (86 10) 8079-8303
E-mail: icd@ncepubj.edu.cn
Website: http://www. ncepu.net.cn

Beijing University of Machinery 北京机械工业学院
Overview:
Beijing University of Machinery is an engineering institute with courses in
mechanical engineering, management engineering, humanities and social sciences.
A Chinese Language programme has been established for foreign students to learn
practical Chinese on short-term and long-term bases.

Courses:
Foreign students can study in both short-term and long-term Chinese programmes
and for HSK testing.

Contact information:
International Student Office, Beijing University of Machinery,
12 East Road Qinghe
Xiaoying, Haidian District, Beijing 100085, PRC
Tel: (86 10) 6293-9325 or 6293-9287
Email: ibmfao@public.bta.net.cn

Beijing Institute of Clothing Technology 北京服装学院
Overview:

The Beijing Institute of Clothing Technology focuses on fibre materials, clothing, arts and crafts, international trade, industrial design and automation. The institute offers both Bachelor and Master degree programmes. Bachelor degrees are for Fashion Design, Ornamental Art and International Trade.

Courses:

Foreign students may study elementary and intermediate level Chinese in both short-term and long-term classes. Bachelor degrees may also be pursued.

Contact information:

Foreign Affairs Office, Beijing Institute of Clothing Technology,
Heping Bei Jie, Chaoyang District, Beijing 100029, PRC
Tel: (86 10) 6428-8257

Beijing Institute of Art and Design 北京艺术设计学院
Overview:

Beijing Institute of Art and Design trains students in the fields of modern art and design, and decorative art. Departments include multi-media design, arts and handicrafts, public environment arts, digital media art and design, visual communications, industrial design, fashion and textiles and various majors related to industrial and interior design.

Courses:

International students can contact the International Cooperation and Exchange Center for further details.

Contact information:

International Cooperation and Exchange Center,
8 Huixin Dong Street, Chaoyang District, Beijing 100029, PRC
Tel: (86 10) 8463-3331 or 8464-7017
E-mail: yanghao@bijad.net.cn

Beijing Materials Institute 北方物资学院
Overview:

Beijing Materials Institute is located in Tongzhou at the northern end of the Grand Canal. Studies include: International economics, business administration, marketing, accounting, financial management, information management and information systems, e-trade, human resource management, labour economics and social security, and logistics.

Courses:
International students can study in short- and long-term Chinese language programmes as well as pursue Bachelor's and Master's degrees.

Contact information:
Foreign Affairs Office, Beijing Materials Institute,
Tongzhou District, Beijing 101149, PRC
Tel: (86 10) 8953-4412
E-mail: wzxyybaa@cj.edu.cn
Website: http://www.bmi.edu.cn

Beijing Physical Education University 北京体育大学
Overview:
Beijing Sports University is a key university aimed at training highly qualified physical education teachers, coaches, athletes, sports science researchers, administrators, and other professional personnel in the field of physical education.

Contact information:
Foreign Students Office, Beijing Sports University,
Zhongguancun Bei Dajie, Haidian District, Beijing 100084, PRC
Tel: (86 10) 6298-9341
E-mail: bupefso@sina.com
Website: http://www.bupe.edu.cn

China Conservatory of Music 中国音乐学院
Overview:
The China Conservatory of Music is a renowned institute for producing outstanding and talented musicians, composers, singers and professors of music. It is also the only institute in China whose mission is to preserve and develop the traditional music of Chinese nationalities. It has eight major departments: Musicology, Composition, Vocal, Chinese Instruments, Music Education, Piano, Conducting and Art Management.

Courses:
Foreign students can study music refresher courses, Chinese Language and pursue degrees in Musicology, Composition and Performance. A short-term Chinese course is also offered in summer.

Contact information:
1 Anxiang Road, Chaoyang District, Beijing 100101, PRC
Tel: (86 10) 6488-7358 or 6388-7359
E-mail: zyywb@yahoo.com/zyywb@public.bta.net.cn

Beijing Institute of Education 北京教育学院

Overview:
The Beijing Institute of Education covers programmes in art, history, psychology, mathematics, physics, chemistry, biology, geography, physical culture, educational technology, educational administration and Chinese language and culture.

Courses:
Short-term and long-term courses in Chinese language and culture, calligraphy and kungfu can be arranged. Tailor-made courses can also be arranged for visiting groups.

Contact information:
Foreign Students Office, Beijing Institute of Education,
2 Wen Xing Street, Xicheng District, Beijing 100044, PRC
Tel: (86 10) 6835-5321
E-mail: bie@bjedu.gov.cn
Website: http://www.bjie.ac.cn

Beijing Dance Academy 北京舞蹈学院

Overview:
Beijing Dance Academy is the only institute of higher learning dedicated to dance. Specialities include: choreography and performance studies in Chinese Classical Dance, Chinese Folk Dance, Ballet, Modern Dance, Musical Theatre, Ballroom Dancing, Fashion Shows.

Courses:
Foreign students take short-term training programmes in Chinese dance as well as pursue Bachelor and Masters degrees in dance and related fields.

Contact information:
Foreign Affairs Office, Beijing Dance Academy,
19 Minzu Daxue Nan Lu, Haidian District, Beijing 100081, PRC
Tel: (86 10) 6893-5859 or 6893-5696
E-mail: bdainter@public.bta.net.cn
Website: http://www.bda.edu.cn

Beijing Film Academy 北京电影大学
Overview:
The Beijing Film Academy is the largest institution for the study of film and television production in Asia. Undergraduate and postgraduate degrees are offered in the following fields of study: Film Literature, Film and Television Production, Performing Arts, Film and TV Photography, Art Design and Advertising, Sound Recording, Management and Distribution, Still Photography, and Animation. Foreign students are welcome to study any field.

Contact information:
International School of Beijing Film Academy,
4 Xitucheng Road, Haidian District, Beijing 100088, PRC
Tel: (86 10) 8204-5433 or 8204-5747
E-mail: guopei@bfa.edu.cn
Website: http://www.bfa.edu.cn

Beijing International Youth University 北京青年研修大学
Overview:
The Beijing International Youth University offers programmes in Chinese language and culture to foreigners on short-term and long-term bases. The University also is a testing site for the HSK exam. Accommodation is available for up to 200 foreign students in a well equipped complex complete with swimming pool, gym, restaurants and tennis courts.

Contact information:
40 Liangmaqiao Road, Chaoyang District, Beijing 100016, PRC
Tel: (86 10) 6466-4803 or 6462-8476
E-mail: iyu@iyu.com.cn
Website: http://www.sevk.com.cn

Peking University Health Science Centre 北京大学医学部
Overview:
Peking University Health Science Centre was established in 1912 and was the first Western medical school in China. It offers a full range of courses in medical sciences, clinical medicine, pharmaceutics, public health, stomatology, and nursing to foreign students. Undergraduate (five years) and postgraduate (three to five years) degree programmes can be pursued. Students must meet admission requirements in Chinese and prerequisite science courses.

Contact information:
Foreign Students Office
Tel: (86 10) 8280-1253
E-mail: fso@bjmu.edu.cn
Website: http://www1.bjmu.edu.cn

Graduate School of the Chinese Academy of Social Sciences 国社会科学院
Overview:
The Graduate School of the Chinese Academy of Social Sciences offers programmes for Master's and PhD students from all over China and the world. There are more than 68 Master's degree programmes and 58 PhD degree programmes available. There are approximately 120 foreign students studying here.

Prerequisites:
Prerequisites for application include a BA degree or above (Master's for PhD students) and reference letters from two associate professors or professors. Applicants must sit for a written and oral examination in late March/early April.

Contact information:
Foreign Students Admission Office, International Exchange and Cooperation Center, Graduate School of Chinese Academy of Social Sciences,
1 Wangjing Zhonghuan nanlu, Chaoyang District, Beijing 1001029, PRC
Tel: (86 10) 6472-2352 or 6472-2390
E-mail: lb@graduate.cass.net.cn
Website: http://www.gscas.ac.cn

Capital University of Medical Sciences 首都医科学院
Overview:
Capital University of Medical Sciences is a key university in China. Its major objective is to educate high-level undergraduates and postgraduates of clinical application. Disciplines include: clinical medicine, stomatology, preventive medicine, nursing, traditional Chinese medicine, paediatrics, rehabilitation, medical iconography, pharmacy, and optometry. Regular student enrolment is about 14,600 students. Foreign students are welcome to study here.

Contact information:
International Exchange Centre, Capital University of Medical Sciences,
10 Xitoutiao, Youanmen, Beijing 100054, PRC
Tel: (86 10) 6305-1065
E-mail: overseas@cpums.edu.cn
Website: http://www.cpums.edu.cn

China Foreign Affairs University 外交大学
Overview:
The China Foreign Affairs University is affiliated with the Chinese Foreign Ministry. It is a leading institution in the field of international studies in China. There are approximately 1,400 Chinese students studying in the fields of Diplomacy, English and International Studies, Foreign Languages (Japanese/French), International Law, and International Studies.

Courses:

The International Exchange Centre offers training in Chinese Language for both short-term and long-term students. Foreign students can also study for degree programmes. During the summer break, courses on China's Foreign Policy, International Relations and Mandarin Chinese are also offered.

Contact information:

International Students Office, China Foreign Affairs University,
24 Zhanlan Road, Beijing 100037, PRC
Tel: (86 10) 6823-3894 or 6823-3348
E-mail: admission@cfau.edu.cn/waiban@cfau.edu.cn
Website: http://www.cfau.edu.cn

Chinese People's Public Security University 中国人民公安大学

Overview:

The Chinese People's Public Security University is the largest university dedicated to training senior police officers. Departments include: Police administration, criminal investigation, law, public order management, police training, international police cooperation, Chinese language and literature, science and technology for public security, traffic control and engineering, and forensic science.

Courses:

Foreign students are welcome study either Chinese or subjects in police science and legal studies.

Contact information:

Foreign Affairs Office, The Chinese People's Public Security University,
Muxidi Nanli, Xicheng District, Beijing 100083, PRC
Tel: (86 10) 8390-3066 or 8390-3067
E-mail: wsb@cppsu.edu.cn
Website: http://www.cppsu.edu.cn